ORIENTALISM

AND MODERNISM

Orientalism

and Modernism

THE LEGACY OF CHINA IN POUND

AND WILLIAMS

ZHAOMING QIAN

DUKE UNIVERSITY PRESS   Durham and London

1995

© 1995 Duke University Press

All rights reserved

Printed in the United States of America on acid-free paper ∞

Designed by Cherie Holma Westmoreland

Typeset in Weiss by Keystone Typesetting, Inc.

Library of Congress Cataloging-in-Publication Data appear

on the last printed page of this book.

FOR MY MOTHER AND

IN MEMORY OF MY FATHER

CONTENTS

LIST OF ILLUSTRATIONS

ACKNOWLEDGMENTS

My largest debt is to Barry Ahearn, who started me on the study of Pound, Williams, and Chinese poetry and gave me counsel at every stage of the book's development. I am grateful to Geoffrey Harpham, who helped me sharpen my mind and extend my learning. To the late Wang Zuoliang and the late Xu Guozhang at Beijing Foreign Studies University I owe my initiation into East-West comparative poetics. I especially would like to thank Hugh Kenner for permitting me access to his own transcripts of Ernest Fenollosa's notes for six *Cathay* poems in the early phase of my investigation. During the early going I was also fortunate enough to have the encouragement of Carroll F. Terrell. I am especially grateful to Donald Gallup for kindly responding to my trying queries and helping me locate materials. I am equally indebted to Charles Norman, A. Walton Litz, James J. Wilhelm, Paul Mariani, Robert J. Bertholf, Peter Schmidt, Anne Farrer, Christopher Date, Jennifer White, and Tang Gaocai for answering my various questions. I owe a special debt of gratitude to Mary de Rachewiltz, who encouraged my research and granted me permission to quote her mother's entry in her notebook. I am especially thankful to Omar Pound for his prompt response to my queries. Thanks must also go to many colleagues and friends who have helped me in various ways across the years: Joseph Cohen, Donald Pizer, the late Philip Bollier, Gerald Snare, Dale Edmonds, Michael Boardman,

Molly Rothenberg, Felipe Smith, Ernest Chachere, Philip Coulter, Rima Reck, Mary FitzGerald, Linda Blanton, Mackie Blanton, John Cooke, Elizabeth Penfield, Richard Katrovas, Miriam Miller, Bob Sturges, John Gery, Cynthia Hogue, William Pratt, Massimo Bacigalupo, Anne Carson, the late Andrew Kappel, Thomas Whitaker, Theodora Rapp Graham, Peggy Fox, Edwin Kennebeck, Shoji Yamana, Ding Wangdao, Lin Xuehong, Dai Ruihui, and Nova Thriffley.

I am especially indebted to the librarians and staff of several institutions. To Patricia C. Willis, curator, and the staff of the Collection of American Literature, the Beinecke Rare Book and Manuscript Library, Yale University, I owe special thanks for giving me generous assistance over a long period of time. I wish to express my gratitude to Robert J. Bertholf, curator, and the staff of the Poetry/Rare Books Collection of the University Libraries, the State University of New York at Buffalo, for their remarkable help in my search through their complete sets of about a dozen periodicals. I would like to thank James Fraser, director, and the staff of the Florham-Madison Campus Library, Fairleigh Dickinson University, for their cheerful assistance in my inspection of their William Carlos Williams Collection.

I am deeply grateful to Tulane University, which granted me a Richard Perrill Adams Award in 1989 and a travel stipend in 1990 that enabled me to begin my researches; to the Beinecke Rare Book and Manuscript Library of Yale University, which awarded me the H. D. Fellowship in American Literature for the period 1992–93 that permitted me to spend a month of research and writing at Yale in the early summer of 1993; and to my home institution, the University of New Orleans, which offered me a Research Council Grant and a Summer Scholar Award in 1993 that gave me the time and support invaluable for the completion of the book. Successive grants from the UNO Office of Research and College of Liberal Arts have helped defray the costs of illustrations and permissions. For all this I am grateful.

Some of the groundwork for this study was laid in previously published articles: a shorter version of Chapter Five appeared in *Paideuma* 19.1 and 2 (1990); Chapters Seven and Eight are based on an article published in *William Carlos Williams Review* 17.1 (1991); and a large portion of

Chapter Six was published in *Twentieth Century Literature* 39.3 (1993). It gives me pleasure to acknowledge permission by Carroll F. Terrell, Peter Schmidt, Brian Bremen, and William McBrien to reprint. I am thankful for the comments and challenges of those who have listened to parts of this study in oral presentations. In particular, I enjoyed reading a paper on Pound and Wang Wei at the 20th Century Literature Conference at Louisville in February 1993 and reading another paper on Pound and Qu Yuan at the 15th Ezra Pound International Conference at Rapallo in July 1993. I received much stimulation from my students. Those who participated in my 1992 and 1994 Modern American Seminars at UNO were a special inspiration.

I particularly wish to thank the readers of this study for Duke University Press—Zhang Longxi and Reed Way Dasenbrock—for encouragement and insights. To the support of Stanley Fish and Reynolds Smith at Duke University Press I owe a great deal. And Jean Brady deserves gratitude for intelligently preparing the manuscript for the printer. Finally, special thanks to you, May, Yuyan, and Yuli, for your interest, confidence, and unfailing support.

Grateful acknowledgment is given to New Directions Publishing Corporation and Faber and Faber Ltd. for permission to quote from the following copyrighted works of Ezra Pound: *The Cantos* (copyright © 1934, 1937, 1940, 1948, 1956, 1959, 1962, 1963, 1966, and 1968 by Ezra Pound); *Ezra Pound and Dorothy Shakespear* (copyright © 1976 and 1984 by the Trustees of the Ezra Pound Literary Property Trust); *Ezra Pound's Poetry and Prose Contributions to Periodicals* (copyright © 1991 by the Trustees of the Ezra Pound Literary Property Trust); *Gaudier-Brzeska* (copyright © 1970 by Ezra Pound); *Literary Essays* (copyright © 1918, 1920, and 1935 by Ezra Pound); *Personae* (copyright © 1926 by Ezra Pound); *Pound/Joyce* (copyright © 1967 by Ezra Pound); *Selected Letters 1907–1941* (copyright © 1950 by Ezra Pound); and *The Spirit of Romance* (copyright © 1968 by Ezra Pound). Previously unpublished material by Ezra Pound and Ernest Fenollosa (copyright © 1995 by the Trustees of the Ezra Pound Literary Property Trust) is used by permission of New Directions Publishing Corporation, agents. Grateful acknowledgment is given to

New Directions Publishing Corporation for permission to quote from the following copyrighted works of William Carlos Williams: *Collected Poems:* Volume I (copyright © 1938 by New Directions Publishing Corporation; copyright © 1982 and 1986 by William Eric Williams and Paul H. Williams); *I Wanted to Write a Poem* (copyright © 1958 by William Carlos Williams); *Imaginations* (copyright © 1970 by Florence H. Williams); *Selected Essays* (copyright © 1954 by William Carlos Williams); and *Selected Letters* (copyright © 1957 by William Carlos Williams). Previously unpublished material by William Carlos Williams (copyright © 1995 by William Eric Williams and Paul H. Williams) is used by permission of New Directions Publishing Corporation, agents. "Dancing" from *Fir-Flower Tablets, The Complete Poetical Works of Amy Lowell* (copyright © 1955 by Houghton Mifflin Co.; copyright © renewed 1983 by Houghton Mifflin Co., Brinton P. Roberts, and G. D'Andelot Belin, Esquire) is reprinted by permission of Houghton Mifflin Co. A 1921 version of "To Po Chü-i" from *The Collected Poems of Babette Deutsch* (copyright © 1969 by Babette Deutsch) is reprinted by permission of Adam Yarmolinsky. Excerpts from *Ezra Pound's Cathay* by Wai-lim Yip (copyright © 1969 by Princeton University Press) are reprinted by permission of Princeton University Press. Excerpts from *The Pound Era* by Hugh Kenner (copyright © 1971 by Hugh Kenner) are reprinted by permission of Hugh Kenner.

Illustrations were provided through the courtesy of the British Museum, the Freer Gallery of Art, the Metropolitan Museum of Art, the Art Institute of Chicago, the University of Pennsylvania Museum, the Baltimore Museum of Art, the Kyoto Chishakuin Temple, the Shanghai Museum, the Beinecke Rare Book and Manuscript Library of Yale University, the Joseph Regenstein Library of the University of Chicago, the Golda Meir Library of the University of Wisconsin-Milwaukee, the Florham-Madison Campus Library of Fairleigh Dickinson University, and Mr. Omar S. Pound.

A NOTE ON

TRANSLITERATION

For the transliteration of Chinese names and words I have followed the pinyin system, which is both most accurate and increasingly widespread. In my quotations from Giles, Waley, and other early writers, however, I have retained their Wade-Giles usage. A short list is given below of those names whose pinyin and Wade-Giles spellings are quite different:

> Bo Juyi = Po Chü-i
> Guanyin = Kwanyin
> Laozi = Lao Tzu
> Li Bo = Li Po
> Qu Yuan = Ch'ü Yüan
> Tao Qian = T'ao Ch'ien
> Yang Guifei = Yang Kui-fei
> Zhuangzi = Chuang Tzu

For those unfamiliar with the pinyin system, it may be useful to remember these general rules for pronunciation: c = ts, q = ch, x = sh, z = dz, and zh = j.

PROLOGUE: THE PLACE OF THE

ORIENT IN THE MODERNIST MOVEMENT

In this study I use the term Orientalism differently from Edward Said *(Orientalism* 1978) in several ways. For Said the Orient is specifically the Muslim Orient. For me it is the Far East, particularly China. If until the early nineteenth century the Orient "had really meant only India and the Bible lands" (Said 4), by the early twentieth century the term came primarily to mean China and Japan. Indeed, for the great Modernists— Yeats, Pound, Eliot, Williams, Stevens, and Moore—it was the Far East rather than the Near East that was a richer source of literary models. Therefore, a study of the Far East's impact on Modernism indisputably has greater significance. For Said "Orientalism is a cultural and a political fact . . ." (13). Accordingly, his study covers all the various dimensions of the complex system. For me the concept is primarily a literary one. I consider literary Orientalism not in abstract terms but in the concrete form of individual Chinese poets—Qu Yuan (Ch'ü Yüan), Tao Qian (T'ao Ch'ien), Li Bo (Li Po), Wang Wei, and Bo Juyi (Po Chü-i)—as discovered and translated by late nineteenth-century and early twentieth-century English and American scholars. It was through Ernest Fenollosa, H. A. Giles, and Arthur Waley that Modernists like Pound and Williams had dialogues with the great Chinese poets. For Said "[t]he Orient was al- most a European invention"; it was the key culture against which the West defined itself (1–2). There are obviously many examples where

Said's model works well. In considering Pound's and Williams' enthusiasm for China, I find, however, that this model has shortcomings. First, Pound and Williams did not seem to believe in Western cultural superiority. Second, what attracted the two poets toward the Orient was really the affinities (the Self in the Other) rather than the differences (the Otherness in the Other). In the chapters that follow, therefore, I will adopt a contrasting Orientalist model—the model of imitation as defined by Reed Way Dasenbrock in *Imitating the Italians: Wyatt, Spenser, Synge, Pound, Joyce* (1991). In this model, China and Japan are seen not as foils to the West, but as crystallizing examples of the Modernists' realizing Self. Dasenbrock has not explicitly articulated the theoretical basis for his approach. In fact, one may find strong support for it in Heidegger's hermeneutics. As Hans-Georg Gadamer, one of the leading proponents of hermeneutics, observes, in the Heideggerian hermeneutic process "interpretation begins with fore-conceptions that are replaced by more suitable ones" (*Truth and Method* 236).

I have begun with the term "Orientalism" because it bears on the question out of which this book has grown: what role did Pound's and Williams' interest in Chinese poetry and culture play in their rapid transition toward high Modernism around 1920? My inquiry has unavoidably brought my attention to an influence in the Modernist movement as a whole that has been underemphasized—the influence of the Orient. (By the Modernist movement I specifically refer to the Anglo-American poetic revolution of the 1910s and 1920s.) Since I will focus my discussion narrowly on Pound and Williams in Part One and Part Two, I feel that I have an obligation to elaborate my broader premise about Orientalism and Modernism in this Prologue.

Critics like Zhang Longxi ("The Myth of the Other: China in the Eyes of the West" 118–19) have noted a strong Chinese influence on the West in the Age of Enlightenment. My own investigation of the early twentieth-century literary scene indicates a far more penetrating influence of the Far East. The first wave came in pictorial art around the turn of the century (see Julia Meech and Gabriel P. Weisberg, *Japonisme Comes to America: The Japanese Impact on the Graphic Arts 1876–1925* [1990]). For Americans of Pound's and Williams' generation, Charles Lang Freer (1854–1919),

Ernest Fenollosa (1853–1908), and the Oriental Wing of the Boston Museum of Fine Arts were the names associated with their initial awareness of the Orient. In England during the same period there were Arthur Morrison (1863–1945), Laurence Binyon (1869–1943), and the Sub-department of Oriental Prints and Drawings of the British Museum. Anglo-American interest in China and Japan was really sparked by a visual and intellectual encounter. Pound's friend John Gould Fletcher chronicled his response to a visit to the Boston Museum of Fine Arts in 1914 that was characteristic of his contemporaries. "The hours I spent then in the Oriental Wing," he observed, "seeing the Sung or Kamakura masterpieces with new eyes, re-educated me in regard to the purposes of a pictorial art close in spirit to my own poetry, and to the function of the poetic artist in reshaping the world. They rededicated me to the vital instinct, and to the soul of nature" (*Life Is My Song* 185).

Note that what attracted Fletcher was the Self rather than Otherness. This sentiment was shared by Wallace Stevens, who observed to Elsie Moll in 1909 that Chinese landscape painting was inspired by impulses similar to his own (*Letters* 137), and by Pound, who wrote Dorothy Shakespear in 1913 that he felt "older & wiser" beholding the Japanese prints of the British Museum (*ED* 177). Notice the dates—1909, 1913, and 1914— precisely the moments of the rise of the Modernist movement in poetry. And notice also what specifically in the Orient drew the English and American poets toward it—a prolonged and rich heritage of intensity, precision, objectivity, visual clarity, and complete harmony with nature—all key elements of Modernism itself. Little wonder that the early Imagists (T. E. Hulme, F. S. Flint, etc.), who began by imitating the French Symbolists, soon fell under the spell of the Orient. First it was the Japanese *haiku* and *tanka*, and then the more sophisticated verse of China represented by Tao Qian, Li Bo, Wang Wei, and Bo Juyi. It was not by accident, then, when Pound's *Cathay*, put together "from the notes of the late Ernest Fenollosa, and the decipherings of the professors Mori and Ariga" (*P* 130), came out in 1915, that almost all the major Modernists— Yeats, Ford, Lewis, Eliot, and Williams—applauded its freshness, elegance, and simplicity. Ford, in particular, remarked, "If these were original verses, then Pound was the greatest poet of the day" (qtd. in Stock

174), which should indicate that the English Modernist writer and critic had perceived affinities between his own and Far Eastern sensibilities.

Under the impact of Pound's *Cathay*, there arose in the late 1910s and early 1920s a vogue of imitating the Orient. Small magazines such as the Chicago *Poetry* and *The Little Review* competed around 1920 in bringing out Chinese poems as well as poems modeled on the Chinese and the Japanese. Amy Lowell, collaborating with Florence Ayscough on a Chinese poetry anthology at that moment, wrote, "Chinese poetry is much in people's minds at present . . . we must work hard and work quickly" (MacNair 76). Yeats, who worked closely with Pound between 1913 and 1916, was also caught up in this "Far East Fever," though his enthusiasm was principally for the Japanese *Noh* drama. Indeed, he claimed in 1916 that "I have found my first model—and in literature if we would not be parvenus we must have a model—in the 'Noh' stage of aristocratic Japan" (*Four Plays for Dancers* 86).

Many imitators of the Orient, like Stevens and Fletcher, later publicly acknowledged their debt to China and Japan. When asked about the Orient's impact on his Modernism, Stevens, for instance, candidly told his interviewer Ronald Lane Latimer, "Yes: I think that I have been influenced by Chinese and Japanese lyrics. But you ask whether I have ever 'tried deliberately to attain certain qualities.' That is quite possible" (*Letters* 291). Others, like Williams and Moore, chose to keep silent about their connections with the Far East. In Part Two, I will produce textual evidence in an attempt to show how Williams, inspired by Pound's *Cathay*, began a serious dialogue with the mid-Tang poet Bo Juyi, first through Giles and then through Arthur Waley, between 1916 and 1921, and how the encounter resulted in an adoption of Chinese notions and methods in his early Modernist *Sour Grapes* and *Spring and All*. As for the Moore-China connection, I have to find another occasion to deal with her "objective approach akin to the Chinese" (Fletcher, *Selected Essays* 79) as well as her numerous references to Chinese motifs. Among the poets of the Modernist camp, Eliot was perhaps one of the few who chose India over China and Japan for the Eastern spirit. But he also showed a high respect for China. Referring to his Harvard professor Irving Babbitt's "addiction to the philosophy of Confucius," he remarked: "I have the highest respect for the Chinese mind and for Chinese civilization; and I am willing to believe that Chinese civilization at its highest has graces and excellences which may make Europe seem crude" (*After Strange Gods* 43). Thus we see that like French Symbolism and Italian culture, Orientalism is a constitutive element of the Modernism of the 1910s and 1920s. In this study I will not try to downgrade the French influence in Modernism stressed by René Taupin (*L'influence du symbolisme français sur la poésie américaine (de 1910 à 1920)* [1929]) and Scott Hamilton (*Ezra Pound and the Symbolist Inheritance* [1992]), nor the Italian influence considered by Reed Way Dasenbrock (*Imitating the Italians: Wyatt, Spenser, Synge, Pound, Joyce* [1991]). Rather, I will argue for a multiculturalist model that recognizes the place of the Orient among all other influences in the Modernist movement. Modernism is a phenomenon of internationalism/multiculturalism. It would be gross insensibility not to perceive the Oriental contribution to its growth.

Though what I am attempting in this book is to assert the place of the Orient in the Modernist movement, I do not claim that the illustrations I am providing here are sufficient. Ideally a comprehensive work on Orientalism and Modernism would cover at least two or three more prominent Modernist figures. But tackling several other major Modernists—Yeats, Eliot, and Stevens, for instance—would create a huge new project and would eclipse the Pound-Williams dichotomy I intend to emphasize in this study. (True, there are other important dichotomies—Yeats-Pound, Pound-Eliot, Pound–H. D., Williams-Stevens, Williams-Moore—at work in the Modernist movement, but the Pound-Williams dichotomy appears to stand at the center.) Fortunately, the Orient's impact on Modernists like Yeats and Eliot has been studied elsewhere (for example, Shiro Naito, *Yeats and Zen: A Study of the Transformation of His Mask* [1984]; Masaru Sekine, *Yeats and the Noh: A Comparative Study* [1990]; P. S. Sri, *T. S. Eliot, Vedanta, and Buddhism* [1985]; Ashok Kumar Jha, *Oriental Influences in T. S. Eliot* [1988]; and Amar Kumar Singh, *T. S. Eliot and Indian Philosophy* [1990]). So, perhaps I can say with more legitimacy that my work, like those earlier treatments of individual Modernists and the Orient, is part of a mutual effort to reassess—beyond the scope of a single book—the role of the Orient in the Modernist movement as a whole.

It may be objected that in treating the legacy of China in Pound and

Williams I have largely ignored Chinese influences in the two Modernists' more important later works. But without suspending these later influences, I would not have been able to concentrate on the rich detail in support of my major thesis about the Chinese contribution to Pound's and Williams' rapid transition toward Modernism in the decade of 1913–23. Besides, previous critics, notably Hugh Kenner (*The Pound Era* [1971]), James Wilhelm (*The Later Cantos of Ezra Pound* [1977]), and John Nolde (*Blossoms from the East: The China Cantos of Ezra Pound* [1983]), have already read the Chinese influences particularly on Pound's epic and later lyrics. Summaries of these would add little to scholarship.

What follows, then, traces and elaborates not only Pound's and Williams' remarkable dialogues with the great Chinese poets—Qu Yuan, Li Bo, Wang Wei, Bo Juyi, and so on—between 1913 and 1923, but the role these encounters played in the two poets' perfection of a Modernist tradition. It explores Chinese influences such as the ethics of pictorial representation, the style of ellipsis, allusion, and juxtaposition, and the Taoist/Chan-Buddhist (Zen-Buddhist)[1] notion of nonbeing/being (formlessness/form) in Pound's pre-Fenollosan Chinese adaptations (1914), *Cathay* (1915), *Lustra* (1916), and Early Cantos (1915–19), and in Williams' *Sour Grapes* (1921) and *Spring and All* (1923).

Though my study relies heavily on historical data (rare and unpublished materials from the Beinecke Rare Book and Manuscript Library of Yale University as well as illustrations from the British Museum, the Freer Gallery of Art, and elsewhere), the real emphasis is on comparing literary works across cultures and periods. A recurring theme in my comparison is that instinctive affinity is the ground of all appreciation and influence. Pound's and Williams' backgrounds in American Transcendentalism, Hellenic culture, and European Modernism—close relatives to Orientalism—adequately prepared them for receiving the Far Eastern heritage in the crucial decade of 1913–23.

Zhaoming Qian   January 1994

I

POUND'S

ROAD TO

CHINA

1 "GETTING ORIENT

FROM ALL QUARTERS": BINYON,

UPWARD, FENOLLOSA

Ezra Pound was no stranger to Oriental art when he met Mary McNeil Fenollosa, the widow of the American Orientalist Ernest Fenollosa (1853–1908), in London in late September 1913. He had been introduced to Chinese and Japanese painting by the English poet and connoisseur of Far Eastern art Laurence Binyon (1869–1943),[1] whose lectures of March 1909 on "Oriental & European Art" gave him a preliminary education in regard to the nature and significance of Oriental paintings (Holaday 29).[2] His bride-to-be Dorothy Shakespear, quite an accomplished watercolorist herself, shared this new interest with him. As frequenters of the British Museum, the two lovers had often ventured into its Department of Prints and Drawings, where Binyon served as Assistant Keeper in charge of its growing collection of Far Eastern paintings and color prints.[3] There Dorothy would amuse herself by drawing pictures after Chinese models (see figs. 1–4)[4] while Ezra would walk around to examine exhibits that appealed to his imagination.

Prominently displayed in Binyon's Oriental Gallery in the Museum's White Wing (1910–12) was one of the most magnificent artworks of Oriental Antiquities, *The Admonitions of the Instructress to Court Ladies*, attributed to the fourth-century A.D. artist Gu Kaizhi (ca. 345–406) (see figs. 5 and 6).[5] Ever since its acquisition in 1903, Binyon had seized every occasion to expatiate upon this monument of Chinese art. It is impossi-

1. Dorothy Pound, *A Dragon*. Omar Pound.

2. Tao Yi
(fl. ca. 1530),
A Dragon.
The British Museum,
London.

3. Dorothy Pound, *An Imperial Palace Tower.*
Omar Pound.

4. Zhu Bang
(fl. ca. 1500),
The Forbidden City.
The British Museum,
London.

5. Attributed to Gu Kaizhi (ca. 345–406), Scene 2 from *Admonitions of the Instructress to Court Ladies*. The British Museum, London.

6. Attributed to Gu Kaizhi (ca. 345–406), Scene 4 from *Admonitions of the Instructress to Court Ladies*. The British Museum, London.

ble that Pound's attention did not go to this masterpiece made up of nine visually stunning scenes, each illustrating a quotation from a Han (206 B.C.–A.D. 220) text dealing with correct court conduct. Indeed, he may have paused a little longer in front of its second scene representing the Han imperial concubine Ban Jieyu, or the Lady Ban, "refusing the Emperor's invitation to ride with him in his palanquin" for fear of distracting him from state affairs (see fig. 5). In November 1913, we are to learn in Chapter Two, he was to adapt a version of the Lady Ban's famous "Song of Regret" into his Imagist "Fan-Piece, for her Imperial Lord."

A 1909 addition to the British Museum Oriental collection, the Buddhist art from Dunhuang's "Cave of the Thousand Buddhas,"[6] is even more likely to have fascinated Pound. Thirty-odd years later, when he began his Pisan Cantos in the DTC, he would recall with vividness the dazzling image of the Bodhisattva of Compassion Guanyin ("and this day the air was made open / for Kuanon of all delights") presented by unknown artists of the Tang (618–907) in *Standing Guanyin* (fig. 7) and other scrolls.[7] The sixteenth-century Japanese painter Shukei Sesson's set of *The Eight Views* (fig. 8),[8] along with two Ming (1368–1644) copies of the same traditional landscape subjects ("Snowy Evening" and "Rainy Evening"), should have called forth Pound's memory of a sequence of similar scenes in a Japanese manuscript book kept in his parents' Wyncote, Pennsylvania, home. In about two decades he was to send for the yellowing book and to produce his own version of *The Eight Views* in his Seven Lakes Canto.

That Pound cherished a fond memory of his visits to the British Museum is evidenced by his referring to his early London years generally as the "British Museum era" in Canto 80 and by his honoring Binyon for his beauty of slowness ("BinBin 'is beauty'. / 'Slowness is beauty.'") in Canto 87.[9] Those happened to be the years in which Binyon was vigorously engaged in promoting the art and aesthetics of the Orient. In 1908 he published *Painting in the Far East*, the first comprehensive study of the subject in English. (Fenollosa's *Epochs of Chinese and Japanese Art* appeared posthumously in 1912.) In 1909 he gave his lectures on "Oriental & European Art." In 1910 he organized the 1910–12 Exhibition of Chinese and Japanese Paintings,[10] which provided the English public with their first opportunity to examine a large collection of Oriental masterpieces covering a period of some fifteen hundred years, from the fourth century to the nineteenth century A.D.[11] In 1911 he published *The Flight of the Dragon: An Essay on the Theory and Practice of Art in China and Japan Based on Original Sources*, which was to be reprinted in August 1914, January 1922, August 1927, June 1935, December 1935, . . . In November 1912, shortly after he became the head of the newly formed Oriental Sub-department, he traveled to the United States to study the Chinese and Japanese art collections in Detroit, Chicago, and New York.[12]

Pound, who regularly lunched in Binyon's group at the Vienna Café near the British Museum ("the loss of that café [in 1914]/meant the end of a B. M. era," wrote Pound in Canto 80), would have many chances to listen to the English champion of Oriental art dilate on his favorite subjects. It was in those conversations that followed his attendance at Binyon's lectures or his inspection of the Far Eastern collection of the British Museum that Pound was forced into the culture of the Orient. By the time Pound met Mrs. Fenollosa, he had most probably studied both Binyon's pioneering work on Far Eastern painting and Fenollosa's equally influential *Epochs of Chinese and Japanese Art*.[13] He would have noticed that a considerable number of the illustrations in the two works were from the British Museum collection (figs. 6 and 8, for example, in the former, and fig. 9 in the latter). In a year and a half he was to review for Wyndham Lewis' *Blast* 2 (July 1915) Binyon's *The Flight of the Dragon*, and to criticize his Far Eastern art mentor's attempt "to justify Chinese intelligence by dragging it a little nearer to some Western precedent" (EPPP 2: 99).

Mary Fenollosa's purpose in seeing Pound, however, was not to hear his praise of her late husband's survey of Far Eastern pictorial art, which had seen print the previous year only because she had toiled on the "most complicated and difficult manuscript" for three years (Fenollosa v). Her aim was rather to find out if the young American poet, whose April 1913 "Contemporania" sequence she had read with delight, might be interested in taking charge of her late husband's notes and unpublished manuscripts on classical Chinese poetry and Japanese *Noh* drama. As a writer and editor,[14] Mary Fenollosa knew that the undertaking demanded a poet, and in Pound she saw one who could possibly act as her husband's literary executor.

7. Anonymous (eighth century), from
Dunhuang, *Standing Guanyin*. The British
Museum, London.

8. Shukei Sesson (1504–89), "Returning Geese Flying over a Mountain,"
Scene 2 from *The Eight Views*. The British Museum, London.

Mary Fenollosa had sought out Pound at the right moment. Spurred
by T. E. Hulme's notion that *"Creative* effort means *new* images" (95) and
armed with Ford Madox Hueffer's point of view that "poetry should be
written at least as well as prose" (*LE* 373),[15] Pound had inaugurated the
Imagist movement over a year before with his friends Hilda Doolittle
and Richard Aldington. Since then, he had succeeded in pushing Harriet
Monroe to publish in her newly established Chicago *Poetry* several
batches of Imagist poems and an Imagist manifesto prepared by him and
signed by F. S. Flint. Once the idea of Imagism had gotten in the air, and
poets like Amy Lowell had been drawn to London for Imagist education,
Pound had felt the need of enriching the discipline with models that
more accurately embodied his poetic ideals. It was for this purpose that
he had, in the previous summer, looked to the French moderns—Cor-
bière, Tailhade, de Gourmont, de Régnier, and Jammes—for discoveries
of principles and techniques. The result of this encounter had been
constructive. As René Taupin puts it, the French experimenters, "who
had similar aims," had "helped Pound to make this discipline more pre-

9. Anonymous (eighteenth century), *The Earthly Paradise.*
The British Museum, London.

cise" (121). To sum up his findings, Pound had written a series of articles
under the general title "The Approach to Paris."[16] While the articles were
still being published in installments in A. R. Orage's *New Age,* however,
Pound had already switched some of his attention to the Far East. It was
inevitable that his next move was toward China. As if knowing of Pound's
intent and need, the shade of Fenollosa appeared on the scene at this
moment with a master key to the gate of the new territory.

One must admit that Pound's knowledge of Chinese literature up to
1913 was still limited. He had read two or three "standard" translations
of Chinese poetry, including Judith Gautier's *Le livre de jade* (1867) and
Marie Marquis d'Hervey-Saint-Denys' *Poésies de l'époque des Thang* (1872)
(Jung 5).[17] The poetry of Li Bo, Du Fu, and Su Dongpo offered in these
versions, however, had left no visible marks on his work prior to 1913.
Nor had Pound, so far as I know, referred to any Chinese poets in his
writings of the period. This should prove that Pound had not, up to this
point, seriously studied Chinese poetry. On the other hand, he had,
in his evolution toward Imagism, benefited by studying and imitating

the Japanese *haiku*. It was probably from T. E. Hulme's Poets' Club that Pound learned the Japanese verse form. As F. S. Flint has written of the Club of 1909, "We proposed at various times to replace [the old-fashioned English poetry] by pure *vers libre;* by the Japanese *tanka* and *haikai;* we all wrote dozens of the latter as an amusement . . . " (71). Pound wrote his first *haiku*-like poem, "In a Station of the Metro," in 1911. The episode of how the poem was made has now become part of the history of Imagism. The Japanese *haiku,* however, was not the only Eastern poetic form Pound had pursued. By 1913 he had also examined the work of the Bengali poet Rabindranath Tagore (1861–1941). Indeed, it was through studying Tagore that he had discovered the spirit that underlies Eastern expression. In a brief essay on "Tagore's Poems," he defines this spirit as "a deeper calm" of the mind and "the fellowship between man and the gods; between man and nature." This calm, he points out, is what "we need overmuch in an age of steel and mechanics" (*EPPP* 1: 109).

It was after these experiments, and after these discoveries, that Pound began to pay more attention to the Chinese. At this moment, he may have recalled what Binyon had said about China's position in Oriental art. "Of all the nations of the East," Binyon emphasizes in *Painting in the Far East*—and presumably also in his lectures of March 1909—"the Chinese is that which through all its history has shown the strongest aesthetic instinct, the fullest and richest imagination" (5). In the same book, Binyon also points out:

The Japanese look to China as we look to Italy and Greece: for them it is the classic land, the source from which their art has drawn not only methods, materials, and principles of design, but an endless variety of theme and motive. (6)

Pound was soon to echo these remarks of Binyon's about China's importance in Eastern Culture. In "The Renaissance," first published in *Poetry* (February, March, and May 1914), he calls China "a new Greece" (*LE* 215). And in his letter to John Quinn, 10 January 1917, he observes: "China is fundamental, Japan is not. Japan is a special interest, like Provence, or 12–13th century Italy (apart from Dante). . . . But China is solid" (L 155). By the fall of 1913, I believe, Pound must already have gotten the message: to seek the permanent and the most advanced in the Eastern literary tradition, one must take the voyage to China.

Indeed, an intimate friend of Pound's, Allen Upward (1863–1926), had already set an example to him in making the voyage. Like Pound, Upward did not know a word of Chinese. He became interested in Chinese literature at the turn of the century under the influence of Lancelot Cranmer-Byng (1872–1945), a poet who had studied Marquis d'Hervey-Saint-Denys' French version of Tang poetry and Professor Herbert A. Giles' English version of Chinese gems. In 1900, Upward and Cranmer-Byng founded a small printing firm in London, which later became the Orient Press that started the "Wisdom of the East" series (Knox 73).[18] By the time Pound was introduced to Upward in London (in 1911), the latter had already made a name for himself as a poet and a writer of original thought. It has been said that his *The New Word*, a "powerful plea for idealism," "aroused England" in 1907 (*Poetry* September 1913).[19] Pound was a fervent admirer of the book both for its "etymological insights into myth" (Bush, *Genesis* 93) and for its reference to Confucian wisdom. In the book, Upward praises "K'ung the Master" for refusing to discuss with his disciples "the appointments of Heaven" (224). "No great teacher who ever lived taught men so little about the Unknown as K'ung," he reiterates in his introduction to "Sayings of K'ung the Master" for *The New Freewoman* (November 1913) (189). ("And [Kung] said nothing of the 'life after death,'" echoes Pound in Canto 13.) Upward's admiration for the ancient Chinese sage may have sparked Pound's lifelong interest in Confucianism.[20] At any rate, from Upward Pound could have learned a fair bit about Confucius. Indeed, he was probably initiated into the Confucian universe even before he had a chance to read the Confucian classics in translation.

This brings us to mid-September 1913, the eve of Pound's meeting with Mary Fenollosa. In his oddly shaped room at 10 Church Walk, Pound had opened the *Poetry* that had just arrived from Chicago. His eyes were fixed upon a sequence of poems—"Scented Leaves from a Chinese Jar"—by his friend Upward. The opening piece was titled "The Bitter Purple Willows":

Meditating on the glory of illustrious lineage I lifted up my eyes and beheld the bitter purple willows growing round the tombs of the exalted Mings. (DI 51)

In the prose poem, Pound saw a state of mind set side by side with an image. The juxtaposition of the two otherwise disconnected concepts had created for him a complex of feelings and images. This method of creation was not new to Pound and his fellow Imagists. But Upward's images had distinct Chinese colors, which Pound had witnessed in the Chinese landscape paintings of the British Museum. The "Genteels" would not accept these as fine poetry. Pound was glad that Miss Monroe had printed them in her magazine. He wrote Dorothy that day (17 September 1913): "The chinese things in 'Poetry' are worth the price of admission" (ED 256). Six days later, he found out from Upward himself how the poems had been composed. "Upward is a very interesting chap," he reported to Miss Monroe. "He says, by the way, that the Chinese stuff is not a paraphrase, but that he made it up out of his head, using a certain amount of Chinese reminiscence" (L 59).

About two years later, Upward, in a verse letter to the editor of The Egoist (1 June 1915), offered a more luminous but not necessarily precise account of how the sequence was made:

In the year nineteen hundred a poet named Cranmer Byng brought to my
    attic in Whitehall Gardens a book of Chinese Gems by Professor Giles,
Eastern butterflies coming into my attic there beside the Stygian Thames,
And read me one of them—willows, forsaken young wife, spring.

Immediately my soul kissed the soul of immemorial China:
I perceived that all we in the West were indeed barbarians and foreign
    devils,
And that we knew scarcely anything about poetry.

I set to work and wrote little poems
Some of which I read to a scientific friend
Who said,—"After all, what do they prove?"

Then I hid them away for ten or twelve years,
Scented leaves in a Chinese jar,
While I went on composing the poem of life.

I withstood the savages of the Niger with a revolver:
I withstood the savages of the Thames with a printing-press:
Byng and I we set up as publishers in Fleet Street, and produced the "Odes
   of Confucius," and the "Sayings."

My own poems I did not produce:
They were sent back to me by the *Spectator* and the *English Review.*
I secretly grudged them to the Western devils.

After many years I sent them to Chicago, and they were printed by Harriet
   Monroe. (They also were printed in *The Egoist.*)
("Correspondence" 98)

Taking a clue from this statement in verse, K. L. Goodwin remarks that
"Scented Leaves" were the "earliest poems claimed by Pound as 'imagis-
tic' " (4). Goodwin's speculation is probably valid. Evidently Pound was
enormously pleased with his discovery of the sequence. Upward had
fused Chinese colors and methods into his verse. Pound wished to do
the same. Thus, under the influence, he exclaims in "A Song of the
Degrees":[21]

> Rest me with Chinese colours,
> For I think the glass is evil.
> (p 95)

And in "Further Instructions," printed along with "A Song of the Degrees"
in the November 1913 *Poetry*, he articulates the same sentiment:

> But you, newest song of the lot,
> You are not old enough to have done much mischief,
> I will get you a green coat out of China
> With dragons worked upon it. . . .
> (p 95)

Pound now began rapidly to absorb things Chinese. Whether by acci-
dent or design, he seemed "to be getting orient from all quarters" (ED
264). He was visiting Upward, his mentor on Chinese things, doing
"shows chinesesques [Exhibitions]," dining in "a new curious & excellent
restaurant chinois," and getting "real japanese prints . . . at Cedar Lawn"

(ED 264). It is true that Fenollosa was to start him on the journey to the Far East. But if one is aware of Pound's Imagist need and the Chinese influence then in his mind, one will agree that he would have taken the voyage to China even without meeting the widow of the American Orientalist.

2 VIA GILES:

QU YUAN, LIU CHE,

LADY BAN

The story of Pound's meeting with Mary Fenollosa has been told many times. Lawrence Chisolm's version follows Mrs. Fenollosa's recollection:

Pound met Mrs. Fenollosa in London, probably through Heinemann or Laurence Binyon, the British Museum's Far Eastern art scholar. Pound questioned her at length about her husband's work and their life in Japan and was so enthusiastic about Fenollosa's literary researches that Mrs. Fenollosa promised, on her return to America, to send him whatever translations and notes she had. (222)[1]

Pound gave a different account in 1960—

Well, I met her at Sarojini Naidu's and she said that Fenollosa had been in opposition to all the profs and academes, and she had seen some of my stuff and said I was the only person who could finish up these notes as Ernest would have wanted them done. Fenollosa saw what needed to be done but he didn't have time to finish it. (Hall 49)

—which is really a confirmation of Eliot's version offered early in 1917 ("Ezra Pound" 177).

With easy access now to the vigorous correspondence between Ezra and Dorothy during that period (thanks to Omar Pound and A. Walton

Litz, who ably prepared *Ezra Pound and Dorothy Shakespear: Their Letters 1909–1914*), we are able not only to verify established versions of the encounter against reliable historical data, but also to construct a more accurate and more detailed chronology of the important event. According to the records Pound entered in his letters to Dorothy, he and Mrs. Fenollosa met no less than three times in London in the fall of 1913. The first meeting took place in the home of the Indian nationalist poet Sarojini Naidu on Monday, 29 September. The conversation between them seems to have focused on Fenollosa's Far Eastern art researches—his *Epochs of Chinese and Japanese Art* and his contribution in assembling the Freer collection. At any rate, in his first entry of the event, Pound still called Ernest Fenollosa "the writer on chinese art, selector of a lot of Freer's stuff, etc." (ED 264). But Mrs. Fenollosa perhaps mentioned on this occasion her husband's enthusiasm for classical Chinese poetry. I suspect she did because right after that first meeting (the following day perhaps), Pound went to the Isle of Wight to visit his Chinese literature tutor Upward. Upward sort of stirred him up to read two books: H. A. Giles' *History of Chinese Literature* (1901) and M. G. Pauthier's *Les quatre livres de philosophie morale et politique de la Chine* (1841).[2] On Thursday, 2 October, Pound observed to Dorothy:

I would have writ before but I went to Ryde to visit [Allen] Upward. . . . Dined on monday with Sarojini Niadu [*sic*] and Mrs Fenolosa [Mrs. Ernest Fenollosa], relict of the writer on chinese art, selector of a lot of Freer's stuff, etc. I seem to be getting orient from all quarters. . . . I'm stocked up with K'ung fu Tsze [Confucius], and Men Tsze [Mencius], etc. I suppose they'll keep me calm for a week or so. (ED 264)

Evidently an appointment for a second meeting had been arranged, where Mrs. Fenollosa would have the leisure to describe to Pound how her husband studied Chinese poetry in Japan. Pound's curiosity was aroused. He couldn't even wait until the fixed date. Before he knew it, he was reading the Chinese ancients as excitedly as he had read the French moderns the previous summer.

The second meeting between the two took place in the Café Royal on the evening of 6 October. The atmosphere of the milieu reminded Pound of his favorite artist James McNeill Whistler. Among the party also were Sarojini Naidu and William Heinemann, the publisher who brought out Fenollosa's posthumous *Epochs* in two volumes. By then, Pound not only had perused Pauthier's French translation of Confucius and Mencius but had gone through the early chapters of Giles' *History*. As a quick digester of an unfamiliar literature, he was already able to make relevant comments here and there while Mrs. Fenollosa narrated her husband's work in Chinese poetry. (One recalls how Pound had replaced F. S. Flint as the chief advocate of modern French poetry after a mere month's intensive reading of the subject.) In his letter to Dorothy of 7 October (the day after the dinner party), Pound mimicked some of the amusing remarks he had made on the occasion: "I find the chinese stuff far more consoling. There is *no* long poem in chinese. They hold if a man can't say what he wants to in 12 lines, he'd better leave it unsaid. THE period was 4th cent. B.C. —Chu Yüan, Imagiste—" (*ED* 267).[3]

Mrs. Fenollosa was undoubtedly impressed. If she had wished to test Pound's sincerity and literary acumen during the first two meetings, by then she was completely satisfied. A third meeting between the two was therefore scheduled. Pound wrote on 11 October: "Madame Fenollosa has had me to two bad plays & to dinner with [William] Heinemann. She seems determined that he shall support me" (*ED* 270). The rest of the story was recalled by Pound forty-five years later:

. . . and after a couple of weeks I got a note: would I come to that hotel in Trafalgar Square—is it Moreley's?—at any rate, it is where my grandfather stayed. There she was, gone like a priestess at an altar, and she merely said, "You're the only person who can finish this stuff the way Ernest wanted it done." Then she sent me his manuscript. . . . (Bridson 177)

Having examined Pound's thoughts and activities before and during his meetings with Mrs. Fenollosa, we can sketch a few points. First, Pound had felt the spell of China before his encounter with the widow of Ernest Fenollosa. Out of his need to perfect Imagism with new models, and owing to the influence of Binyon and Upward, Pound would begin his Chinese exploration anyway between 1913 and 1914. Second, his meeting with Mrs. Fenollosa accelerated the pace of his approach toward the "Eastern classic land." In fact, no sooner was the first meeting over than Pound had begun reading versions of classical Chinese literature. Third, during that period, Pound mainly relied on Giles' *History* to study Chinese poetry. The impact of the work on him remained active long after he received the bulk of Fenollosa's notes and manuscripts in mid-December 1913. (Pound worked on the "more polished" *Noh* plays first after he got Fenollosa's treasures, and it was not until November 1914 that he turned his attention to the Chinese poetry notebooks.) Since it was Giles' *History* rather than Fenollosa's notebooks that first introduced Pound to Chinese poetry, a detailed examination of Pound's encounter with that book is necessary.

A History of Chinese Literature by Herbert Allen Giles (1845–1935), professor of Chinese at the University of Cambridge and former H.B.M. Consul at Ningbo, China, had appealed to many young minds in England and America in the early decades of the twentieth century. Among those who had been influenced by the book before Pound were Upward, Binyon, and John Gould Fletcher,[4] the young poet from Arkansas, whom Pound had been seeing a fair bit of since the late spring of 1913. Indeed, Binyon and Fletcher could also have recommended the title to Pound around 1913. In any case, Pound was most probably delighted to read in the preface of the green-coated volume: "This is the first attempt made in any language, including Chinese, to produce a history of Chinese literature." He was perhaps more pleased to learn next that "a large portion of this book" was devoted to translation. So, he would be enabled to hear the Chinese poet "speak for himself" (Giles v). Giles certainly knew his reader's need. His *History* would keep Pound calm for far more than a week.

Giles wouldn't have been able to attempt the survey of so vast a subject as Chinese literature if he hadn't read a large amount of Chinese literary works during his prolonged diplomatic sojourn (from 1867 to 1892) in China. In fact, before he took up the comprehensive work, he had already brought out several books of translation, of which the two-volume *Gems of Chinese Literature* published in Shanghai in 1884 contributed a good many versions toward his more influential work.[5] Giles' aim in writing *A History* was to offer to his audience an introduction to a "great field which lies beyond" (v). His approach, accordingly, was to suggest, rather than demonstrate in detail, the range and sweep of the panorama by covering in a single volume as many authors of worth as possible. The book, stimulating as it is, is so full of synoptic treatments of individual figures and works that it tends to bewilder a Western reader as much as it enlightens. Pound, however, refused to be bewildered. His early training in the comparative study of Romance literature had adequately prepared him for approaching unvisited literary domains. Besides, he had a clear mind about what he would do with the material. He was not just to get the general knowledge of Chinese literature offered by Giles, but, more importantly, to extract from the book whatever was valuable to his Imagist ideal. It is doubtful if Pound ever got beyond the fourth part of Giles' eight-part *History.* (He never referred to any poet later than the Tang period, covered in the fourth part.) And within the first four parts, he seems to have carefully studied but half a dozen authors whose poetry had appealed to his Modernist imagination.

Giles' *History* commences, as do all other histories of Chinese literature, with a series of summaries of Confucian classics. It seems Pound overlooked this section of the book perhaps because he had had enough of the subjects from reading Pauthier. As he turned to the fifth chapter, however, a passage may have caught his attention:

For poetry has been defined by the Chinese as "emotion expressed in words," a definition perhaps not more inadequate than Wordsworth's "impassioned expression." "Poetry," they say, "knows no law." And again, "The men of old reckoned it the highest excellence in poetry that the meaning should lie beyond the words," and that "the reader should have to think it out." Of these three canons only the last can be said to have survived to the present day. But in the fourth century B.C., Ch'ü Yüan and his school indulged in wild irregular metres which consorted well with their wild irregular thoughts. Their poetry was prose run mad. It was allusive and allegorical to a high degree, and now, but for the commentary, much of it would be quite unintelligible. (50)

Two things in this passage seem likely to have struck Pound as particularly congenial to his Imagist sensibility: one was the Chinese critics' emphasis on suggestion, and the other was the fourth-century B.C. poet Qu Yuan's (Ch'ü Yüan) adoption of "wild irregular metres" for "wild irregular thoughts." Of these, suggestion happens to be a quality Pound had most fervently admired in the Provençal and Tuscan poets. In *The Spirit of Romance* (1910), Pound pays an extraordinary tribute to the troubadour poet Arnaut Daniel's "terse vigor of suggestion" (33). In a few years, when he had studied more Chinese poetry, he was to observe that the Chinese were greater masters of the technique that had "occasionally broken out in Europe, notably in twelfth-century Provence and thirteenth-century Tuscany . . . " (EPPP 3:85).

As for meter, Pound had always believed that it should correspond "exactly to the emotion or shade of emotion to be expressed" (LE 9). In order to reform the English meter, he had first turned to the Greek and the Provençal poets, and much later to the French moderns—Henri de Régnier, in particular, as René Taupin tells us—for techniques. It was after countless experiments that he had, quite late, attained what Yeats calls "real organic rhythm" in a poem like "The Return" ("American Poets" 48). In that poem, as Kenner perceptively notes, "every line has a strongly marked expressive rhythm but no two lines are alike, it is actually the rhythm that defines the meaning" (189). Now from Giles' *History*, Pound learned, to his great amazement, that the Chinese poet Qu Yuan had made a similar discovery and achieved a similar success over two thousand years earlier. "The poet never ends his line in deference to a prescribed number of feet, but lengthens or shortens to suit the exigency of his thought," speaks Giles of Qu Yuan's metric variations. "The reader, however, is never conscious of any want of art, carried away as he is by flow of language and rapid succession of poetical imagery," he elaborates (54). As we see this quotation (actually an exaggeration about Qu Yuan's art), we begin to understand why Pound was drawn to Qu Yuan in his late 1913 exploration of Chinese poetry.

Indeed, by engaging himself in Qu Yuan (ca. 340–ca. 278 B.C.), Pound had engaged himself in China's first great poet. As all scholars agree, Chinese poetry originated from two early anthologies: *The Book of Songs* (*Shi jing*), supposedly compiled by Confucius in the sixth century B.C., and *The Songs of Chu* (*Chu ci*) by Qu Yuan and his imitators, who

10. Zhao Mengfu (1254–1322), "Portrait of Qu Yuan," from *Illustrations for The Nine Songs*. The Metropolitan Museum of Art, Fletcher Fund, 1973.

flourished from the fourth century B.C. onward.[6] Considering that Qu Yuan embodies one of the two origins of Chinese poetry, Giles has done no justice to him by alloting him three pages. (By contrast, the mid-Tang poet Bo Juyi (Po Chü-i) is generously covered in eleven pages.) In this limited space, Giles does, though, provide a brief biography. Qu Yuan (see fig. 10) was "a loyal Minister," he reports, who fell out of favor with his Prince owing to rivals' slanders, and who composed in disappointment and anguish the epic elegy *Li sao*, or "Falling into Trouble" (also translated "Encountering Sorrow"). Sinking into further rejection and banishment, he finally committed suicide by drowning himself in the Miluo River, a tributary of the Yangtze. The event gave rise to the modern Dragon-Boat Festival (on the fifth day of the fifth month), which is supposed to be a search for the national poet's body (50–52).

Several essential facts must be added to Giles' account of the poet's life and career, however.[7] First, Qu Yuan lived in the southern state of Chu, on the Yangtze and Han rivers, in a period of war and disruption. As a minister, he advised his king to unite with the peaceful state Qi in resistance to the militant power Qin. His insightful position was, however, ignored. Eventually, he lived to see his beloved kingdom fall before the invading troops of Qin. Second, born in an aristocratic family, Qu Yuan was immersed in the Chu upper-class culture, that is, their court poetry, dance, and music. His duties to receive state visitors and to serve as an envoy, moreover, enabled him to become familiar with the culture of the northern neighbors. Accordingly, his poetry prior to his banishment was already marked by a feature we now call biculturalism.

Third, his prolonged exile in southern Chu on the banks of the River Xiang and the River Yuan (in present-day southwestern Hunan province) actually gave him the rare opportunity to come into contact with the primitive culture of the region. The bizarre dialects, the unfamiliar legends, and particularly the *wu* (shaman) songs and dance that played an important role in the southern Chu people's religious and cultural life,[8] provided Qu Yuan with a variety of new images, motifs, and verse forms. Thanks to his study of the remarkable and fascinating culture of what was then China's deep South, Qu Yuan was able to create a verse style suitable for expressing complicated thoughts and emotions.[9] In composing his most impressive later work, *The Nine Songs* (*Jiu ge*),[10] he is believed to be directly imitating the *wu* (shaman) songs sung by the natives in sacrificial rites to bring gods or goddesses down from heaven. Giles, who makes no reference to these biographical details, does offer a prose translation of a specimen from the charming *Nine Songs*. Since it was in this version, which Giles calls "The Genius of the Mountain" (*Shan gui*), that Pound first discovered Chinese Imagism, it is worth our while to quote it in its entirety:

Methinks there is a Genius of the hills, clad in wistaria, girdled with ivy, with smiling lips, of witching mien, riding on the red pard, wild cats galloping in the rear, reclining in a chariot, with banners of cassia, cloaked with the orchid, girt with azalea, culling the perfume of sweet flowers to leave behind a memory in the heart. But dark is the grove wherein I dwell. No light of day reaches it ever. The path thither is dangerous and difficult to climb. Alone I stand on the hill-top, while the clouds float beneath my feet, and all around is wrapped in gloom.

Gently blows the east wind: softly falls the rain. In my joy I become oblivious of home; for who in my decline would honour me now?

I pluck the larkspur on the hillside, amid the chaos of rock and tangled vine. I hate him who has made me an outcast, who has now no leisure to think of me.

I drink from the rocky spring. I shade myself beneath the spreading pine. Even though he were to recall me to him, I could not fall to the level of the world.

Now booms the thunder through the drizzling rain. The gibbons howl around me all the long night. The gale rushed fitfully through the whispering trees. And I am thinking of my Prince, but in vain; for I cannot lay my grief. (52–53)[11]

James Liu might point out that Giles' version has ignored Qu Yuan's musical sense, embodied in his characteristic seven-syllable lines divided in the middle by a meaningless *xi* sound. David Hawkes will complain that "[l]ike most of Giles' translations from the Chinese," this is "elegant and extremely readable, but free in a rather arbitrary way . . . " (*Ch'u Tz'u* 215). While all this is true, Giles deserves credit for having preserved in his rendering Qu Yuan's symbolic language, pictorial analogies, and love and fertility motifs borrowed from primitive cults. Evidently, these elements correspond precisely to what Pound had held to be essential in Imagist poetry. For one thing, as Giles' version has shown, this poem is about the human state of mind, or states of mind. Pound was too familiar with the use of masks or personae to have mistaken the ancient poem for the utterance of a Chinese mountain deity. Qu Yuan as a discarded minister obviously had in mind his political situation when recasting the shaman song. For another, the speaker communicates exclusively through concrete, natural symbols. (In fact, almost all of Qu Yuan's speakers communicate through natural symbols. James Liu is not exaggerating when he calls Qu Yuan the "poet who made most extensive use of symbolism in Chinese" (126–27).) The flowers ("orchid," "azalea," etc.), the plants ("wistaria," "ivy," etc.), the animals ("red pard," "wild cats," etc.), and the phenomena of nature ("clouds," "rain," etc.) that she refers to are not colorful ornaments, but essentials of the lyric's emotional complex. In Pound's terms, these images accurately indicating the speaker's changing emotions—her joy and anxiety on the prospect of meeting her "Prince" and her disappointment and frustration when her "Prince" fails to descend—are "[t]he statements of 'analytics'" (GB 91), "lords over fact, over race-long recurrent moods, and over to-morrow" (92).

This latter quality Pound also calls equation. Ever since he became involved with T. E. Hulme's school of the Image, Pound had held the notion that "Poetry is a sort of inspired mathematics, which gives us equations, not for abstract figures, triangles, spheres, and the like, but equations for the human emotions" (SR 14). Hulme, who had introduced Pound to this concept, considered it the first principle of modern poetry (73). Ironically, however, Pound had found this mode of expression most vividly exemplified in ancient Greek songs. In The Spirit of Romance, he has, moreover, demonstrated the restoration of the technique with a new vigor in twelfth-century troubadour songs. "[I]n most Provençal poetry," he remarks, "one finds nature in its proper place, i.e. as a background to the action, an interpretation of the mood; an equation, in other terms, or a 'metaphor by sympathy' for the mood of the poem" (31). Now Giles' version of the ancient Chinese song had shown to Pound, quite surprisingly, how Qu Yuan had developed to perfection the method he had admired in the Greek and the Provençal poets—the method he now considered the Doctrine of the Image. Little wonder that upon reading Giles' version Pound should call Qu Yuan a fourth-century B.C. "Imagiste."

But Qu Yuan, as revealed in Giles' version, had some other attraction for Pound. For all his cultural differences, the Chinese poet resembles the Greek and the Provençal poets evidently more than just in the choice of a poetic mode. As has been stated above, Qu Yuan's "The Genius of the Mountain," like his other poems in The Nine Songs, is generally held to be an elegant remolding of a wu (shaman) song sung by southern Chu natives during fertility rites. Even though no reference to such critical detail is made in Giles' introduction, the version's likeness to Greek and troubadour songs in its portrayal of an erotic deity-mortal encounter and its excessive use of fertility symbols is unlikely to have escaped Pound's acute attention. Indeed, Hugh Witemeyer, in discussing the Greek and the Chinese influence on Pound, has noted that "What might have caught Pound's eye in this passage is its resemblance to a Bacchic procession" (127). There is of course no depiction of a Bacchic procession in Qu Yuan's poem. But Giles' presentation of the Chinese deity "clad in wistaria, girdled with ivy . . . riding on the red pard" with "wild cats galloping in the rear" is strongly suggestive of the vision of Dionysus and the voice of a female worshiper. The striking parallel between the two myths, coupled with other Imagistic qualities that the two traditions happen to share, may well have inspired Pound to adapt Giles' version of the Chinese fertility song into "After Ch'u Yuan":

> I will get me to the wood
> Where the gods walk garlanded in wistaria,
> By the silver blue flood
>   move others with ivory cars.
> There come forth many maidens
>   to gather grapes for the leopards, my friend,
> For there are leopards drawing the cars.
>
> I will walk in the glade,
> I will come out from the new thicket
>   and accost the procession of maidens.
> (P 110)

Here we see that the Imagist spirit of Qu Yuan has entered Pound via Giles as the American poet opens himself to the Chinese influence. Superficially, as K. K. Ruthven has noted, Pound has ignored Qu Yuan's grief theme and borrowed but a few striking images from Giles' version, such as the deity "clad in wistaria," the chariot drawn by "the red pard," the dark grove, and the tangled vine (31). In essence, however, Pound has not only taken vivid phrases from the Chinese model, but, more importantly, followed Qu Yuan's mythical vision and objective approach. It is true that Pound had learned the latter qualities from his earlier models. But it was in the Chinese example that he really saw what Hulme had called a continuous "choosing and working-up of analogies" (85).

As we have seen, Qu Yuan's art was one of perfect equilibrium between a succession of selected images and a succession of selected emotions. To recreate this art would require not only skill, but a redefinition of the Image as a "VORTEX," that is, "a radiant node or cluster . . . , from which, and through which, and into which, ideas are constantly rushing" (GB 92). For the moment, nonetheless, Pound had not fully developed this idea, and so had to be satisfied with his original notion of the Image as "an intellectual and emotional complex in an instant of time" (LE 4). Accordingly, in his adaptation of Giles' version, he had chosen to leave to Qu Yuan the deity's grievous moment, and reproduce only the instant of her glory and happiness. The result of this choice is a loss of resourcefulness, but a gain in concentration. He had taken from the Chinese only the typical and the usable, that is, its pictorial manner, its supernatural overtone, and its fertility motif. As the Chinese primitive cult embodied in the song quite resembled its Greek counterpart, Pound could not resist the temptation of "increas[ing] the Greek overtones of the original by adding maidens and grapes" (Witemeyer 127). Steeped in the Greek classics, Pound probably had in mind *The Homeric Hymn to Dionysos* and Euripides' *Bacchae*. *The Homeric Hymn to Dionysos*, one will recall, sings: "There is a certain Nysa, a lofty mountain overgrown with trees, / far from Phoinike and near the flowing stream of the Aigyptos" (Athanassakis 1). And in the opening scene of the *Bacchae*, we hear a voice that echoes Qu Yuan's speaker,

> Who lingers in the road? Who espies us?
> He shall hide him in his house nor be bold.
> Let the heart keep silence that defies us;
> For I sing this day to Dionysus
> The song that is appointed from of old.

which is followed by the chorus of all the maidens,

His head with ivy laden
    And his thyrsus tossing high,
    For our God he lifts his cry;
"Up, O Bacchae, wife and maiden,
    Come, O ye Bacchae, come;
    Oh, bring the Joy-bestower,
    God-seed of God the Sower,
    Bring Bromios in his power
        From Phrygia's mountain dome;
    To street and town and tower,
        Oh, bring ye Bromios home!"
(Murray 82–83)[12]

Ironically, Pound's merging of images from Chinese and Greek myths in "After Ch'u Yuan," which is generally seen as a disruptive endeavor, will find support in current Qu Yuan criticism. The subject of Qu Yuan's *Shan gui* ("The Mountain Spirit") is traditionally held to be a female deity rather than a male god. In his illustration for "The Mountain Spirit" (fig. 11), the fourteenth-century artist Zhao Mengfu, for instance, portrays a woman-like figure sitting on a leopard shading beneath a pine tree. The seventeenth-century painter Xiao Yuncong, in his version of "The Mountain Spirit" (fig. 12), likewise delineates a lady-like character with ivy around her forehead riding a leopard, flanked by a lynx and a gibbon. Qu Yuan critic Gu Chengtian, in *A Commentary to* The Nine Songs, takes the mountain deity to be the Goddess of Wu (the Lady of Gaotang), a goddess of fertility, above the Yangtze gorges, which opinion has been followed by most modern commentators. Taiwan critic Su Xuelin was perhaps the first to contradict this established view by asserting that the mountain spirit is the effeminate male god Dionysus.[13] Sacred to Dionysus, he argues in *Qu Yuan yu Jiu ge* (Qu Yuan and *The Nine Songs*),[14] are the vine, the ivy, the leopard, and the lynx. Qu Yuan's mountain genius characteristically has all these (the vine in the form of the wistaria, though).[15]

The Greek word "Dionysus" literally means the god of Nysa or the god of the sacred mountain. Qu Yuan's *Shan gui* virtually contains the same

11. Zhao Mengfu (1254–1322), "The Mountain Spirit," from *Illustrations for The Nine Songs*. The Metropolitan Museum of Art, Fletcher Fund, 1973.

meaning. Dionysus was worshiped by maidens on top of forested mountains in ancient Greece. So was Qu Yuan's mountain genius in ancient China (495–98). As for where Qu Yuan heard about the Dionysian cult, Su offers the following explanation. The cult, originally Western Asian, was probably brought to China along with the second wave of immigration from Western Asia during the period of the Warring States (475–221 B.C.). The Han historian Sima Qian (A.D. 145–90), in the "Biogra-

12. Xiao Yuncong (1596–1673), "The Mountain Spirit,"
from *Illustrations for* The Nine Songs.

phies of Mencius and Xunzi," gave an account of how a visiting scholar
called Zou Yan stunned all the princes and lords of the state of Qi by
imparting to them his crafts and learning. Su argues that Qu Yuan, who
served as an envoy in Qi for four or five years during that period, could
have met this distinguished guest and heard from him about the myths of
Dionysus and his other deities (102–04).

While an overview of current scholarship on the Dionysian cult confirms many of the things said by Su Xuelin (Danielou, Evans, Carpenter, etc.), we find his supposition about where Qu Yuan heard about the myth of the god of ecstasy less convincing. As archeological studies have shown, the fertility rites depicted by Qu Yuan in *The Nine Songs* were observed in southern Chu (in what is now southwestern Hunan province) prior to Qu Yuan's own time (Chang 48). His text, moreover, reveals a knowledge about the music and dance of the rites keener than what might have been taken from a verbal description. Since Dionysus has left archeological evidence of his manifestations in many places in Europe, Africa, and Asia, one has reason to suspect that his cult was spread to South China, the region of rivers, lakes, and forested mountains, with an earlier wave of immigration (the first wave of immigration from Western Asia, as Su himself has referred to),[16] and gradually became merged with the local shaman rites. The Chinese *Shan gui* and the Greek Dionysus could have shared the same descent. But Qu Yuan's poem was, after all, modeled on a Chu shaman song.

Pound's very first attempt to invent China, we are to see, prefigures much of what was to come in *The Cantos*: his preoccupation with ancient and medieval myths, his tendency to link the Greek culture with the Chinese culture, and his talent for the style of allusion, ellipsis, and juxtaposition. Moreover, the Dionysian vision of "After Ch'u Yuan" was to appear in a new guise in Canto 2:

> And Lyaeus: "From now, Acoetes, my altars,
> Fearing no bondage,
>   fearing no cat of the wood,
> Safe with my lynxes,
>   feeding grapes to my leopards,
> Olibanum is my incense,
>   the vines grow in my homage."
> (CA 8–9)

Carroll Terrell is perceptive in identifying *The Homeric Hymn to Dionysos* and Euripides' *Bacchae* as Pound's sources for the fascinating Dionysian passage (4). But we can now add that Pound may also have had in mind Qu Yuan's "The Mountain Spirit" while composing the episode.

Pound was searching for fellow Imagists as he went through the pages of Giles' *History* in October 1913. Qu Yuan gave him an example that seemed both to fortify his early Imagist canons and to suggest a revision toward what was to become his Vorticist principles. The discovery of this fourth-century B.C. Chinese Imagist stimulated Pound to trace the development of his art in the hands of his imitators. To his satisfaction, he found among the half dozen Han poets (206 B.C. – A.D. 220) sketchily treated by Giles a true descendant of Qu Yuan. (In a few years he was to dig up Qu Yuan's most brilliant pupil, Song Yu or "Sō-gioku," among Fenollosa's Chinese poetry notes and to echo a whole passage from the latter's exquisite "Wind Poem" in Canto 4.) The name of this poet—Liu Che—has now entered Modernist literature through the medium of Pound. Not only has he called his version of the poet's work "Liu Ch'e," but he has referred to the poet in two of his seminal articles. In his 1914 essay on "Vorticism,"[17] he actually exploits Liu Che's and Ibycus' names to define Imagist verse: "The other sort of poetry is as old as the lyric and as honourable, but, until recently, no one had named it. Ibycus and Liu Ch'e presented the 'Image'" (GB 83). And in his 1915 essay "The Renaissance,"[18] he even envisages a literary revival of Liu Che, Qu Yuan, and Li Bo in twenty-first century: "Liu Ch'e, Chu Yuan, Chia I, and the great *vers libre* writers before the Petrarchan age of Li Po, are a treasury to which the next century may look for as great a stimulus as the renaissance had from the Greeks" (LE 218).

The extraordinary tribute Pound pays to the Chinese lyric tradition certainly sounds flattering to a Chinese reader. But that he should praise Liu Che in the same breath with Qu Yuan and Li Bo—not to mention placing him before Qu Yuan—will also amaze him. To a Chinese mind, Qu Yuan and Li Bo truly represent two glorious peaks in the history of Chinese poetry, whereas Liu Che, for all his enthusiasm for literature and art, was chiefly a powerful ruler whose fame rests on his conquest of the fierce northern tribes, the Xiongnu, and the opening of the famous "Silk Route" to the West.

Nevertheless, to say that Liu Che (156–87 B.C.), or Emperor Wu of the Han, was not a first-rate poet does not mean that he deserves no mention in the study of Chinese literature. His role in Han-dynasty

China was rather like that of Sigismondo Malatesta (1417–68) in Renaissance Rimini, a symbol for civilization and creative powers. It was during his prolonged reign (140–87 B.C.) that the new literary genre *fu*, coming after Qu Yuan's *Li sao* style, began to flourish. Among the brilliant *fu* writers who filled his court were the Confucian scholar Dong Zhongshu, the man of letters par excellence Sima Xiangru, the courtier Dong Fang-shuo, and the historian Sima Qian. And it was under his personal instructions that the *Yue fu*, or the Music Bureau, was expanded into a major government office in charge of collecting and refining folk songs. With the development of this institution, folk melodies were introduced into court poetry and a vigorous poetic form, *Yue fu* ballads, was born. As a great lover of literature, Liu Che occasionally brought forth excellent lines, which unavoidably combined influences of *fu* writings (or rhyme prose) and *Yue fu* ballads. Giles furnishes translations of two specimens in his *History*, and it was the second piece that fascinated Pound:

> The sound of rustling silk is stilled,
> With dust the marble courtyard filled;
> No footfalls echo on the floor,
> Fallen leaves in heaps block up the door. . . .
> For she, my pride, my lovely one, is lost,
> And I am left, in hopeless anguish tossed.
> (Giles 100)

To know what qualities in the version may have impressed Pound, one just has to quote what he has said of Li Bo's "The Jewel Stairs' Grievance" in his 1918 essay "Chinese Poetry," for the two lyrics really belong to the same heritage and evince a very similar beauty:[19]

I have never found any occidental who could "make much" of that poem at one reading. Yet upon careful examination we find that everything is there, not merely by "suggestion" but by a sort of mathematical process of reduction. (*EPPP* 3: 85)

Just as Pound has demonstrated the circumstances behind the vivid expressions in "The Jewel Stairs' Grievance," he must have perceived the circumstances behind the vivid expressions in this elegy:

First, "the marble courtyard"; therefore the scene is in a palace. Second, "rustling silk"; therefore the subject is a harem lady. Third, "The sound is . . . stilled" and "dust . . . filled"; therefore the beloved lady is gone. Fourth, "Fallen leaves . . . block up the door"; therefore the speaker is grieving over the loss of a past love. Indeed, it was with the vision of the circumstances, and with the appreciation of the Imagist method, that Pound was able to bring out a version closer to the Chinese original in spirit:

> The rustling of the silk is discontinued,
> Dust drifts over the court-yard,
> There is no sound of foot-fall, and the leaves
> Scurry into heaps and lie still,
> And she the rejoicer of the heart is beneath them:
>
> A wet leaf that clings to the threshold.
> (P 110–11)

Hugh Kenner is perfectly right in claiming that "'A wet leaf that clings to the threshold' simply applies Imagist canons, the mind's creative leap fetching some token of the gone woman into the poem's system." But he is inaccurate in asserting that "No wet leaf clings in the Chinese, and there is no indication that Pound supposed one did; he simply knew what his poem needed" (197). Sanehide Kodama has already pointed out that Pound's concluding line is a rewrite of "the fourth line of the original Chinese poem" (94). To this assertion I must make two further points. First, Pound's line is, after all, derived from Giles' "Fallen leaves in heaps block up the door." What he has done is simply to turn Giles' plural "Fallen leaves" to his singular "A wet leaf," Giles' colorless "block up" to his emotionally vivid "clings to," and Giles' general "door" to his concrete "threshold." Second, the fourth line in the original poem, *luo ye yi yu chong jiong* 落葉依於重扃, literally means "[A] fallen leaf leans on [the] doubled outer door-bar." Pound is able to catch Liu Che's vivid imagery precisely because he and the Chinese emperor-poet see things from the same point of view. For him, as for Liu Che, every word in the line is a painterly equation for sorrow. The "fallen leaf," or the "wet leaf," stands for the lady who has gone. (Number is absent in Chinese. Giles' plural form obliterates the symbol whereas Pound's singular form brings it into the light.) And as such, it "clings to" rather than "blocks up" the threshold reminiscent of many scenes of past love. Liu Che has picked the Chinese verb phrase *yi yu* for exactly the same reason that Pound has chosen the English verb phrase "clings to": it presents a picture of the mistress who has gone—Li Fu-jen, or Lady Li, as Arthur Waley's version (*Chinese Poems* 70) has revealed—lovingly holding on to him, and it communicates the sensation of her clutching onto his heart.

Pound calls this kind of verb a "picturesque verb." In *The Spirit of Romance*, he has demonstrated its value by citing examples from Arnaut Daniel. "Three times in this stanza," Pound observes after quoting from Arnaut, "the Provençal makes his picture, neither by simile nor by metaphor, but in the language beyond metaphor, by the use of the picturesque verb with an exact meaning" (33). The first half of Giles' version, with verbs such as "stilled," "filled," and "echo," quite adequately shows to Pound that the Chinese poet was a foster father of Arnaut Daniel. When he finds Giles' fourth line in need of a more painterly verb to suggest accurately the speaker's deep sorrow, he simply supplies one of his own, thus regaining the emotional strength of the original line.

A wet leaf, therefore, clings in Chinese. (Even "wet" is implied in the original image, for a dry leaf obviously cannot lean on an outer door-bar.) What is really invented by Pound here is his isolating the line from the main strophe and placing it at the bottom, perhaps "in conformity with his notion of superposition" (Kodama 94). Amusingly, the Chinese poet is also aware of the need of throwing light on his central image. Unlike Pound, who places "A wet leaf" in a separate line at the bottom—which is a French device exploited by him in the contemporaneous "April" and "Gentildonna"—Liu Che highlights "A fallen leaf" in his title, *Luo ye ai chan qu*, which literally means "Cicada's Elegy for a Fallen Leaf."[20]

Liu Che is undoubtedly a Poundian hero, like Sigismondo Malatesta. His *Luo ye ai chan qu* is just another "Tempio Malatestiano to Isotta."[21] Accordingly, it is most fitting that Pound should call forth the Han monarch-poet's pure image in Canto 7, the canto that immediately precedes the Malatesta Cantos:

We also made ghostly visits, and the stair
That knew us, found us again on the turn of it,
Knocking at empty rooms, seeking for buried beauty;
And the sun-tanned, gracious and well-formed fingers
Lift no latch of bent bronze, no Empire handle
Twists for the knocker's fall; no voice to answer.
A strange concierge, in place of the gouty-footed.
Sceptic against all this one seeks the living,
Stubborn against the fact. The wilted flowers
Brushed out a seven year since, of no effect.
Damn the partition! Paper, dark brown and stretched,
Flimsy and damned partition.
                    Ione, dead the long year
My lintel, and Liu Ch'e's lintel.
(CA 25)

The reference here is to the near past as well as to the remote past, where Liu Che revisited his mistress' empty chamber with a heavy heart. In the passage Pound has replaced his earlier "threshold" with "lintel." His preference for metonymy—"threshold" or "lintel" or "latch" or "Empire handle" or "knocker" for "door"—is shared by the Chinese emperor-poet, for the effect of Liu Che's *chong jiong* 重扃 ("doubled door-bar") is also to secure a greater concreteness in the image. It is precisely the shared taste that has drawn Pound to Liu Che, and it is precisely the common point of view that has made the communication between the Han monarch and the twentieth-century American poet easier than assumed.

But in October 1913, Pound had dialogues with other Han literary geniuses as well. Mei Sheng's "Green grows the grass upon the bank" (Giles, *History* 97), whose solitary speaker is copied in a 1910–12 British Museum exhibit, *A Lady Meditating by a Lake* (fig. 13), apparently caught his eye. A year later, when he came upon Fenollosa's version of the same poem, he was to make "The Beautiful Toilet" for *Cathay* using Giles' date and Giles' spelling of the poet's name (Kenner 195). Ban Jieyu, or the Lady Ban, may have appeared a familiar name to Pound by the fall of 1913. The figure is a subject in the most imposing monument of Chinese

13. Anonymous (after Qiu Ying) (ca. 1510–52),
A Lady Meditating by a Lake. The British Museum, London.

painting at the British Museum, *Admonitions of the Instructress to Court Ladies,*
attributed to the fourth-century A.D. artist Gu Kaizhi (ca. 345–406).[22]
The masterpiece, originally preserved in the Imperial Palace in Beijing,
was lost during the "Boxer Rebellion" of 1900. In 1903, the British Mu-
seum announced that it had "[become] possessed of" the Chinese paint-
ing (Binyon, *Painting in the Far East* 37). According to Binyon, in the 1910–
12 Exhibition of Chinese and Japanese Paintings, this approximately 9"
× 11' handscroll consisting of nine impressive illustrations to a Han
didactic text by a certain Zhang Hua (232–300) occupied the most
prominent position—Slope One directly facing the entrance to the Gal-
lery (*Guide* 8 and 14).

Pound, being a fervent admirer of Chinese art, certainly couldn't have missed contemplating this rarity, which presents a whole series of drama and movement in early Chinese court life by means of fine linear rhythms. Moreover, Binyon, who was put in charge of the painting, devotes a whole chapter of *Painting in the Far East* to discussing its significance and extraordinary artistic value. Speaking of the Lady Ban's scene in the masterpiece (see fig. 5), he informs us that it shows the imperial concubine "refusing the Emperor's invitation to ride with him in his palanquin. 'In days of old,' she is reported to have answered, 'only ministers rode beside their monarch'" (40). In the scene, the rhythm of Gu Kaizhi's linear style is vividly displayed in the flying scarves of the Lady Ban as she moves forward to decline the Emperor's invitation. An account of the same episode is given in Giles' *History*. Giles, however, goes on to tell us that this favorite of Emperor Cheng of the Han (32–6 B.C.) "was ultimately supplanted by a younger and more beautiful rival." In disgrace and anguish, Lady Ban, whom W. A. P. Martin calls "the Sappho of China" (82), made a fan poem titled "Song of Regret" (*Yuan ge xing*) for the heartless Emperor, which subsequently got into various anthologies as an exquisite example of the Han *Yue fu* ballads:

> O fair white silk, fresh from the weaver's loom,
> Clear as the frost, bright as the winter snow—
> See! friendship fashions out of thee a fan,
> Round as the round moon shines in heaven above,
> At home, abroad, a close companion thou,
> Stirring at every move the grateful gale.
> And yet I fear, ah me! that autumn chills,
> Cooling the dying summer's torrid rage,
> Will see thee laid neglected on the shelf,
> All thought of bygone days, like them bygone.
> (101)

What might have struck Pound in this longish version by Giles is the Lady Ban's powerful equation of a woman's fate with that of a white silk fan. He increased the intensity of the equation by reducing the ten lines in pentameter from Giles to a *haiku*:

> *Fan-Piece, for her Imperial Lord*
> O fan of white silk,
>   clear as frost on the grass-blade,
> You also are laid aside.
> (*P* 111)

Pound had experimented with the Japanese form in other poems, but this appears to be more like a genuine *haiku*. Not only has it followed the 5–7–5 syllabic pattern more rigorously, but it has an authentic Far Eastern content. (By contrast, his "Metro" poem has a contemporary French subject, and "Alba" contains a Provençal overtone.) It is worth remarking here that Lady Ban's poem is written in *wuyan* (pentasyllabic lines), a blood brother of the Japanese *haiku*. According to C. W. Luh, the latter is a variant of the former (106.)[23] At any rate, both verse forms are characterized by pithy, short lines. (A more literal rendering of the opening couplet would be: "Newly cut white silk, / Clear as frost and snow.") So, by adopting *haiku*, Pound had actually adopted a form most appropriate for the Chinese original.

Upward had shown Pound that Chinese poems could be invented as well by writing from one's "Chinese reminiscence." The idea may well have inspired Pound to make his "Ts'ai Chi'h":

> The petals fall in the fountain,
>   the orange-coloured rose-leaves,
> Their ochre clings to the stone.
> (*P* 111)

Although the poem has no definite identity (Achilles Fang 236), its images can be traced to separate lines in Giles' *History*. The "fountain" image, for example, is in Tao Qian's (T'ao Ch'ien) celebrated title "Peach-blossom Fountain" (130). And "The petals fall" appears in Du Fu's line, "A petal falls!—the spring begins to fail" (157). A closer scrutiny reveals, however, that Pound's poem is really an attempt to imitate the Chinese art of equating color with mood. Giles' *History* furnishes nothing distinctly representative of this technique, but a slender volume of Chinese poems published in 1913 offers a lyric with striking parallels in this respect to Pound's "Ts'ai Chi'h":

Peach blossom after rain
  Is deeper red;
The willow fresher green;
  Twittering overhead;
And fallen petals lie wind-blown,
Unswept upon the courtyard stone.
(Waddell 33)

Even though the title and the original poet's name are not given, we are able to identify the piece as a freehand rendering of a six-syllable quatrain (*liuyan jueju*) by the Tang painter-poet Wang Wei (599–659), who brought to perfection the art of equating color with sentiment. We have no evidence to prove that Pound had actually been influenced by this version in Helen Waddell's *Lyrics from the Chinese*. But we do know that three or four years later he was to go to a great deal of labor in order to make a fine version out of Fenollosa's approximation of that same poem. I will return to Pound's encounter with Wang Wei in Chapter Six. Here suffice it to observe that Pound's version of that poem, which appears in the November 1918 *Little Review* under the title "Dawn on the Mountain," retains an emphasis on color and projects the image of "fallen petals" also. The picturesque verb "clings to" and the image of "fountain" that occur in "Ts'ai Chi'h" are missing in Pound's version. But referring to that poem in a 1919 essay, he picks them up again: "The mist clings to the lacquer. His [de Gourmont's] spirit was the spirit of Omakitsu [Wang Wei]; his *pays natal* was near to the peach-blossom-fountain of the untranslatable poem [Wang Wei's poem]" (*LE* 343).

3 CHINA CONTRA

GREECE IN *DES IMAGISTES*

Pound had another scheme on his mind while he was meeting Mrs. Fenollosa and exploring Chinese poetry via Giles in October 1913: the making of *Des Imagistes*. Since some critics have stated that Pound shipped the manuscript of *Des Imagistes* to the United States for publication in the summer of 1913 (Gallup 137; Kenner 178), I have to clarify a few points before I can go on to show the connection between Pound's discovery of Chinese Imagism and the completion of the first Imagist anthology.

Des Imagistes: An Anthology was published in February 1914 as the fifth number of the short-lived New York periodical *The Glebe*. It was reissued as a book in March 1914 by Albert and Charles Boni, who sponsored *The Glebe*, and in April 1914 by the Poetry Bookshop in London. In his autobiographical *Troubadour* (1925), Alfred Kreymborg offers a detailed account of how he founded the little magazine with his artist friends Man Ray and Samuel Halpert, and how they received the manuscript of *Des Imagistes* from London while awaiting their printing press. He also recalls that originally they planned to put the anthology in their very first issue, but that Albert and Charles Boni, who took over the financing of the magazine in the early fall, had them change the plans (202–05). Supported by excerpts from Pound's letters and card, Kreymborg's account of the episodes sounds quite convincing. Though he supplies no specific dates (no dates for Pound's letters and card either), what he has explicitly said implies that the manuscript of *Des Imagistes* arrived in New York in the summer of 1913.

Thanks to Charles Norman, who took the trouble to inspect the complete set of *The Glebe* (ten issues starting from September 1913) and to interview Albert Boni, one of its two publishers, we are now able to see "some of the errors that crept into [Kreymborg's] account, and thence into *The Little Magazines: A History and a Bibliography*, the authors of which, having placed their reliance on Kreymborg's *Troubadour*, perpetuated his errors" (112). *The Glebe* may not have been founded by Kreymborg, Man Ray, and Sam Halpert. Internal evidence only shows that the former became editor of the magazine with the second number (November 1913).[1] Writing "a dozen years after the events he describes," Norman explains, "it is probable that [Kreymborg], like others before him, has merged two periods—that of *The Glebe*, of which he was not the founder, and that of *Others*, of which he was" (112).

That Kreymborg began editing *The Glebe* in the fall of 1913 rather than in the summer of 1913 is confirmed by John Cournos, "[o]ne of the first men to whom he appealed for material" (Kreymborg 203). According to the Russian-born poet and art critic, who "was directly instrumental" in the publication of *Des Imagistes*, he received Kreymborg's letter inviting him to contribute to "the Glebe series of short books" before he set sail to see his girlfriend in the U.S. in the winter of 1913–14.[2] He "happened to mention Kreymborg's request to Ezra Pound, who was compiling *Des Imagistes: An Anthology*. Thus the first Imagist anthology came to be published" (Cournos 269–70).

Cournos has not told us exactly when he mentioned to Pound Kreymborg's request for contribution to *The Glebe*. The actual date may well have been after the middle of October 1913 because there is evidence that Pound set out to put together the Imagist anthology in late October 1913. Norman discovered in the Houghton Library of Harvard University a letter from John Gould Fletcher, dated 7 September 1913, warning Amy Lowell against going into Pound's Imagist volume (110–11). The fact that Fletcher mentions in that same letter that Richard Aldington and H. D. are just married (" . . . (he [Richard Aldington] has just married H. D. another 'arriviste') . . . ") precisely proves that he wrote that letter not in early September 1913 but in late October—or even early November—1913, for Richard Aldington and H. D. were married after 18 October 1913.[3]

Pound's letter to Amy Lowell, asking for permission to use her poem in the anthology, written, according to D. D. Paige, on an unspecified date in November 1913, further confirms that Pound was putting together the manuscript of *Des Imagistes* between late October and early November 1913: "I'd like to use your 'In a Garden' in a brief anthology *Des Imagstes* that I am cogitating—unless you've something that you think more appropriate" (*L* 61). I believe that Pound must have finished editing the Imagist collection by early November 1913 because, on 7 November 1913, he wrote Harriet Monroe: "By the way *The Glebe* is to do our Imagiste anthology. There'll be various reprints from *Poetry*" (*L* 62). The quote clearly indicates that Pound had gotten word from Kreymborg that the latter was to issue his anthology as a *Glebe* book. If he had not yet sent out the manuscript of *Des Imagistes* to New York by that date, he was to do so pretty soon.

The publication of the first Imagist anthology was indeed delayed, for if the manuscript of *Des Imagistes* really reached New York by early November 1913, it should have been able to catch at least the January 1914 number of *The Glebe*. Kreymborg would have to write to Pound accounting for the delay, since he may have promised him to bring out the anthology as soon as possible. Here we can trust Kreymborg's memory. He may indeed have received a card from Pound with the terse phrase, "All right, we can wait" (205). But the waiting, on the other hand, gave Pound the opportunity to add to his Imagist volume one more impressive piece, James Joyce's "I Hear an Army." We are not certain if it was Yeats or Pound himself who unearthed "I Hear an Army," the last poem in Joyce's *Chamber Music* (1907). Norman thinks that since Pound was "a frequenter of Elkin Mathews's bookstore on Vigo Street he would have seen" copies of Joyce's *Chamber Music* there (107). At any rate, on 26 December 1913, Pound wrote the Irish writer, who was residing in Trieste: "Yeats has just found your 'I hear an Army' and we are both much impressed by it. This is a business note from me and compliments from him. I want permission to use the poem in my anthology of Imagists" (*PJ* 18–19).

Now we see that F. S. Flint's description of the event in his 1915 "History of Imagism" is precise:

Towards the end of the year [1913] Pound collected together a number of poems of different writers, Richard Aldington, H. D., F. S. Flint, Skipwith Cannell, Amy Lowell, William Carlos Williams, James Joyce, John Cournos, Ezra Pound, Ford Madox Heuffer and Allan [*sic*] Upward, and in February– March 1914 they were published in America and England as "Des Imagistes: An Anthology," which, though it did not set the Thames, seems to have set America, on fire. Since then Mr. Ezra Pound has become a "Vorticist". . . . (71)

Kreymborg's account of the episode, though containing a lot of intriguing details, is loose in dates. By proving that the bulk of *Des Imagistes* was put together not in the summer of 1913, as Kreymborg has implied, but in the fall of 1913, or, to be more precise, between late October and early November 1913, we have revealed an immediate relation between Pound's initial Chinese exploration and his final effort to promote the Imagist movement.

Indeed, in early September 1913, Pound was already planning the first Imagist anthology. On September 6 of that year he wrote his mother: "am thinking of publishing a small anthology of *les jeunes*."[4] His casual remark—"*les jeunes*"—reveals a French orientation for the volume. Since August 1913 Pound had been reading Corbière, Tailhade, de Gourmont, and Jammes; and until mid-September of that year he was writing "The Approach to Paris" articles. (In that same letter to his mother, he mentions that he had "only 1½ more articles to do for N. A.") Should Pound have set out to edit the Imagist volume in September 1913, he would have brought into it more French elements. There are several poems with French tones in his "Contemporania" sequence that could have been selected to represent his Imagist ideals in the anthology. But it happened that the making of *Des Imagistes* was postponed to late October 1913. By then he could no longer edit the Imagist anthology in the way he would have done earlier. His meeting with Mary Fenollosa on 29 September 1913 opened up a new phase in his career—the phase marked by his Chinese studies. In the Chinese models provided by Giles (notably Qu Yuan and Liu Che), Pound found an art more objective than the Greek, more suggestive than the Provençal, more precise than the modern French, and more brilliant and resourceful than the medieval Japanese. To illustrate his Imagist theories now, he would have to include, among other things, the Chinese voice.

Commenting on the first Imagist anthology, Norman observes that "Two things strike a reader at once—the many poems, including four of Pound's six, which are adapted from the Chinese or formed on Chinese models, and many, including Pound's other two, which are influenced by Greek art, thought and poetry" (113). The Greek-Chinese combination indeed reflects what Pound was thinking at the moment when he edited *Des Imagistes*. While reading Giles' translations of classical Chinese poetry, he was struck by an affinity between the two ancient traditions. He must have seen that "Hardness of outline, clarity of image, brevity, suggestiveness, freedom from metrical laws—these and other imagist ideals could be drawn from Greek as well as from Hebrew or Chinese" (Hughes 4). Thus, in compiling the first Imagist anthology, he gave prominence only to poems modeled on the Greek and the Chinese.

Contributing to the Greek tone of *Des Imagistes* are, first of all, H. D.'s and Richard Aldington's poems. These include the two Hellenists' earliest Imagist verses: H. D.'s "Hermes of the Ways," "Priapus" ("Orchard" or "Spare Us from Loveliness"), and "Epigram," and Aldington's "Choricos," "To a Greek Marble," "Au Vieux Jardin," and "To Atthis (After the Manuscript of Sappho now in Berlin)." It was by these poems that Pound was inspired to set up the Imagist club with H. D. and Aldington in the late spring or the early summer of 1912. It was with these poems in his mind that he set forth the three Imagist principles:

1. Direct treatment of the "thing" whether subjective or objective.

2. To use absolutely no word that does not contribute to the presentation.

3. As regarding rhythm: to compose in the sequence of the musical phrase, not in the sequence of a metronome. (*LE* 3)

Pound's admiration for H. D.'s poems is expressed in a letter of October 1912 to Harriet Monroe: "This is the sort of American stuff that I can show here and in Paris without its being ridiculed. Objective—no slither; direct—no excessive use of adjectives, no metaphors that won't permit examination. It's straight talk, straight as the Greek!" (*L* 45). His enthusiasm for Aldington's earliest Imagist work is shown in his persistence in publishing the latter's "To Atthis." Harriet Monroe, who received the four poems by Aldington along with Pound's recommendation in October 1912, printed the first three in the November 1912 *Poetry*. But she rejected the last piece, "To Atthis," on the ground that Chicago scholars "wouldn't stand for" something so far from the original (qtd. in Kenner 55). To Pound, however, Aldington's version was a beautiful restoration of Sappho's capacity for equating imagery with human emotion. Kenner has noted in the poem a charm shared by "The Jewel Stairs' Grievance" of *Cathay*, which "is especially prized because [the speaker] utters no direct reproach" (57). The same charm produced by suggestion is visible in "Liu Ch'e," Pound's earlier imitation of a Chinese puzzle. One has only to recall Pound's "A wet leaf that clings to the threshold" to know how deeply he may have appreciated Aldington's "And the dew is shed upon the flowers" in "To Atthis" (*DI* 19).

The Greek influence is present also in William Carlos Williams' contribution to the volume, "Postlude." The poem was taken from Pound's college pal's second book of verse, *The Tempers*, brought out by Pound's English publisher Elkin Mathews in mid-September 1913. Although Pound had been promoting Williams' poetry since summer 1913, there were but two poems in *The Tempers* that he could really put up with: "Hic Jacet" for its "new, sardonic tone" (Mariani 100), and "Postlude" for its "classical allusions" and "a new rhythm, closer to [his] own advanced metrical experiments" (105).

To further increase the Greek tone of the anthology, Pound tossed in his "Δώρια" and "The Return." The two "Greek" poems were created before Pound formed the Imagist club with H. D. and Aldington,[5] but they foreshadowed much of what was to come out of Pound in the programmatic year of 1913–14. Indeed, Pound not only includes the two pieces in *Des Imagistes*, but employs them in his 1914 essay on "Vorticism" as examples to redefine the "Image." As Witemeyer (115) has noted, Pound clearly has "Δώρια" in mind when he remarks in "Vorticism": "By the 'image' I mean such an equation; not an equation of mathematics, not something about *a, b*, and *c*, having something to do with form, but about *sea, cliffs, night*, having something to do with mood" (*GB* 92). And about "The Return," he observes in that same article, "Secondly, I made poems like 'The Return,' which is an objective reality and has a complicated sort of significance, like Mr. Epstein's 'Sun God,' or Mr. Brzeska's 'Boy with a Coney'" (85).

If the "Greek" poems in *Des Imagistes* are in the main early Imagist work, what constitutes the new face of the volume is the group of verses modeled on the Chinese. Among these are Allen Upward's "Scented Leaves from a Chinese Jar," which first sparked Pound's enthusiasm for Chinese colors, and Pound's "After Ch'u Yuan," "Liu Ch'e," "The Fan-Piece, for her Imperial Lord," and "Ts'ai Chi'h." Sanehide Kodama suggests that "Pound probably worked on [the four 'Chinese' poems] as a kind of exercise or étude while awaiting the arrival of the notebooks of Ernest Fenollosa" (62). While this assumption is admissible, I also suspect that Pound wrote these poems especially for the first Imagist anthology. My clue is again from the personal correspondence between Ezra and Dorothy in late 1913. Omar Pound told me that his mother Dorothy started learning Chinese about 1901.[6] Between 1911 and 1912, as I stated previously, Dorothy regularly visited the British Museum to draw pictures after Chinese models.[7] And in 1913 she resumed her Chinese lessons using Sir Walter Caine Hillier's *The Chinese Language and How to Learn It* as a teach-yourself book (ED 298 n). As Dorothy had such a passion for Chinese culture, Pound shared with her virtually everything remarkable in Giles' *History*. In a letter to Pound dated 9 October 1913, Dorothy asked about "the 4th Cent. B.C. Chinese" (ED 269). Two days later Pound responded: "you can have [Herbert] Giles' 'Hist. of Chinese Lit' . . . " (270).

Curiously, between late October and early November 1913, there was no correspondence exchanged. And then, on 20 November, Dorothy wrote Pound asking: "Can *I* have any of the Chinese poems to read—some time?" (275) The next day word came from Pound: "I will copy those [poems]—no I won't I'll bring 'em on Wednesday. Them Chineze (Chinese poems). They are only very small 3½ poems" (276). The "3½ poems" Pound speaks of here are no doubt "After Ch'u Yuan," "Liu Ch'e," "Fan-Piece, for her Imperial Lord," and "Ts'ai Chi'h." It seems most likely that Pound made these adaptations in early November 1913 while he was collecting together *Des Imagistes*.

By bringing in the Chinese poems in the first Imagist volume, Pound had actually pointed out to the Imagist movement a new direction and a new possibility—the possibility of drawing on the robust Imagistic tradition of the Chinese. It is true that the qualities Pound admired in the Chinese masters are the same qualities he had sought in his earlier models. But to him China was a crystallizing influence. It was through the examples of Qu Yuan and Liu Che that Pound most accurately defined what he believed to be the Doctrine of the Image. Objectivity, precision, and intensity had always been Pound's poetic ideals. But now that he had studied Giles' History, he realized that the poetry he was building up had a strong kinship to the spirit of China. It is not surprising, then, that he made an effort to bring to his Imagism a further intensity and suggestivity. As a result, the Chinese influence was to be visible in a considerable number of poems written during this period.

In response to Kate Buss' review of his 1916 Lustra, Pound denied the impact of Fenollosa's Chinese poetry notes on that book (L 154). It is true that most of the poems subsequently included in Lustra had been written before Pound began his Cathay translations. But it is also true that the Lustra poems were mostly written after he had taken up Chinese studies with Giles. The only pre-Gilesian poems in Lustra, one will notice, are the "Contemporania" sequence and the "Song of the Degrees" grouping. If in the "Metro" poem one discerns but a devious influence of China, in "Heather," "Epitaphs (Fu I; Li Po)," "Meditatio," and "The Seeing Eye"[8] one is sure of identifying a more direct impact of the Chinese lyric tradition—the color, the imagery, and the "hard" style, if not the prosodic pattern, which is Pound's own. René Taupin, who has examined Pound's transition toward Modernism with the acutest eye, notes that "Toward 1914, a new crystallization was taking place in [Pound's] poetry. There was still to be seen in Ripostes a 'softness' which was not to be seen in Lustra . . . " (129). To be sure, the "hardness" of a considerable number of Lustra poems is due to Pound's pre-Fenollosan Chinese studies.

But the impact of Pound's initial Chinese exploration was to be felt beyond Lustra. Indeed, it intellectually conditioned him for his 1914–15 Modernist venture. As has been shown previously, Pound was to continue to rely on the Chinese examples provided by Giles to illustrate his Vorticist notion of the "Image." And he was to use Giles' History as a guide in his endeavor to carry on his dialogue with the Chinese via Fenollosa.

4 THE POUND-FENOLLOSA VENTURE:

AN OVERVIEW

In a letter to his father, dated 5 December 1913, Pound entered the following résumé of his activities:

The glebe—96 Fifth Ave—is publishing "Des Imagistes" an anthology in Feb. 1914.—write for prospectus.

I think I wrote that I am to have Prof. Fenollosa's valuable *mss.* to edit & finish a book on the Japanese drama & an anthology of chinese poets.

It is a very great opportunity, as not only Fenollosa but two authorities of the Japanese imperial court have prepared the stuff, & been at great expense in gathering the materials.

If you get Fenollosa's "Epochs of Chinese & Japanese Art", you'll get some idea of what his work means, & of his unique opportunity.

Richard [Aldington] has taken on the N. F. [*New Freewoman*] so I'm fairly free to go to work on the Fenollosa *mss* when it arrives.

Like everything worth having it has come out of a clear sky without any effort on my part.[1]

It is evident from this letter that Mary Fenollosa had described to Pound the content of her forthcoming gift: it consisted of her husband's notes and unpublished manuscripts on Japanese *Noh* drama and Chinese classical poetry prepared under "two authorities of the Japanese imperial court." (Mary Fenollosa most probably had in mind Professor Mori and

Mr. Ariga when she mentioned to Pound the "two authorities" involved in her husband's Oriental studies.) Pound's road to the Orient was charted. He knew what he would do with the treasures coming "out of a clear sky." He was to "edit & finish a book on the Japanese drama & an anthology of chinese poets."

Pound's joy and excitement grew when, about ten days later, the bulk of the promised legacy arrived. On 19 December 1913, Pound wrote William Carlos Williams from Yeats' Stone Cottage: "I am very placid and happy and busy. Dorothy is learning Chinese. I've all old Fenollosa's treasures in mss." (L 65).

In considering the Pound-Fenollosa venture, it is necessary first to take a look at the general contours of the Fenollosa notebooks. Thanks to Hugh Kenner, researchers now have a reliable guide and time-saver in their effort to reexamine the notoriously complicated document. The following account is taken from Kenner's *The Pound Era*:

The notebooks record [Fenollosa's] five years' furious quest for the facts which should underlie a grasp of the poetry. Three sessions with a Mr. Hirai in September 1896 yielded detailed if sometimes vague glosses on 22 poems by Wang Wei and Li Po ("Omakitsu," "Rihaku"; all the proper names in the notebooks are in Japanese form). With a Mr. Shida two years later he studied T'ao Ch'ien ("To-Em-Mei"). Then in February 1899 he commenced two years' intensive work with Professor Mori (1863–1911), a distinguished literary scholar and himself a practitioner of the delicate art, called in Japan *kanshi*, of writing poems in Classical Chinese. Mori spoke no English, and though Fenollosa's Japanese was adequate he often brought with him to their private sessions his own former philosophy student Nagao Ariga, who had at one time written out for him texts and translations of early Chinese poems. Ariga, one surmises, helped Fenollosa be sure he understood Mori's discourse when the talk got technical.

For a year and a half they worked through "Rihaku"; two very large notebooks contain cribs, glosses, comments, scholarly apparatus for 64 poems. (These furnished the backbone of *Cathay*.) Toward the end of this time Fenollosa was also working at early and Taoist poems with another teacher. Finally, on his last sojourn in Japan (April–September 1901) he commis-

sioned from Mori a course of systematic lectures in literary history, com-
mencing with the legendary invention of the written characters. A Mr.
Hirata interpreted. They filled three notebooks; the last entry (19 Sept.
1901) is dated just days before Ernest Fenollosa left Japan for ever.

And the record of all this study, eight notebooks in all, plus the volumes of
notes on *Noh* drama, plus the books in which he was drafting his lectures on
Chinese poetics, plus a sheaf of loose sheets, all these his widow in late 1913
transferred to Ezra Pound, some in London, some later by mail from Ala-
bama. So it came about that the opportunity to invent Chinese poetry for
our time fell not to some random modernist but to a master. The 14 poems in
the original *Cathay*, selected from some 150 in the notebooks, were the first
vers-libre translations not derived from other translations but from detailed
notes on the Chinese texts. (198)

More recent scholarly investigations have yielded many new findings
about Pound's encounter with the "Fenollosa Papers." Insofar as the basic
facts are concerned, however, Kenner's description of the Fenollosa
notebooks still appears to be the most dependable.[2] Ronald Bush, in a
discussion of Pound's parleyings with Li Bo (701–62), for example, pro-
vides "A List of the Poems of Li Po in Fenollosa's Two 'Rihaku' Note-
books" ("Pound and Li Po" 56–59). In the list, Bush takes the trouble to
match his own number (1–48) with Pound's in parentheses (104–50)
followed by the first line of the poem in Fenollosa's translation. Sure
enough, the list has indicated a Pound number which "corresponds to no
poem,"[3] and it has included three poems unnumbered by Pound. But it
has illegitimately left out the first seventeen numbers (87–103) assigned
by Pound. Bush is undoubtedly correct in pointing out that "On the
inside covers of the two notebooks, Pound continued his running count
of poems from earlier volumes," but he is wrong to state that Pound
"numbered the first of the Li Po poems . . . 104" (56). Pound numbered
the first few poems in the first "Rihaku" notebook 87 to 103, but they
somehow slipped Bush's searching eye.[4] In his description of the two
"Rihaku" notebooks, Kenner has wisely eluded such detail. By saying that
the two notebooks "contain cribs, glosses, comments, scholarly appara-
tus for 64 poems," he simply follows Pound's original count. Whether
Pound has made any mistakes in his counting seems unimportant.

Anne S. Chapple was perhaps the first critic to give serious attention to Pound's selection procedure. Her essay "Ezra Pound's *Cathay*: Compilation from the Fellonosa Notebooks," based on an admirably conducted investigation, is also not without misrepresentations. She informs us, for example, that the "150 or so poems" Pound numbered are "in twelve separate notebooks and folders" (11). Here again, it is Kenner who has given us the precise information. The "150 poems" are recorded not in twelve but in eight separate notebooks—1 to 29 in Notebook 7 (record of sessions with Hirai and Shida), 30 to 37 in Notebook 17 (record of sessions with a Mr. Kakuzo[5]), 38 to 77 in the three volumes of Notebook 11 (record of Professor Mori's lectures), 78 to 86 in Notebook 8 (texts and translations of early Chinese poems—Song 167 ["Song of the Bowmen of Shu"] from *The Book of Songs*, Qu Yuan's *Li sao* and other poems from *The Songs of Chu*—written out by Ariga), and 87 to 150 in Notebooks 20 and 21 (the two "Rihaku" notebooks). It is true that there are a number of other Chinese poetry notebooks, but they are either Fenollosa's books of notes on Chinese poetry (Notebooks 12, 13, 14, and 16) or Pound's notes for new editions of Mori's lectures and Ariga's texts prepared in subsequent years (Notebooks 9, 10, and 18) and sheaves of loose sheets in which he was drafting new translations (Notebooks 15 and 19).[6]

Chapple, nevertheless, has done an impressive job in shedding light on how Pound worked through Fenollosa's Chinese poetry notebooks in late 1914 and how he made choices for *Cathay* from the "150 or so poems." Relying upon Pound's unpublished material—his notes, jottings, and drafts of translations included among the "Fenollosa Papers"—she demonstrates that "Pound's selection methods may be traced to personal tastes which stemmed from his own imagist 'doctrine' and earlier, related interests" (11). Since Pound's move toward *Cathay* was contemporaneous with his move toward Vorticism (Dasenbrock, *Literary Vorticism* 109), Chapple might as well claim that Pound's selection processes were to a certain extent influenced by his Vorticist notion of the Image.

In fact, some of Chapple's own arguments quite eloquently back up this revised contention. Speaking of Pound's "The Jewel Stairs' Grievance," for instance, Chapple argues that "the poem doesn't seem to contain a conspicuous 'Image,' if [one] define[s] 'Image' as 'that which presents an intellectual and emotional complex in an instant of time" (17). Through careful analysis of published and unpublished material (Pound's gloss for the poem in his 1918 "Chinese Poetry" essay and Fenollosa's gloss for the poem in Notebook 20), she demonstrates that Pound was drawn to this famous lyric by Li Bo precisely because it "represents a kind of delayed Image" (20). Apparently, the "delayed Image," which Chapple defines as that which "does not permit 'instantaneous' appreciation of its emotional element" (19), contributes to Pound's Vorticist notion of the Image. In Chapter Five, I will furnish more examples from *Cathay* that illustrate Pound's Vorticist inclinations. Here, suffice it to stress two points. First, Pound's Vorticism was essentially a perfection of his Imagism rather than a departure from it. As Donald Davie recalls, "the two movements were, in Pound's sense of the matter, really one" (40). From this perspective, Chapple can legitimately refer to Pound's poetic ideals in 1914–15 as his "imagist 'doctrine.' " Second, while Pound's Vorticism colored his Chinese endeavor, his Orientalism also contributed to his Vorticist ideas. According to Dasenbrock, "Pound himself saw the compatibility of the two influences, and in the period of Vorticism he constantly drew parallels between his two sources of inspiration" (*Literary Vorticism* 108).

The heart of Chapple's essay, however, is a challenge to the validity of Kenner's claim that Pound's 1915 *Cathay* was a war book. Chapple makes her stance clear in the beginning by stating that "No written evidence exists to substantiate such claims" (10). Although I agree that Pound chose poems from Fenollosa's notebooks largely according to his Imagist/Vorticist sentiments in late 1914, I should also point out that he made important adjustments in early 1915, which eventually reinforced the antiwar theme of the volume. Bush, who has examined the issue with the greatest care, informs us that Pound's *Cathay* had gone through two rearrangements before it was brought out by Elkin Mathews in April 1915. Originally, the sequence was made up of eleven poems,[7] of which only one was about war ("Song of the Bowmen of Shu").[8] The "Cathay" typescript at the Beinecke Library shows that Pound had added four poems (none of which is about war) to the original eleven when he submitted the sequence to Elkin Mathews. However, in the last minute, "perhaps because the war became more oppressive," Pound "suppressed the four appended poems and added 'Lament [of the Frontier Guard]' and 'South-Folk [in Cold Country].'" And in early 1916, when Pound incorporated "Cathay" into *Lustra*, he restored the four suppressed poems (Bush, "Pound and Li Po" 60 n). Thus we see that Bush is precise in stating that "*Cathay*, though in 1915 very much a reflection of the war, did not start out that way nor did it remain so for long" (36).

Insofar as our investigation of the Pound-Fenollosa venture is concerned, one thing yet remains to be recognized. That is how well Pound was prepared for his 1914–15 Chinese endeavor. In *Make It New* (1935), Pound recalls that "Fenollosa's work was given me in manuscript when I was ready for it" (8). A statement to the same effect is to be found in his 1935 typescript of notes on Mori's Chinese poetry lectures: " . . . and even at that time [1914] I had certain qualifications which are possibly not the common property of every philologist" (Notebook 9). I think I have evidence now to prove that Pound's remarks had reference not only to his early training in the comparative study of Romance literature (Nolde 13 n) and his search in 1912–13 for a language "for the Chinese poetry" (Eliot, "Ezra Pound" 180), but, more specifically, to his quest in late 1913 for facts about Chinese literature.

Indeed, the previous year's study of Giles' *History* had done Pound a lot of good. For one thing, when he went through the Fenollosa Chinese poetry notebooks in November 1914, he was capable of filling the pages with informed critical marginalia and submarginalia. Examples of this kind are available in Chapple's "*Cathay*" article. For another, he was able to match Fenollosa's Japanese forms of the names for Chinese figures with Giles' forms of the names, using whatever clues he may have found in the notes and translations. In the three notebooks for Mori's lectures on Chinese poetry (vols. 1 to 3 of Notebook 11), therefore, one finds that a considerable number of the Japanese forms of the names are glossed by Pound in red pencil with Giles' names and dates. Thus for "Toemmei" is given "365–427 ad (p. 128) T'ao Yuan Ming or T'ao Ch'ien"; for "Rihaku" "Li Po"; for "Hakurakuten" "Po Chü-i"; and for "Kantaishi" "Han Yu or Han Wen Kung." "Omakitsu," however, due to uncertainty for the moment on Pound's part, is given as "Wang Wei" with two question marks ("??"). And so is "Meng Hao-jan" with one question mark ("?") for "Mo Konen." The simple fact that Pound was able to gloss such lesser-known Chinese literary figures as the Tang emperor Xuanzong (Ming Huang) and his favorite lady Yang Guifei (Yang Kui-fei) indicates that he had a copy of Giles' *History* at his elbow. Giles' *History* has an author index, which should have made Pound's search for biographical data easy.

In Notebook 15, titled "Chinese Poetry: Notes by Pound, including translations," one may find the typescript of a columnar list of names and dates prepared by Pound for his own reference:

2 Confucius b. 551 b.c.

1 King Wan (Bun O). 1184–34 b.c. (Wen Wang)

4 Mei Sheng (Baijo) d. b.c. 140

  Rafu poem. folk song. 2. cent B.C.

5 Han Shojo   Lady Pan B.C. 32–6

3 CHU YUAN, Kutsugen, fourth century B.C.

        Li Sao. (Ri-so)

6 To em mei, Tao yuan Ming 365–427

  Mokonen, Ming Hao Jan 689–740

7 Omakitsu, Wang Wei 699–759

  Toshimi = *Tu-fu* 712–770

8 Rihaku, Li Po, 705–762

  Kantaishi, Han Yü, 768–824

  Budda-Bone. Han Wên Kung

        768–824

  Po Chü I. 772–846. Hakurakulen

  Biwa Ko

It should be noted that the numbers preceding the names and the italicized items in the list were subsequently added by Pound in black ink ("= To-fu 712–770," however, was done in red pencil). Apparently, it was after going through the Fenollosa Chinese poetry notebooks that Pound made the list. His purpose, it seems, was to bring together a few figures that had received prominence in both Giles' *History* and Fenollosa's notes for Mori's lectures. From the original list of twelve poets (including the anonymous bard of the *Yue fu* ballad "Rafu" [Pound's "The Mulberry Road"], but excluding Bo Juyi), it may be noticed, Pound picked out eight and numbered them in chronological order. As can be seen, this short-list, precisely reflecting Pound's preferences of the moment, designates his choice for *Cathay*. With the exception of Qu Yuan and Lady Ban, whose poetry Pound had adopted a year earlier, every figure numbered has received a place in the sequence. Wen Wang (King Wen) and Confucius are assumed to be jointly represented by an ancient song ("Song of the Bowmen of Shu").[9] Mei Sheng, Tao Qian (Tao Yuanming), and Wang Wei are each embodied by a piece ("The Beautiful Toilet," "The Unmoving Cloud," and epigraph to "Four Poems of Departure," respectively). And Li Bo alone has eleven poems to his name.

It is appropriate that Pound should introduce his 1915 *Cathay* with these words: "For the most part from the Chinese of Rihaku [Li Po], from the notes of the late Ernest Fenollosa, and the decipherings of the professors Mori and Ariga" (*P* 130). His 1914–15 encounter with Fenollosa was essentially an encounter between himself and Li Bo via Fenollosa-Mori-Ariga. But Pound's decision to give Li Bo such prominence in *Cathay* was endorsed not only by Fenollosa-Mori-Ariga, who provided him with the "64 poems" of the Tang master, but by Giles as well. After all, it was from Giles that Pound first learned that "By general consent Li Po himself (A.D. 705–762) would probably be named as China's greatest poet" (*History* 151).[10] Kenner has noticed an echo of Giles in the note to the "Exile's Letter" first published in the April 1915 *Poetry*: Li Bo is "usually considered the greatest poet of China" (206–07). The note must have been prepared by Pound himself, for in his 1918 essay on "Chinese Poetry," he is found to be saying more or less the same thing: "By fairly general consent, their greatest poet is Rihaku or 'Li Po,' who flourished in the eighth century A.D." (*EPPP* 3: 85).

As planned, out of the Fenollosa notebooks Pound extracted enough material to complete "an anthology of chinese poets." But he made two repeated attempts to introduce the Japanese *Noh* drama: *Certain Noble Plays of Japan* in 1916 and *Noh or Accomplishment* in 1917.[11] In addition, after two and a half years' sniffling and squabbling, he managed to have

Fenollosa's essay on "The Chinese Written Character" published in installments in *The Little Review* (September–December 1919). In 1935, it is worth noting, he returned once more to the Fenollosa notebooks and endeavored to bring out an edition of Mori's lectures. "As a fund or fountain of wisdom applicable to the criticism of ANY poetry, that is to say world poetry or the poetry of any nation, they have a value that no one but an ass can deny. They contain considerably more wisdom than I noticed when I first read through them 20 or so years ago . . . " (Notebook 9). So he wrote of Mori's lectures in his "foreword" to an unfinished book. In late 1958, in his tower room at Brunnenburg, he revisited Fenollosa's turn-of-the-century notes for the last time. It seems that after thirteen years of exile in Washington his mind was again fixed on his failed attempt to publish Mori's lectures. "I now tackle Fenollosa's penciled record of Mori's lectures on the History of Chinese Poetry, with the intention of transmitting them as *his* view of the subject . . . " (Notebook 10). The typescript ran on for eighty-four leaves, and then it was dropped. Was Pound torn away by the final typescript of *Thrones*? Or could it be that he realized that an edition of Mori's lectures was no longer necessary since he had transmitted their value into *Cathay* and was further transmitting it into the last Cantos? The answer remains to be explored.

5 VIA FENOLLOSA:

TAOISM VERSUS VORTICISM IN *CATHAY*

Ever since T. S. Eliot made the influential remark that "Pound is the inventor of Chinese poetry for our time" (Introduction xvi), Pound criticism has shown a tendency to praise his *Cathay* as an invention rather than a translation. Most critics, it seems, agree that *Cathay* has a freshness, elegance, and simplicity that are rarely seen in English and American poetry.[1] Yet, surprisingly, few will acknowledge that *Cathay* is first and foremost a beautiful translation of excellent Chinese poems that exhibit freshness, elegance, and simplicity.

Indeed, to what extent can *Cathay* be read as a translation? How much of its charm is transformed from the Chinese original and how much of it is actually invented by Pound? To seek an answer to these questions, one has to compare carefully Pound's *Cathay* poems with the corresponding Chinese texts and Fenollosa's notes, which served as intermediary when Pound did the rendering. In the 1960s, Wai-lim Yip made a pioneering effort at examining the "triple relation."[2] To his brilliant *Ezra Pound's Cathay* (1969) I owe a debt. Here we may as well begin our investigation with "Taking Leave of a Friend" (Li Bo's *Song you ren*), a piece Yip has considered in his study. Whereas Yip's focus is on the syntactic aspect, I will direct more of my attention to the aesthetic and thematic concerns in my comparison.

Let us first quote Pound's version of the poem:

> Blue mountains to the north of the walls,
> White river winding about them;
> Here we must make separation
> And go out through a thousand miles of dead grass.
>
> Mind like a floating wide cloud,
> Sunset like the parting of old acquaintances
> Who bow over their clasped hands at a distance.
> Our horses neigh to each other
>   as we are departing.
>   (P 141)

Li Bo's original text, at which Fenollosa worked with Mori and Ariga on 3 July 1900 (his notes are presented in Appendix I), actually consists of two pentasyllabic quatrains (*wuyan lushi*). It runs as follows with Yip's word-for-word translation next to each line:

Green mountains lie across the north wall.	青山橫北郭
White water winds the east city.	白水繞東城
Here once we part,	此地一為別
Lone tumbleweed, a million miles to travel.	孤蓬萬里征
Floating clouds, a wanderer's mood.	浮雲游子意
Setting sun, an old friend's feeling.	落日故人情
We wave hands, you go from here.	揮手自茲去
Neigh, neigh, goes the horse at parting.	蕭蕭班馬鳴

(Yip 212)

If we compare the two, we immediately notice that they share a distinct terseness and formal beauty. Pound's short lines, concrete words, and parallelism as seen in lines 1 and 2 and lines 5 and 6 are all approximations of Li Bo. More importantly, the pictorial quality that we perceive in "Taking Leave of a Friend" is unmistakably from the Chinese original. Notice that in both versions each line represents a self-contained scene, and joined together they form a unified whole.

The images—"mountains," "walls," "river," "cloud," "Sunset," "hands," "horses," and so on—are all literal translations. By themselves they are familiar rather than foreign to Pound's audience. Nevertheless, the way they are combined or juxtaposed is exotic. "Blue mountains" and "White river," for example, are rare collocations in English. In fact, the color word *qing* 青 in classical Chinese can mean "blue," "green," "grey," or "black" according to the context. Yip is certainly not mistaken to gloss it "green." However, as readers of Chinese poetry, we must be aware of the fact that Chinese landscape poetry grew up hand in hand with Chinese landscape painting and that in Chinese landscape painting mountains in the far distance are depicted as blue rather than green to show a "linear perspective." This is because, as one Chinese art critic explains, "the air is not entirely transparent. Therefore the densely-wooded mountains in the near distance are deep green while those in the far distance look pale blue or violet; further away still they are even paler until they become void of colour and their outlines obscure" (Jin 169). Thus, in Li Bo's contemporary Wang Wei's lines,

Morning rain wets Weicheng's light dust;   渭城朝雨浥輕塵
The inn-yard willows look greener and fresher.   客舍青青柳色新

the character *qing* 青 would signify to a Chinese reader the color green rather than blue or grey. Pound's rendering of the second line catches the precise shade of color in the Chinese poetic scene:

> The willows of the inn-yard
> Will be going greener and greener,
> (*P* 140)

for after the morning rain, the willows right before one's eyes naturally look very green. By contrast, in Li Bo's

The Three Hills half visible beyond the pale sky,   三山半落青天外

qing tian 青天 should mean "pale sky" or "dim sky." More precisely, the phrase refers to the distant grey mist that obscures a full view of the "Three Hills." So, in "The City of Choan," Pound legitimately omits the word "blue" in Fenollosa's paraphrase,

The triangle mt is half disappearing beyond the blue sky[3]

and introduces the word "far" into his

> The Three Mountains fall through the far heaven,
> . . . . . .
> (P 142)

As for "White river" in "Taking Leave of a Friend," one has only to know Wang Wei's famous line "At sunset rivers and lakes gleam white" (qtd. in Jin 165) to understand that the whiteness of the water actually specifies the hour of the parting scene in the poem. So, the color words here as well as in other classical Chinese poems really have the power of suggesting distance, time, and atmosphere. Whether Pound had, through examining Chinese landscape painting in the British Museum (see fig. 18, for example), acquired an understanding of the aesthetic value and significance of Chinese art, and so was conscious of the visual suggestivity of these images, we are still not quite sure. But one thing is reasonably certain: these unexpected collocations initially kept in Fenollosa's notes ("Where blue mt. peaks are visible toward the Northern suburb / And white water flows encircling the East of the city") must have appealed to Pound's poetic sensibility, and therefore he has deliberately preserved them to evince the Chinese flavor.

With the same sensibility and the same deliberation, Pound has also managed to reproduce Li Bo's efficient style. Notice the sharp transition from objective to subjective in line 3:

> Here we must make separation.

Fenollosa renders this as:

> At this place we have for once to separate.

And Shigeyoshi Obata, whose translation of Li Bo has won some admirers, has this to offer us:

> Here we part, friend, once forever.
> (94)

Both Fenollosa and Obata have translated the meaning but missed the overtone. Pound alone, by using the English modal verb "must," has brought out the sharpness and, in addition, conveyed the subtle implication in the original: the speaker has accompanied his friend outside the gate of the city still reluctant to part with him.

When we come to the next couplet, however, we discern inconspicuous deviations within overall resemblance. Read Pound's

> Mind like a floating wide cloud,
> Sunset like the parting of old acquaintances

side by side with Li Bo's

Floating clouds, a wanderer's mood.　　浮雲游子意
Setting sun, an old friend's feeling.　　落日故人情

One is struck by the affinity in imagery and sentence structure. But a closer scrutiny reveals that Pound has ingeniously reversed Li Bo's order of the images in the first juxtaposition. Moreover, he has inserted the connective "like" in both lines perhaps in order to achieve clarity and a poetic flow. In effect, however, the intended ambiguity and simultaneity in Li Bo's lines are ruined.[4]

In line 7, we notice a more conspicuous discrepancy: *hui shou* 揮手 in the original is rendered as "bow over their clasped hands." A look at Fenollosa's notes reveals that Mori and Ariga have provided two glosses for the phrase: "Shaking hands" and "Brandishing [hands]." Pound obviously finds neither meaning culturally appropriate in the context. For Yip, as for all other speakers of modern Chinese, *hui shou* simply means "wave hands." Pound's "bow over their clasped hands" is therefore a forced dramatization. An illustration for "Taking Leave of a Friend" available in the "Dalian" edition of *Three Hundred Poems of the Tang (Tang shi san bai shou,* 1992) (fig. 14) shows, however, that Pound is not alone in dismissing the accepted meaning of *hui shou.* J. Hillis Miller states, in *Illustration,* that illustrations tend to add "something more, something not in the text" (102). He argues from the deconstructionist perspective that "What they bring to light they also hide" (150). (In Richard Poirier's words, "A canonical text . . . generally . . . does not want to clarify itself" [140].) To a certain extent, translations are like illustrations. They, too, illuminate abstractions while they darken them. In the case of "Tak-

14. Chen Youmin, "Taking Leave of a Friend." Reproduced in *Tang shi san bai shou* (Three Hundred Poems of the Tang) (Dalian, 1992).

ing Leave of a Friend," what Pound has brought into the open is the culturally correct (or what he believes to be culturally correct) detail suggesting silent communion. Pound is most probably aware of Li Bo's use of the Taoist "poetics of silence,"[5] for in his version, we can still sense the electricity of emotions: the two friends are utterly at a loss what to say when the time has come for them to separate.

The subtle awareness, however, is articulated by the neighing of the

parting horses. This ingenious treatment that we find in Li Bo's conclud-
ing line is parroted in Pound's rendering. Notice that the communion
between men is followed by the communion between humanity and
nature. The poetic situation is characteristic of Chinese landscape poetry
that obtains its energy from Taoism and Chan Buddhism (or Zen Bud-
dhism). In it Pound seems to have found a way to make his Imagism
"more intense" and "more dynamic" (GB 90), "a way to be Vorticist"
(Dasenbrock, *Literary Vorticism* 109). Indeed, despite his expressed con-
tempt for Taoism in the China Cantos, in his 1914–15 effort to translate
Li Bo, he has rarely failed to respond to the Tang poet's Taoist sensibility,
and rarely has he shrunk from toiling to reproduce his Chan-like (or
Zen-like) communion that aptly demonstrates the dynamic force of the
universe. Thus, in "The Jewel Stairs' Grievance," we find Pound's court
lady, like Li Bo's, "let down the crystal curtain / And watch the moon
through the clear autumn" (P 136). Meanwhile, the solitary moon is also
watching the court lady with silent compassion. And in the "Exile's Let-
ter," Pound's poet-speaker, like Li Bo's, verifies his Taoist awareness of the
power of silence in saying, "What is the use of talking, and there is no end
of talking, / There is no end of things in the heart" (139).

For readers well-versed in *The Book of Songs*, Li Bo's closing line has
another aspect of charm. It alludes to a resonant line in Song 179:
蕭蕭馬鳴 ("*xiao xiao* the horses neigh").[6] Li Bo here has simply in-
serted one character *ban* 班 ("parting"), but by inserting that character,
he has given the classical line a new life. As the Chinese character *ban* can
mean "stray," "wandering," "separating," or "separated," his stress is ob-
vious. Thus with a single stroke, Li Bo has brought out the theme of
human pathos in the poem. This Taoist emphasis appears uncertain in
Fenollosa's crib. Pound, with his keen sensibility, however, must have
perceived from the context the intensification of the speaker's sense of
loss in the concluding line, and, therefore, he has managed to reproduce
the effect in his own way. He resorts to the typographical device of
breaking the line into two,

> Our horses neigh to each other
> as we are departing.

allowing a brief pause in between. The technique is characteristically Poundian.[7] The effect, however, is fully in accord with the Chinese original.

Thus, in "Taking Leave of a Friend," one is sure of perceiving a silent communion between scene and sentiment, objective and subjective, nature and human being. The tranquil images ("misted mountains," "the winding river," "drifting grass," "wandering mind," "floating cloud," "the setting sun," etc.) have the force of inciting the readers to build up in their imagination the undepicted detail in the landscape and reconstruct what remains unsaid by the speaker. If these images—or "Vortex" in Pound's 1914 concept—capable of inciting thoughts and emotions are the charm that has appealed to Pound's audience, then they are all there in Li Bo's original verse. But Pound as the translator deserves to be given credit for his success in bringing Li Bo's Taoist spirit across by his Vorticist means.

It is true that not everything in Li Bo's original is kept intact in Pound's version. But we have to see that perfection is out of the question for translation. This is particularly true when one deals with a language and culture so drastically different. The translator in such a case has to decide what to preserve and what to sacrifice. For Pound, what matters most in rendering Chinese poetry are the fresh images and the sophisticated presentation, and what is less important and so can be sacrificed are the "music," the "[f]ancy styles," and things of "local 'taste'" (MN 159–60). In his 1918 essay "Chinese Poetry," Pound makes it clear to us that he translates Chinese poems precisely "because Chinese poetry has certain qualities of vivid presentation; and because certain Chinese poets have been content to set forth their matter without moralizing and without comment . . ." (EPPP 3: 84). "Vivid presentation" is a strength Chinese poets have derived from Taoism, and "without moralizing and without comment" is a typical Taoist attitude. As Yip observes, these traits also "echo . . . the imagist credo: 'Direct treatment of the thing' (Summer, 1912, LE, 3), 'Don't be viewy' (1913, LE, 6), and many related points" (34). So, it is the parallel of Taoism and Pound's Vorticist sensibility that has inspired him to make a painstaking effort to mimic Li Bo's philosophical way of presenting poetical ideas. And it is also the parallel of Taoism and

Pound's Vorticist sensibility that has ensured his triumph in bringing out the Chinese quintessence.

If Pound is essentially imitative in "Taking Leave of a Friend," and the beauty of the poem should first be ascribed to Li Bo, he is more inventive in the "Song of the Bowmen of Shu." It is accordingly more difficult for us to determine how much of the charm in *Cathay*'s opening piece is from the Chinese text and how much is Pound's creation.

. The first four lines of Pound's "Song of the Bowmen of Shu" is worth quoting:

> Here we are, picking the first fern-shoots
> And saying: When shall we get back to our country?
> Here we are because we have the Ken-nin for our foemen,
> We have no comfort because of these Mongols.
> (P 131)

The Chinese text, which in late 1914 yielded Pound his "Song of the Bowmen of Shu," is Song 167, *Cai wei* ("Pick Ferns") from the *Shi jing* or *Book of Songs*. Here is the opening stanza that corresponds to the passage above. The approximation given here is again Yip's.

Pick ferns, pick ferns,	采薇采薇
Ferns are sprouting.	薇亦作止
Return, return,	曰歸曰歸
The year is dusking.	歲亦莫止
No house, no home,	靡室靡家
The Hsien-yün are the sole cause.	玁狁之故
No time to rest,	不遑啓居
The Hsien-yün are the sole cause.	玁狁之故

(Yip 182)

The discrepancies between the two versions are apparent. For one thing, Pound has combined every two lines in the original (as written out by Ariga) into one, thus forming longer lines with more complicated syntactic and rhythmical structures. For another, he replaces the internal repetitions that occur in lines 1 ("Pick ferns, pick ferns"), 3 ("Return,

return"), and 5 ("No house, no home") with a more varied repetition that disperses through the lines ("Here we are . . . / . . . / Here we are because . . . / . . . because . . .), thus eliminating the choppy rhythm of the original, which would sound much too light for the depressing tone of the ancient song if rendered into English.[8] In other words, Pound's approach here is to assimilate the meaning of the original and then reproduce it as a whole in his own poetic manner. Thus, in the "Song of the Bowmen of Shu," we read the complaint of an ancient Chinese frontier guard in the form of a natural modern English verse. There is, of course, Eastern coloration, reminding one that it is a Chinese poem. But, unlike "Taking Leave of a Friend," the charm of the "Song" doesn't reside in the literal translation of the images. Rather, it exists in the English rhythmic flow and the melancholy atmosphere gradually imbued in it. This is particularly true when the "Song" draws to its close with a rhetorical question:

> When we set out, the willows were drooping with spring,
> We come back in the snow,
> We go slowly, we are hungry and thirsty,
> Our mind is full of sorrow, who will know of our grief?
> (P 131)

As Bruce Fogelman notes, the "anguish" of the soldier is drastically intensified here by "the dense and varied repetition of o sounds . . . " (65–66). In fact, one may as well notice the effect of the equally dense and varied repetition of w sounds.

All this is evidently Pound's invention. Now the question is whether Pound's meddling in mode and detail has effected a drastic change in the original theme and mood. For Sanehide Kodama, the answer is yes. In his discussion of Cathay and the Fenollosa Notebooks, Kodama states that "'Ts'ai wei' [Cai wei] as a whole is an 'inspiring' poem. It was written, 'reputedly by Bunno [Wen Wang or King Wen],' to encourage rather than discourage his soldiers" (63). But "By emphasizing the sorrow, uncertainty, and anxiety of the soldiers throughout the poem, Pound is building an antiwar poem from the Chinese war poem" (69).

Here we have to clarify two points. First, the attribution of Cai wei to

King Wen (Bunno) has proven to be invalid. As some scholars have shown, the expeditions to resist the northern tribes of Xianyun (Hsienyün) referred to in the "Song" were undertaken in the time of King Xuan of the Zhou (827–781 B.C.).[9] This has convincingly placed *Cai wei* between the late ninth and early eighth centuries B.C. King Wen, who had lived about two centuries before (in the eleventh century B.C.) certainly could not have composed the song. Second, Kodama's assertion about *Cai wei* being a war poem is based on the Mao edition's Preface. Master Mao, the earliest commentator on the *Shi jing*, is quoted in various subsequent editions as saying: "At the time of King Wen there were the threats of the Kunyi from the West and of the Xianyun from the North. King Wen as the Son of Heaven gave the order to dispatch troops to guard the Middle Kingdom and composed *Cai wei* to encourage his frontier soldiers."[10] Mao's opinion was blindly followed until the eighteenth and nineteenth centuries, when critics like Yao Jiheng and Fang Yurun seriously began to question its validity. After a century's debate, I think scholars have reached a consensus now with regard to this song. In fact, as my investigation of some dozen editions has shown, the tendency since the 1950s is to regard this text as a song of complaint.[11] To give a typical example of a contemporary view, Taiwan scholar Wang Jingzhi contends in his edition of the *Shi jing:* "If this song were meant to encourage the frontier soldiers, it wouldn't have said 'No house, no home,' and 'Our hearts are bitter, / We went, but never return.' These lines would destroy rather than boost soldiers' morale. Therefore, we should have no doubt that this poem was a frontier soldier's complaint" (348).

It is amazing that Pound, who knew nothing about the debate, should form an opinion so close to twentieth-century *Shi jing* scholarship. But with a more radical attitude, he has to a considerable degree intensified the grievance of the original, and, moreover, modified certain details that appear inappropriate for the antiwar motif. A notorious example is his alteration of Fenollosa's (or rather Ariga's) "The horses are tied already to the chariot"[12] to "Horses, his horses even, are tired."

Indeed, the depiction of the general's chariot and steeds in the fourth and fifth stanzas is not quite in agreement with the overall mood of the ancient song. According to Yip, this section of the poem actually functions to turn "the mounting sorrow subterranean until it comes out piercingly again in the atmosphere of a most miserable moment" (119). His explanation sounds plausible. But I suspect that these lines were later added rather than originally created by the anonymous bard(s). As the Han historian Sima Qian informs us, the ancient Chinese songs "amounted to more than 3,000"; Confucius "selected in all 305 pieces, which he sang over to his lute, to bring them into accordance with the musical style of the Shaou, the Woo, the Ya, and the Sung" (qtd. in Legge 1). My speculation is, therefore, that these colorful phrases, which Marcel Granet aptly calls "descriptive auxiliaries" (88), were probably introduced into the song by refiners like Confucius in their effort to improve its musical effect. Circumstantial evidence supporting this assumption can be found in the text of the *Shi jing*. Lines such as *jia bi si mu* ("The four steeds are yoked") and *si mu kui kui* ("The four steeds, eager and strong"), like musical refrains, ring not only in Song 167, *Cai wei* (Legge 260; Karlgren 110–12), but in Song 162, *Si mu* ("My Four Steeds") (Legge 249; Karlgren 105–06), Song 179, *Che gong* ("Our Chariots Were Strong") (Legge 289; Karlgren 123–24), and Song 191, *Jie nan shan* ("The Lofty Southern Hill") (Legge 313; Karlgren 132–34).

Since Pound may have detected the prosodic rather than thematic function of the phrases, it seems probable that he has deliberately suppressed them in order to restore the consistent tone of the ancient song. In 1911, one will recall, Pound had made a similar revisionary effort in reworking the Anglo-Saxon "Seafarer."[13] Dealing with a text sixteen to seventeen centuries older, it may have occurred to him that he had more right to be suspicious about its confusing lines.

When we turn to Pound's "The River-Merchant's Wife: A Letter," however, we are overwhelmed by a loveliness and simplicity that outshine "Taking Leave of a Friend" and the "Song of the Bowmen of Shu." The special appeal of this poem resides in the charming image of the speaker, a lonely teenage wife. In Ford Madox Ford's opinion, the image of this young woman is able to "stir your emotions; so you are made a better man; you are softened, rendered more supple of mind, more open to the vicissitudes and necessities of your fellow men" (Homberger 221). His comment explains why "The River-Merchant's Wife" should rank among the most anthologized of Pound's poetic works.

The poem is a dramatic monologue—a form in which Pound finds himself most at home—by the Chinese teenage wife—a kind of personality he is quite unfamiliar with. Nevertheless, he manages to produce the youthful Chinese woman's voice—simple, naive, and straightforward:

> While my hair was still cut straight across my forehead
> I played about the front gate, pulling flowers.
> You came by on bamboo stilts, playing horse,
> You walked about my seat, playing with blue plums.
> And we went on living in the village of Chokan:
> Two small people, without dislike or suspicion.

Notice the choice of images: "hair," "forehead," "pulling flowers," "playing horse," "playing with blue plums," and "Two small people, without dislike or suspicion"—all connoting loveliness and innocence.

Nevertheless, the speaker's tone of voice is constantly changing, signifying a curve in her mental development over the years (or, in Pound's 1914 terms, "a VORTEX, from which, and through which, and into which, ideas are constantly rushing" [GB 92]). For a time it is modest and shy:

> At fourteen I married My Lord you.
> I never laughed, being bashful.
> Lowering my head, I looked at the wall.
> Called to, a thousand times, I never looked back.

For another, it is full of love and affection:

> At fifteen I stopped scowling,
> I desired my dust to be mingled with yours
> Forever and forever and forever.
> Why should I climb the look out?

But before the poem comes to its end, it becomes anxious, sorrowful, and finally almost despairing:

And you have been gone five months.
The monkeys make sorrowful noise overhead.

. . . . . .

The paired butterflies are already yellow with August
Over the grass in the West garden;
They hurt me. I grow older.
If you are coming down through the narrows of the river Kiang,
Please let me know beforehand,
And I will come out to meet you
                As far as Cho-fu-Sa.
(P 134)

    So this is the image of the River-Merchant's Wife that Pound presents in his version, which has the power of touching the reader's heart. The question that concerns us is whether we shall find the same charming image in the Chinese text. One has only to quote the corresponding lines for a comparison. Li Bo's original poem *Chang=gan xing* ("Song of Chang-gan")[14] is indeed a song of love, separation, and longing, written in the form of a dramatic monologue. It opens in the same direct, sincere, artless voice of the sixteen-year-old River-Merchant's Wife:

My hair barely covered my forehead.	妾髮初覆額
I played in front of the gate, plucking flowers,	折花門前劇
You came riding on a bamboo-horse	郎騎竹馬來
And around the bed we played with green plums.	繞牀弄青梅
We were then living in Ch'ang-kan.	同居長干里
Two small people, no hate nor suspicion.	兩小無嫌猜

All the lovely images are there, blended with the speaker's nostalgic feelings. Pound's "Two small people, without dislike or suspicion," in particular, has improved upon Fenollosa's "And we two little ones had neither mutual dislike or suspicion,"[15] which translates the meaning but doesn't capture the simple voice.

    Then there is a shift of the tone to tenderness and timidity,

At fourteen, I became your wife.	十四為君婦
I seldom laughed, being bashful.	羞顏未嘗開

I lowered my head toward the dark wall. 　　　低頭向暗壁

Called to, a thousand times, I never looked back. 　千喚不一回

followed by an outburst of passionate love:

We wished to stay together like dust and ash. 　願同塵與灰

If you have the faith of Wei-sheng. 　　　　　常存抱柱信

Why do I have to climb up the waiting tower? 　豈上望夫台

Notice that the image of "dust" is there. Indeed, Pound's rendering of the line is emotionally closer to the original than Yip's ("to stay together like dust and ash") or Fenollosa's ("to be with you even as dust, and even as ashes partially together"), for Pound's choice of the word "mingled" brings out the Taoist implication of "becoming one body and soul" in the original, whereas Yip's "stay together" or Fenollosa's "be with you" does not. Also note the difference in the following lines; here Li Bo's River-Merchant's Wife becomes allusive, referring to a legendary personality and place ("have the faith of Wei-sheng") where Pound's Wife sounds Shakespearean ("Forever and forever and forever") (Ruthven 205). Yet, aside from this, we perceive in both voices the same sincere, fervent love.

In the latter half of the poem, nonetheless, the dominant tone changes to one of worry, longing, sorrow, and slight resentment:

The unpassable rapids in the fifth month 　　五月不可觸

When monkeys cried against the sky. 　　　　猿聲天上哀

. . . . . .

In the eighth month, butterflies come 　　　八月蝴蝶黃

In pairs over the grass in the West Garden. 　雙飛西園草

These smite my heart. 　　　　　　　　　　感此傷妾心

I sit down worrying and youth passes away. 　坐愁紅顏老

When eventually you would come down from 　早晚下三巴
　　the Three Gorges.

Please let me know ahead of time. 　　　　　預將書報家

I will meet you, no matter how far, 　　　　相迎不道遠

Even all the way to Long Wind Sand. 　　　直至長風沙

(Yip 192 and 194)

Again, the same images and the same moods. Pound's version is not without misrepresentations. For example, he improvises Fenollosa's "5 month," meaning "the fifth month," into "five months," thus lengthening the period of separation by over one month. There is also deliberate intensification of the tone of complaint in the original.[16] However, one has to admit that the whole image he presents in "The River-Merchant's Wife" is that of Li Bo's creation. Its charm, simplicity, and power of stirring emotions all exist in the original.

How about the style of language, then? How much affinity and how much difference are there between the two versions? Kodama in his comparison argues that Li Bo, by using an elevated diction, makes "the speaker appear to be a prudent woman," whereas Pound in his translation presents "the image of a young wife, full of love but naive and simple . . ." (76). One of the examples he gives in support of his argument is Li Bo's choice of the word *qie* 妾 for the speaker to refer to herself ("the first person singular pronoun 'I'") and the word *lang* 郎 to refer to the person addressed ("the second person singular"). He explains that *lang* was used here "to denote the husband with a tone of reverence," and *qie* "was used to show the wife's humility toward her husband" (76).

Apparently, Kodama has gotten the dictionary meaning right but misread the overtone in the context. As a matter of fact, in the Tang period (A.D. 618–907), *qie* and *lang* were used not only by married women to indicate themselves and their husbands, but also by unmarried women to denote themselves and their lovers. In colloquial usage, moreover, the two words carry different overtones in different contexts. In Li Bo's *Qie bo ming* ("Wretched Me, Flimsy Fate"),[17] a dramatic monologue by an imperial concubine that has fallen out of favor, for example, the speaker calls herself *qie* with a miserable tone (hence "wretched me" rather than simply "me" in my rendering). In Li Bo's *Yang pan'r* ("Rebellious Yang"), a song of love between two unmarried people, we hear the female speaker chant:

> *You* (my dear) sang "Rebellious Yang"
> And *I* poured the *xin feng* wine
>
> . . . . . .
>
> *You* (my dear) drunk, stayed overnight in *my* home.[18]
> (Emphasis added)

The young woman calls her lover *jun* 君 (a synonym of *lang*) and herself *qie* apparently with much tenderness and affection.[19]

In *Mo shang zeng mei ren* ("To a Beautiful Girl on the Street"), still another poem by Li Bo, the speaker (very much the poet himself) ran into a beautiful young woman, who

> . . . smiling, pulled aside a pearl-strung portiere.
> Pointing to a red abode beyond, "That's *my* home."[20]
> (Emphasis added)

Sure enough, the flirt on the street denotes herself with the word *qie* in a frivolous tone. Similarly, the word *lang* also carries different overtones in different situations.

With this understanding, we realize that in "The River-Merchant's Wife," Li Bo chooses these words precisely because he wants to let the teenage wife speak in an intimate and loving tone. Pound gets this right from the context where Fenollosa and others fail to do so because they depend on a literal reading.

Another problem Kodama finds in Li Bo's language is allusiveness. He contends that by putting allusions into the young wife's mouth, Li Bo has made her sound like "an educated woman who is well versed in classical Chinese literature" (76). This is again an anachronistic reading. In fact, the allusions which Kodama calls literary were in household use in medieval China. By saying "have the faith of Wei-sheng,"[21] the River-Merchant's Wife simply means "have an eternal faith," or in Pound's phrase, "Forever and forever and forever." She doesn't necessarily know all the details of the legendary story about Wei-sheng. Similarly, when she says "climb up the waiting tower," she actually means "look out for my husband to return with no real hope." This is just like a housewife in thirteenth- or fourteenth-century England alluding to Greek myths or parables in the Bible. If Chaucer's Wife of Bath's copious biblical allusions do not sound particularly cultivated to the English audience, neither does Li Bo's River-Merchant's Wife with her legendary references appear so well-versed in classical literature to the Chinese reader.

Kodama, however, also finds Li Bo's geographical references unfitting for the naive speaker. He wonders why the teenage wife "strangely has full knowledge about Kuto [Qutang Gorge] and Enyotai [Yanyu Reef]" up the Yangtze River (78). The reason is in Chinese reality. In the eighth century A.D., Nanjing on the lower Yangtze River (or Jiankangfu as it was then called) was already a flourishing city, and about two miles south of it was a district called Chang-gan, or "Ch'ang-kan," where a high percentage of the population relied on traveling along the river to make a living. The teenage wife, who grew up in this district, must have from early girlhood heard a hundred times from adults about how "The monkeys [made] sorrowful noise overhead" when they traveled through the narrows, and how boats were smashed against the Yanyu Reef and swallowed up in the torrent. Indeed, until the ominous huge rock at the entrance of Qutang Gorge was blasted away in 1958, Yangyu Reef remained a synonym of peril to the people living along the Yangtze River for centuries. Therefore, it was only natural for the River-Merchant's Wife to think of these perilous spots and, moreover, refer to them with fear and apprehension when her own husband had gone to that area on business.

In Pound's rendering, "You went into far Ku-to-en, by the river of swirling eddies," we find that the two place names—"Ku-to" and "Yen-yotai"—from Fenollosa's notes are conflated into one, while words like "far" and "the river of swirling eddies" are added to indicate the distance and danger of the locality. Kodama believes that Pound's coinage of the new place name has an effect of "molding [the speaker's] character as an innocent, modest, helpless, and lonely woman" (79). But the fact of the matter is that even if Pound has such an intention, his audience will not be able to sense it as Kodama has, for whether the place name is coined or real, it sounds all the same to them. On the other hand, the words added by Pound will surely convey a message, which is indeed the association that the Chinese reader will get from the geographical names.

There is no question, then, that "The River-Merchant's Wife" is a thing of "a supreme beauty"[22] whether considered as a verse or as a translation.[23] What about the "Exile's Letter," the piece that Pound in 1920 called one of his "major personae" (qtd. in Bush, "Pound and Li Po" 42)? Can it be relied on as a translation as well? Bush has sought to answer this question by comparing it to the Fenollosa text without reference to Li

Bo's original.[24] Not surprisingly, he has found Pound arbitrarily inventive in his reworking. He is unaware that many of these "inventions" actually serve to restore "for the English readers something close enough to the 'power' and 'effect' of the original" (Yip 87).[25]

Bush, for example, accuses Pound of magnifying Li Bo's nostalgia for "a single friendship" to include one for "a poetic community" by inserting "without authority" the pronouns "we" and "they" into lines 4, 5, 7, 9, and 10 in the opening section of the poem ("Pound and Li Po" 42–43). The accusation is unjustified first because the idea about a poets' club is provided by Fenollosa in the immediate context. From his note on line 6,

From all parts of the Empire came flocking wise and great guests in prosperous court life (to me while I was there)[26]

any reader can reasonably infer that it was not Li Bo alone who was "drunk for month on month, forgetting the kings and princes." Nor was it he or his closest friend alone who "made nothing of sea-crossing or of mountain-crossing" (P 137) for those joyous gatherings.

Second, this notion about "a poetic community" is also supported by Fenollosa's notes for the next section of the poem, where the poet-speaker recollects how he and his closest confederate were welcomed by "The governor of Kanchu" and "the sennin of Shiyo" to a terrific feast that allowed them to forget all social norms of behavior and drink and sing and dance to their hearts' content. From this Pound can legitimately conclude that Li Bo's reminiscence is not merely about "a single friendship."

Further, the keynote of Li Bo's original text for the "Exile's Letter" is exactly his nostalgia for a past when poets could speak out their "hearts and minds . . . without regret." This theme is, however, bemuddled by Fenollosa's effort to introduce the pronoun "I" into his "(And) once drunk for months together I despised Kings + princes" and the pronoun "you" into his "(You) considering it nothing even if you had to roll over mts. . . . " (Agents are absent in Li Bo's original lines. This feature is indicated in Fenollosa's gloss.[27]) Pound's interference, while failing to preserve the intended ambiguity that invites both interpretations, has brought back for us the overall force and style in Li Bo's masterpiece. Arthur Waley, an early critic of Pound's translation of Li Bo, apparently sees eye to eye with him on this point. In his 1918 retranslation of the "Exile's Letter" ("a shot meant for Pound," according to Achilles Fang[28]), he simply follows Pound's way to introduce the pronouns "we" and "they" into the corresponding lines.[29]

Comparing the "Exile's Letter" only to Fenollosa's notes, Bush also argues that the passage starting with line 47 ("And you would walk out with me to the western corner of the castle") in the third section contains "some of [Pound's] finest inventions" (44). Amusingly, to my mind what Bush calls fine "inventions" represent some of Pound's most admirable practices, in which he pierces beneath Fenollosa's crippled notes to Li Bo's original consciousness.

Bush, for example, notices that Pound has "subtracted agents and agency from Fenollosa's line, 'we floated a boat and played with the water.'" "Through a series of present participles," he goes on to explain, "Pound's lines convey a privileged moment in which . . . the human world and the world of the landscape reflect each other, and the equilibrium suggests the permanent ministry of poetry" (44–45). Readers of Li Bo are aware that the harmony Bush admires as Pound's "invention" exists in his original lines. In the memorable passage, it may be noted, the poet-speaker's spirit is at its height, and he spontaneously begins to activate vision upon vision without resorting to naming their agents and agency. It is amazing that from Fenollosa's virtually impossible gloss (rather than his readable literal translation),

making–	boat	play	water	month	drum	sing
float		with		organ		play out
						make noise

Pound should have captured something close to the Tang poet's original impulse and manner. In reworking the version, therefore, he chooses to link the visionary images with present participles and not to introduce any agents or agency. By doing so he has in fact reproduced for the English-speaking readers something proximate enough to Li Bo's effect.

The next line (line 43 in Li Bo's original text and line 51 in the "Exile's Letter") will serve to illustrate Pound's dramatic resurrection more effectively. Li Bo's *wei bo long lin suocao lu* 微波龍鱗莎草綠 is a perfect example of his robust poetic imagination. Fenollosa's notes show he doesn't understand that *long lin* 龍鱗 and *suocao lu* 莎草綠 embody two reflexive visionary processes (turning dragon-scales + going grass green) rather than two isolated visionary images:

faint waves dragon scales water-floating grass green ripples
The small ripples resembled the scales of dragons, and the water grass
   was green.

With his Vorticist sensibility, Pound was, however, able to go beneath Fenollosa's fragmented gloss to "a radiant node or cluster" in the original poetry, and his "With ripples like dragon-scales, going grass green on the water" (P 138) recaptures for us both Li Bo's visual imagination and his poetic energy. For Bush, this line exhibits another "fine invention" by Pound. But by noting that Pound's "go grass green on the water" telescopes "the greening power of nature with the metamorphic power of poetic vision" (45), he has in fact testified to Pound's resurrection force.

As Li Bo's poem draws to its close, it reveals that all the poet-protagonist's recollections about genuine companionship are intended to build up a sense of grievance beyond human expression. As Bush observes, Pound extracting from Fenollosa's crib for the last four lines gives an ending still more dismal than Fenollosa's already dismal literal translation:

> What is the use of talking, and there is no end of talking,
> There is no end of things in the heart.
> I call in the boy,
> Have him sit on his knees here
>   To seal this,
> And send it a thousand miles, thinking.
> (P 139)

In this Bush recognizes a distinctive Poundian voice. His judgment is precise. Yet, I have to add: turning the conclusion Poundian in this case does not cause it to be any less like Li Bo, or his poet-speaker for that matter; quite to the contrary, it has the happy effect of making it closer to the original sensibility. Li Bo's masterpiece can be appropriately summed up by two words: nostalgia and grievance. Pound's ending word "thinking," like Li Bo's *yao xiang yi* 遙相憶 , hits both the aspects with emphasis on the emptiness of the heart and silence whereas Fenollosa's "we think of each other in (at a) distance" with many explanatory words only confuses the reader.

Yip, in *Ezra Pound's Cathay*, asserts that "even within the limits of free improvisation and paraphrase in the 'Exile's Letter,' [Pound] sometimes tends to come closer in sensibility to the original than a literal translation might" (93). To illustrate this sensitive opinion he cites precisely the above-quoted passage side by side with his own version and Waley's version of the corresponding lines.[30]

In the 1960s Yip was given access to the reproductions of Fenollosa's notes for only a few *Cathay* poems.[31] He was able to defend passionately Pound's "Lament of the Frontier Guard" as a translation of Li Bo (84–88) precisely because he had inspected Fenollosa's notes for that poem. Had he had access to Fenollosa's crib for the "Exile's Letter," I am confident, he would have given the centerpiece of *Cathay* more credit than having to yield to Waley's biased assessment ("a brilliant paraphrase") (83).

Indeed, after consulting Fenollosa's text one will see that Pound's improvised phrase "smothered in laurel groves" in line 13, a notorious instance for dismissing the centerpiece as a translation, is in fact closer in undertone to the original than Fenollosa's confusing "climbed the laurel trees." Fenollosa's instructor Mori apparently did not know that the Chinese idiom *pan guizhi* 攀桂枝 actually means "visiting Taoists and becoming a hermit" (Xiao 289) (hence Fenollosa's faulty crib "climbed the laurel trees (they are abundant there and there is a poem of ???? empire by old king of ????) and a poetical way of saying he had to go there"). Nor does Waley, who mistakenly renders the expression as "to pluck my laurel-branch," and elaborates in a footnote, "i.e. to marry Miss Hsü?" (*Li Po* 13). Of the three versions in question, Pound's is clearly the only one that doesn't mar the original sense and sentiment. Similarly, after examining Fenollosa's crib, one will hesitate to blame Pound for misrepresenting "The governor of Kanchu" as "The foreman of Kan Chu," for, as Bush notes in his transcript, "in Fenollosa's hand, this word [governor] looks much like 'foreman'" ("Pound and Li Po" 50).

In April 1915, the "Exile's Letter, from the Chinese of Rihaku (Li Po)" was singled out by Pound for special appearance in the Chicago *Poetry*. Pound had every reason to prize this piece and to look upon it as one of his "major personae." The original text of the "Exile's Letter," as he must have detected from Fenollosa's fragmented notes, bespeaks not only the Tang poet's but to a considerable degree his own personality and impulse. In Giles' *History* he had first learned that Li Bo's "wild Bohemian life, his gay and dissipated career at Court, his exile, and his tragic end, all combine to form a most effective setting for the splendid flow of verse which he never ceased to pour forth" (151). Through going over the "64 poems" in Fenollosa's two "Rihaku" notebooks he had managed to secure a firm grip of the Tang poet's spirit and style. It was in Li Bo's masterpiece, however, that he had come to see most vividly how the Other mirrored the Self: Li Bo's poet-speaker was a perfect Poundian hero, and Li Bo's Taoist sensibility epitomized Pound's Vorticist insight virtually in all detail.

"The Pound of 'The Flame' . . . like the earlier Pound of 'Hilda's Book' . . . and the later Pound of Canto 47 . . . and the 60-year-old Pound who wrote in Pisa that 'the sage delighteth in water' . . . was Taoist in his deepest impulses," wrote Kenner (456). So, it was the parallel of Li Bo's Taoist sensibility and Pound's Vorticist insight that ensured the triumph of *Cathay*.[32] But Pound himself also benefited from translating Li Bo and other Chinese poets. He found a way to clarify and enrich his Vorticist poetics. By doing so he succeeded in deepening the poetic revolution he had endeavored to inaugurate.

6 IMITATING WANG WEI:

TOWARD *THE CANTOS*

Pound's contact with Chinese poets did not come to an end with the publication of *Cathay,* however. The appearance of the book in April 1915 rather marked the beginning of his persistent effort to draw on Chinese sources for Modernist inspiration. An immediate proof of this is his inclusion of two Chinese adaptations in his contribution to Wyndham Lewis' *Blast* 2 (July 1915). As Chapple notes, Pound "produced drafts for far more poems than he actually finished or incorporated into the *Cathay* volume" (12). The two Chinese poems he contributed to *Blast* 2 were chosen from his unused drafts for *Cathay.* The first, "Gnomic Verses," is an improvisation he produced after working on Fenollosa's notes for Li Bo's quatrain "Calm Night Thought."[1] Chapple calls it "a silly parody of what Pound must have considered rather obtuse poetry" (20). The second, "Ancient Wisdom, Rather Cosmic," is, however, a fine adaptation of Li Bo's *Gu feng* ("Ancient Airs"), no. 9:

> So-shu dreamed,
> And having dreamed that he was a bird, a bee, and a butterfly,
> He was uncertain why he should try to feel like anything else,
>
> Hence his contentment.[2]
> (P 123)

The source of this poem is in Fenollosa's first "Rihaku" notebook (no. 110, "Shoshu dreamed of being a butterfly"). Though Pound probably knew (from reading Giles) that the dreamer in Li Bo's poem was the fourth-century B.C. Taoist philosopher Zhuangzi (Chuang Tzu) (ca. 369–ca. 286 B.C.),[3] he retained Fenollosa's Japanese spelling of his name "So-shu"[4] as he had retained "Rihaku" for Li Bo and "To-em-mei" for Tao Qian (T'ao Ch'ien). In Li Bo's presentation of Zhuangzi's Taoist vision of the freedom of metamorphosis between the human world and the natural world, Pound may have perceived a resemblance to his youthful faith in the truth of Greek myths (SR 92). In "The Tree" for "Hilda's Book," he had sung,

> I stood still and was a tree amid the wood,
> Knowing the truth of things unseen before;
> (P 3)

and in *The Spirit of Romance,* he had expressed a belief in the Greek hypothesis "that the little cosmos 'corresponds' to the greater, that man has in him both 'sun' and 'moon'" (94). Now Chinese lyrics influenced by Taoist teachings seem to have revealed to Pound a wisdom greater than that of the Greek ancients. The Chinese, as presented in these verses, were capable of not only uniting humanity with nature, but, more amazingly, ignoring all distinctions between the two worlds.

If in his 1914–15 Chinese exploration, Pound appeared to be a fervent lover of Li Bo, he was to become a wholehearted admirer of Li Bo's contemporary Wang Wei ("Omakitsu") (699–759) in the ensuing years when he began writing and rewriting his Ur-Cantos. I take for proof of this neglected encounter Pound's own statements made on various occasions between mid-1916 and early 1919. The first of such statements is to be found in Pound's letter to Iris Barry, dated 24 August 1916: "I have spent the day with Wang Wei, eighth century Jules Laforgue Chinois" (L 144). With it we can determine the approximate date when Pound began his serious dialogue with Wang Wei. In addition, we are enabled to see the reason why Pound should at this point show such an enthusiasm for the Tang painter-poet: he saw in him a modern sensibility and a likeness to the French Symbolist Jules Laforgue. Pauline Yu contends that "Wang Wei's work is a fulfillment of several key Symbolist aims" (*The Poetry of Wang Wei* 22). To illustrate this, she enumerates as many as four poetic notions shared by the Tang poet and the Symbolists (22–28).[5] Thus Pound's comparison of Wang Wei to Laforgue confirms his critical perceptivity. In Wang Wei he apparently discovered the possibility of further modernizing his style by combining the French and Chinese influences.

Pound made a second statement about Wang Wei in his letter to Kate Buss, dated 4 January 1917. There he agains emphasizes Wang Wei's modernity and his resemblance to the French Symbolists: "Omakitsu is the real modern—even Parisian—of VIII cent. China—" (*L* 154). This seems to indicate that Pound was continuing his study of Wang Wei in early 1917, when he was almost ready to publish Ur-Cantos 1–3 ("Three Cantos"). Nevertheless, it was not until November 1918—when he was rewriting Ur-Canto 4—that he finally brought out a version of Wang Wei's poem in *The Little Review*:

Dawn on the Mountain

Peach flowers turn the dew crimson,
Green willows melt in the mist,
The servant will not sweep up the fallen petals,
    And the nightingales
Persist in their singing.

                        Omakitsu

(*EPPP* 3: 217)

This poem we mentioned in passing in Chapter Two, when discussing Pound's pre-Fenollosan "Ts'ai Chi'h." Apparently Pound was not satisfied with his translation, for he remarked in an essay on Rémy de Gourmont in the February 1919 *Little Review*: "I do not think it possible to over-emphasize Gourmont's sense of beauty. The mist clings to the lacquer. His spirit was the spirit of Omakitsu; his *pays natal* was near to the peach-blossom-fountain of the untranslatable poem" (*LE* 343). Here Pound is of course comparing de Gourmont's sense of beauty to that of Wang Wei.

"The mist clings to the lacquer" is an image from "Dawn on the Moun-
tain," which, in Pound's view, vividly sums up de Gourmont's—and per-
haps also Laforgue's and the Prufrock Eliot's—sensibility.

Wang Wei's spirit indeed entered Pound's Ur-Cantos along with other
influences of the period. In a fragment among his early drafts for Canto 4,
Pound laments for his lost adolescence, using Wang Wei's sensual image
as an analogy:

> When you find that feminine contact
>   has no longer the richness
>   of Omakitsu's verses,
> Know then, o man,
>   that the Cytherean has turned from you,
>   fugges!
> When the smoke no longer
>   hangs
>   clings upon the laquer,
> When the night air no
>   longer clings
>   to your cuticle,
> When the air has in it no
>   mystery about her,
> . . . . . .
> Know then that the days
>   of your adolence [sic] are
>   ended
>   fugaces, fugges, fugus
> (qtd. in Froula 103)

Christine Froula, in her study of the genesis of Canto 4, takes pains to
show how Pound created the "Seven enigmatic lines [that] follow the
wind poem" ("Smoke hangs on the stream, / The peach-trees shed bright
leaves in the water, / Sound drifts in the evening haze, / . . . " [CA 16])
by fusing the "smoke" image with other images from Wang Wei's poetry.
According to her, the other images in the passage—"the stream," "The
peach-trees," "The bark," "the ford," "an open field," and so on—are taken

from Fenollosa's version of Wang Wei's "Peach Source Song" (40–41),
and her assertion is certainly correct.

"Peach Source Song" (*Tao yuan xing*)[6] is known in Chinese literary
history as a superb rewriting of Tao Qian's prose masterpiece "Peach-
blossom Fountain" (*Tao hua yuan ji*) by the then only nineteen-year-old
Wang Wei.[7] In Tao Qian's original work, the narrator recounts how a
fisherman lost his way among a grove of peach trees and found "a new
world of level country, of fine houses, of rich fields, of fine pools, and of
luxuriance of mulberry and bamboo." He was told that the ancestors of
these people, some five hundred years before, had taken refuge to escape
tyranny and war and that "they had remained, cut off completely from
the rest of the human race." After being feasted for several days, the
fisherman returned to tell of his experience, and inevitably the Governor
sent out troops to find the valley, but mysteriously the "Peach-blossom
Fountain" had disappeared (Giles, *History* 130–31).

Since its appearance in the fifth century, Tao Qian's "Peach-blossom
Fountain" has enjoyed an unparalleled popularity. The classic has given
rise to countless imitations and rewritings in art and literature. Two
brilliant artists, Qiu Ying of the sixteenth century and Shi Tao of the
seventeenth century, have been particularly successful in their endeavors
to bring the great recluse's Taoist paradise alive with their ink and brush.
Their scroll paintings share the same title, *The Peach Blossom Spring*. A late
sixteenth- or seventeenth-century copy of Qiu Ying's masterpiece (fig.
15) is now hanging in the Art Institute of Chicago,[8] whereas the original
Peach Blossom Spring by Shi Tao (figs. 16 and 17) has been in the Freer
Collection since 1882.[9] Though we are unaware of any visit of Pound to
the two galleries that held these artworks, we are reasonably certain that
he studied Giles' version of Tao Qian's allegory in late 1913. He must
have detected the derivative nature of Wang Wei's "Peach Source Song,"
for in his 1919 article he refers to the Tang poet's work by his precursor's
title in Giles' translation ("the peach-blossom-fountain of the untranslat-
able poem").

Pound was introduced to the Chinese painter-poet much earlier than
the summer of 1916. Indeed, he may already have heard about Wang
Wei in 1909 from his friend Laurence Binyon. Moreover, he may have

contemplated in Binyon's Oriental Gallery two visually imposing Chinese landscape paintings: *Landscape in Blue and Green Style,* said to be done by Wang Wei (fig. 18), and *Landscape of the Wang River,* a copy of the Tang master's artistic recreation of his country home by the Yuan artist Zhao Mengfu (1254–1322) (fig. 19).[10] In *Painting in the Far East,* Binyon describes Wang Wei as the "founder of the southern school" of Chinese landscape painting, who was "even more famous for his poetry than for his painting." "Of Wang Wei," Binyon notes, "it was said that his poems were pictures, and his pictures poems" (74). Even if Pound hadn't read *Painting in the Far East* (which is unlikely), he would have heard all about this from Binyon himself while viewing the above-mentioned scroll paintings.

Pound could also have learned something about Wang Wei from Fenollosa's *Epochs of Chinese and Japanese Art* (which he probably read shortly before his meeting with Mrs. Fenollosa in the fall of 1913). There the American Orientalist not only offers a brief account of Wang Wei's outstanding achievements in art (119–20), but includes among his illustrations a reproduction of the "Famous Painting of a Waterfall, said to be an original by Omakitsu (Wang Wei)" (fig. 20).

It was not until October 1913, when Pound began reading Giles' *History,* that he got a chance to examine versions of Wang Wei's poetic work. Giles, nevertheless, seems to have a rather low opinion of Wang Wei, granting him only a single page and offering versions of but two of his short lyrics (150).

In contrast to Giles, who ranks Wang Wei conspicuously below such Tang poets as Li Bo, Du Fu, Han Yu, and Bo Juyi, Fenollosa, in his Chinese poetry notebooks, gives the Tang painter-poet sufficient attention. In September 1896, when Fenollosa began taking Chinese poetry lessons with Hirai, he concentrated on just two poets: Wang Wei and Li Bo. His Notebook 7, a record of his sessions with Hirai and Shida, contains nine poems of Wang Wei ("Omakitsu"), which Pound numbered 1 to 9 in blue pencil when he leafed through the pages in November 1914. It was apparently due to Fenollosa's influence that Pound put Wang Wei among the top eight figures in his 1915 list of major Chinese poets, a list showing his choice for *Cathay.* If Pound presented only one

15. Anonymous (after Qiu Ying) (ca. 1510–92), detail of
The Peach Blossom Spring. The Art Institute of Chicago,
Kate S. Buckingham Fund, 1951.

Below: 16. Shi Tao (1641–ca. 1717),
The Peach Blossom Spring. The Freer Gallery of Art,
Washington, D.C.

17. Detail of 16 (below).

18. Anonymous (after Wang Wei) (699–759), *Landscape in Blue and Green Style*. The British Museum, London.

19. Zhao Mengfu (1254–1322) (after Wang Wei), detail of *Landscape of the Wang River,* 1309. The British Museum, London.

poem by Wang Wei in *Cathay* (epigraph to "Four Poems of Departure"), it was because his 1914–15 Chinese endeavor was essentially an encounter between himself and Li Bo, and *Cathay* is a book mainly devoted to "Rihaku's" work.

Pound did turn his attention to Wang Wei, though. In fact, we have evidence not only that he studied Wang Wei's poetry in August 1916 (and probably also in 1917 and 1918), but that he made painstaking efforts to rework Fenollosa's versions of Wang Wei as well, between 1916 and 1918. As Froula has demonstrated, Pound worked on no. 2 of Fenollosa Notebook 7, a version of Wang Wei's "Peach Source Song," in 1916 or 1917, and produced a fragmented passage for Canto 4 (40–41). The

20. Attributed to Wang Wei (699–759), *A Waterfall.*
The Chishakuin Temple, Kyoto.

"Seven enigmatic lines" of Canto 4 ("Smoke hangs on the stream / The peach-trees shed bright leaves in the water / . . . "), while alluding to Tao Qian's "Peach-blossom Fountain," have actually conflated images from two of Wang Wei's poems in Fenollosa Notebook 7: no. 2, "Peach Source Song," and no. 5, "Farm Field Pleasure" (Pound's "Dawn on the Mountain").[11] The effort is reminiscent of Pound's earlier conflation of two separate poems of Li Bo in *Cathay's* "The River Song." It is also indicative of the evolution of Pound's "ideogrammic method" for *The Cantos,* a method characterized by concrete and fragmentary presentations.

Furthermore, among one of the three sheaves of leaves in the Beinecke folder labeled "Chinese Poetry, Notes by Pound, including translations" (Notebook 15), one will find Pound's typed drafts for eight of Wang Wei's poems. The sources of these drafts are easily identifiable because their numbers correspond to those given to Fenollosa's versions contained in his Notebook 7. (No. 2, "Peach Source Song," is unfortunately missing.) By special permission, they are presented in Appendix II as Pound typed them, but with the incorporation of his autograph revisions in italics, some adjustment of spacing and indentation, and my correction of his typographic errors in square brackets.[12]

Although no date is given anywhere, we can still determine that these drafts came after *Cathay*, because for no. 6, the *Cathay* piece, Pound gives not a translation but a brief note, in which the Latin phrase "vide Cathay" betrays a date later than *Cathay* (see Appendix II).

On 24 August 1916, Pound observed to Iris Barry, "I have spent the day with Wang Wei, eighth century Jules Laforgue Chinois" (L 144). A week later, on 31 August 1916, he wrote his mother, "I have nearly finished with the Chinese part of Fenollosa stuff rec'd" (YCAL). From these remarks, we can safely infer that between late August and early September 1916 Pound was waging a new attack on the Fenollosa Chinese poetry notebooks. The result of this endeavor was evidently the aforementioned typescript, which includes among other things his drafts for eight (or all nine) of Wang Wei's poems.[13]

It is worth noting that in Chinese literary history, Wang Wei is known not only as a painter-poet, but, more importantly, as a poet with strong Taoist/Chan-Buddhist leanings. Despite the high positions he held at court (the emperor's adviser at one time), he studied Taoism and Buddhism seriously. For about ten years, it is said, he kept visiting a Chan monk. Accordingly his poetry turned manifestly Taoist/Chan-Buddhist after he acquired the Wang River estate miles east of the Tang capital, Chang'an, where he had the privilege to lead a double life as high official and recluse.[14] It is true that a number of other Tang poets (notably Li Bo, Meng Haoran, and Bo Juyi) also show to varying degrees the influence of Taoist/Chan-Buddhist thinking. But it is in Wang Wei's work that we find the full development of a poetics based on the Taoist/Chan-Buddhist conceptions of nonbeing as being, emptiness as form, and the transcendence of the duality between self and world. Fenollosa, who had studied Taoism/Buddhism in Japan, was obviously aware of some of the religious implications in Wang Wei's poems. To his gloss and literal translation of the seventh poem, "Painful Heat" ("Suffering from Heat"), for instance, he appends this note: "There must be some Buddhist-Zen conception here, not nearly Confucian. Possibly derived from Roshin [Laozi]" (Fenollosa Notebook 7). The piece turns out to be Wang Wei's most cited

Buddhist lyric. Pauline Yu (*The Poetry of Wang Wei* 124) and Willis Barn-
stone (lii–liii), in discussing Wang Wei's religious dimension, both refer
to this same poem.

What might first have caught Pound's eye in these versions of Wang
Wei, however, are their distinct Imagist-Vorticist qualities—their paint-
erliness, their conciseness, their suggestivity, and their detachment. (In
fact, Wang Wei derived all these strengths from Taoism/Chan-Bud-
dhism.) When Pound began making his modern epic, Imagist-Vorticist
works still had a strong fascination for him. In a note to his "Vorticism"
article, he indicated that he would like to write "a long vorticist poem"
(*GB* 94). We have reason to believe, therefore, that he had the intention
of borrowing certain Imagist-Vorticist colors for his Ur-Cantos as he
studied Wang Wei in 1916 and 1917. Pound obviously equates Wang
Wei's Taoism/Chan-Buddhism with his Imagism/Vorticism. This is possi-
ble, as Dasenbrock observes, "perhaps, only in a cosmos organized by
Ezra Pound . . ." (*Literary Vorticism* 226). "Farm Field Pleasure," a version
of Wang Wei in Fenollosa Notebook 7, which Pound was to work and
rework, shows this:

> Farm field pleasure   7 poems
> 1 of them
>
> encloses
> Peach crimson also contains inn rain
> from night
> Peach blossoms are crimson, and also contain the rain
> that has lodged there (in the night) (in the petals)
>
> also
> Willow green nearly belts spring smoke
> Willow is green, and also belts in with its silhouette
> this spring mists
> (parallelism of words of these lines)
>
> Flower falling house servant not yet sweep
>
> Uguisu crying mountain guest still sleeps
> Nightingale   (the person who lives here)
> (another couplet parallelism)

> All Chinese poems have rhyme, but their rhyming varies with different stanza.

Earlier, Pound had successfully reworked several poems of nature and of scenery with Taoist implications by Li Bo; three examples that immediately come to mind are "Taking Leave of a Friend," "The City of Choan," and portions of the "Exile's Letter." He had also tried his hand at translating at least one of Wang Wei's picture poems (epigraph to "Four Poems of Departure"). When he set his eyes on the notes above in August 1916, he couldn't have failed to be stricken by a similar beauty and simplicity. In fact, he probably immediately went to great labor. The effort is evidenced by a draft in his hand that I have unearthed among Pound's and Fenollosa's notes for "The Chinese Written Character" and the typed version in Notebook 15, to which I have just referred.

Pound's first draft for Wang Wei's "Farm Field Pleasure" (no. 6 of *Tian yuan le*) is penciled on the verso of a typed sheet cut in two, in Notebook 28. It is in fact a crib:

	pink		holds	water	
peach	~~red~~	also		after	rain
blossom	crimson	again	peep	holds	
			customer		
bird	cry	mt.	people	steal	sleep
	sing		sightsee		
	just		peach		
willow	green	more	clots	delicate	smoke
		than			
		~~intensified colour~~			
flower	falls				
			house servant		
	wont		~~still~~		
		~~not yet~~		sweep	
				up.	

By then, Pound had studied Fenollosa's unfinished essay "The Chinese Written Character as a Medium for Poetry,"[15] and, moreover, he was learning Chinese characters from his Morrison's Chinese-English Dictionary and Dorothy's Chinese language handbook.[16] He was therefore able to gloss two words—"peach" and "rain" in the first line—with Chinese characters, which turn out to be the characters that Wang Wei uses in the poem. Also, he was able to figure out from Fenollosa's crib that the original poem was a quatrain of six characters. His first draft is precisely an attempt to match each character in the original with a single English word. For certain words, such as Fenollosa's "belts" and "crying," he offers alternatives ("clots" and "sing") that prove to be closer equivalents to the corresponding Chinese characters. As for the line sequence, Pound cannot resist rearranging it. Thus Wang Wei's second line becomes the third, the fourth line becomes the second, and the third line becomes the last.

Probably during the same week in late August 1916, Pound typed out drafts for eight (or all nine) of Wang Wei's poems. No. 5 is "Farm Field Pleasure," for which he first produced the above crib:

> Peach flowers hold up the dew that shows crimson
> The green willows belt in the smoke-mist,
>> making lines in its denseness.
> Servant has not swept up the fallen petals,
> The guest of this mountain,
>> sleeps through the nightingales noise.

Here Pound is obviously trying to imitate Wang Wei's unique sense of color and form. He has restored Wang Wei's line order. And in doing so he triumphs in recapturing the contrast and parallelism that are in the original. His rendering of the last line is excellent, for it has successfully brought out the speaker's passive attitude. His translation of the first couplet, however, is not as satisfactory, for in order to achieve clarity he has destroyed Wang Wei's special charm, which resides chiefly in his brevity and elusiveness.

Pound evidently became dissatisfied with his typed draft version when he returned to the poem in 1917 or 1918, for he has left subsequent penciled revisions and deletions in the draft. One will observe from the typescript in the Beinecke Library (fig. 21) that he has substituted "turn the dew crimson" for "hold up the dew that shows crimson" in the first

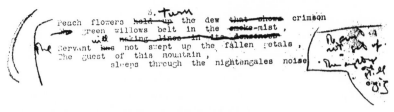

Above: 21. Ezra Pound, typed draft for "Dawn on the Mountain." The Beinecke Rare Book and Manuscript Library, Yale University. *Below:* 22. Ezra Pound, autograph draft for "Dawn on the Mountain." The Beinecke Rare Book and Manuscript Library, Yale University.

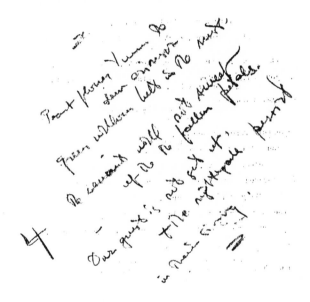

line, and deleted "smoke" and "making lines in its denseness" in the second line. And more important, on the verso of the previous typed leaf, one will notice yet another draft in his hand for Wang Wei's elusive quatrain (fig. 22):

> Peach flowers turn the
> dew crimson,
> Green willows belt in the mist,

> The servant will not sweep
> up the fallen petals,
> Our guest is not yet up,
> the nightingales persist
> in their singing.
>
> (Fenollosa Notebook 15)

A comparison with the published text of "Dawn on the Mountain" reveals that this is the draft closest to Pound's final product. But before submission, he apparently made one final effort to improve the concluding line. Thus, "Our guest is not yet up, / the nightingales persist / in their singing" is shortened to "And the nightingales / Persisting in their singing." It seems that Pound toiled to preserve everything essential, but every time he gained something he lost something else. In the first couplet, for instance, Pound brings across Wang Wei's visual clarity (his color contrast in particular) along with his formal terseness, but he has no way to recapture his simultaneity and mutual reflexiveness. (Chinese syntax allows agents to act as recipients as well, and vice versa. Thus in the first line, "peach blossoms" at once turn the "dew" pink and are turned glossy by the "dew.") And in the concluding line he has difficulty in highlighting both the natural/human dramas and their interrelation in succinct terms. To preserve concision, Pound is forced to sacrifice the human action ("Our guest is not yet up"), and hence the man-nature correspondence fundamental in Wang Wei's poetic world also.

Pound must have been deeply aware of his inadequacy in translating Wang Wei, for he never reprinted "Dawn on the Mountain." Moreover, upon referring to Wang Wei in the 1919 essay on de Gourmont, as we have seen, he calls his work "untranslatable" (*LE* 343). Wang Wei is indeed difficult to translate. Yu is substantially correct when she attributes the difficulty to the profound philosophy that underlies his poetry: " . . . his poems possess a surface simplicity. . . . Yet paradoxically, on second glance, his works reveal disturbingly elusive philosophical underpinnings, grounded in Buddhist metaphysics . . . " ("Wang Wei" 219).

Pound's failure to reproduce Wang Wei's whole art, however, has been potent, generative, ironically influential. First, he was exposed to a poetics firmly based on the nondualistic notions of Taoism/Chan Buddhism. Though Pound may not have been able to grasp Wang Wei's Taoist/Chan-Buddhist philosophy, he was by that point both intuitively and conceptually conditioned to appreciate the Tang poet's Taoist/ Chan-Buddhist art. In Yu's description, this art, perfected in Wang Wei's hand, is characterized by "its concentrated vision and form; its precise yet evocative imagery; its preference for the concise and concrete as opposed to the discursive and abstract; its mode of presentation which places as much value, if not more, on what is implied as on what is stated directly" (*The Reading of Imagery* 187). Apparently these traits corresponded precisely to Pound's Imagist/Vorticist doctrine. By imitating Wang Wei, he crystallized a critical insight that enabled him to expand subject and method.

Furthermore, Pound's encounter with Wang Wei began at the moment when he was composing and recomposing Ur-Cantos 1–3 ("Three Cantos"), and it continued through the years in which he became increasingly disenchanted with the uncertain manner with which he opened his modern epic. In *The Genesis of Ezra Pound's Cantos*, Bush has examined the influence of James, de Gourmont, Laforgue, Eliot, and Joyce on Pound's refashioned style for the Ur-Cantos of 1917–19. To these we must add the art of Wang Wei that contributed to the poetic breakthrough Pound made during this period. Bush is undoubtedly correct in emphasizing the dominant impact of de Gourmont,[17] who directed Pound to unify his long poem's "rag-bag" of subject matter by "the inflections of a single sensibility" (*Genesis* 159). However, it was through comparing him with Wang Wei ("His spirit was the spirit of Omakitsu . . . ") that Pound rediscovered de Gourmont's true value, and it was by drawing on Wang Wei's imagery ("The mist clings to the lacquer") that he found the most precise and the most vivid terms to redefine de Gourmont's sensibility. Moreover, in his attempt to imitate de Gourmont in the Ur-Cantos, Pound began by imitating Wang Wei, whose art he considered an equivalent of the French Symbolist's. Thus, in Ur-Canto 4 (now Canto 4), which marks Pound's turning away "from the uncertain Browningesque pastiche of 'Three Cantos' to the creation of a modern style" (Froula 5), we notice that the force which holds together his "rag-bag" of subject matter is a sensibility borrowed from Wang Wei.

In the Gourmontian context provided by Bush we can see clearly that the "Smoke-peach-trees" passage of Canto 4 that grew out of Pound's repeated experiments with Wang Wei is intended "precisely to display the complex subjectivity of a mind" (*Genesis* 202). As has been demonstrated previously, the sensory images of the passage are culled from two versions of Wang Wei's poems; "Peach Source Song" communicates a youthful yearning for Tao Qian's imaginary realm of the "Peach-blossom Fountain," where people live in abundance and in peace with nature and their environment, and "Farm Field Pleasure" celebrates the tranquil life of a Taoist/Chan-Buddhist recluse. Pound has made no attempt to follow the original designs of Wang Wei's poems. (In fact, I believe that he was rather relying on reminiscence sustained from reworking versions of Wang Wei to compose these lines.) Yet, by conflating key elements— sensual images and a serene manner that unmistakably bear the Tang poet's imprint—from the two lyrics, he has miraculously reproduced the single, deep, and unified emotion that is depicted in "Peach Source Song" and "Farm Field Pleasure."

The "[s]even enigmatic lines" of Canto 4 are thus a beautiful imitation of a sensibility. Behind "Smoke hangs on the stream, / The peach-trees shed bright leaves in the water, / Sound drifts in the evening haze, / . . . " stands unquestionably a mind, an intellect like Wang Wei's, that expresses serenity and leisure, a peace and harmony with nature. It is important to note that in this concrete and fragmentary depiction of a single sentiment Pound saw a method, a force capable of stitching together his "rag-bag" of subject matter. He did this by allowing the sensibility of the "Smoke-peach-trees" passage to underlie the different episodes of the poem. Thus the "Palace in smoky light" scene that opens Canto 4 is intended to be sustained in the reader's mind until it is juxtaposed with the "Smoke-peach-trees" passage. The echo of the "smoke" image is to set up a contrast that releases a complex of emotions involving visions of Trojan glory and wreckage repeated in modern European history. The "Ityn/Cabestan" episode with lines such as "And she went toward the window, / the slim white stone bar / Making a double arch . . . " is meant to be set side by side with the final two of the "[s]even enigmatic lines"—"Three steps in an open field, / Gray stone-posts leading. . . . " The Buddhist ideal suggested is to create a remarkable balance to the speaker's disgust with past and present impurity.

Kenner is perhaps the first critic to have an insight into Pound's early intention of building his long epic around certain concrete forms of Eastern spirits. For him, one such form that ideally fulfills Pound's purpose is the sacred twin pines of Takasago and Sumiyoshi (529). ("[W]hen [Pound] sent the three Ur-Cantos to Miss Monroe," Kenner notes, "he had said that his long poem's theme was ('roughly') *Takasago*'s theme . . . " [284].) Needless to say, the *Noh* image first referred to in Canto 4 evokes precisely the same Taoist/Chan-Buddhist consciousness of sincerity, peace, and eternal bond as lies behind the "Smoke-peach-trees" scene of Wang Wei. So does the vision of Père Henri Jacques conversing with the Sennin on Rokku. So does the "wind poem" that precedes the "[s]even enigmatic lines." True, the "wind poem" opens with Sō-Gyoku's (or rather Song Yu's) un-Taoist-like statement—"This wind, sire, is the king's wind. . . . " But the disciple of Qu Yuan's flattery is, after all, quoted only to be refuted by a more eloquent voice—"No wind is the king's wind"—which indubitably concurs with the poem's single unifying sentiment.

Significantly, the Taoist voice of Canto 4 rings again seventy cantos later in the first Pisan Canto—"The wind is part of the process / The rain is part of the process" (449)[18]—and again, another forty or so cantos later, in a fragment—"Do not move / Let the wind speak / that is paradise" (816)—just as the Chan-Buddhist images of Wang Wei recur many more times in the modern epic. Kenner is certainly right in maintaining that in Pound's long epic, "Wars, ruins, destructions—a crumbling wall in Mantua, smoke over Troy—these are never far out of mind . . . " (416). But to this statement we might add: superimposed upon the "evil things" of the world is an "eternal consciousness" often expressed by recurrent paradisiacal images from Eastern sources. This pattern is followed most visibly in Canto 16, where the speaker journeying from hell to Mount Purgatory has alternate visions of a pastoral region with Wang Wei's "calm field," "quiet air," and "fountain" (69) and of the Franco-Prussian War and the First World War. Wang Wei's "Smoke-peach-trees" scene, one must perceive, changes to "blossoms of the apricot" in Canto 13, "rain in the twilight," "Autumn moon," "the monk's bell," "Wild geese," and so on in Canto 49, and "Mt Taishan" and "Kuanon" in the Pisan Cantos. All these Pound first encountered in the culture-making artworks of the British Museum. In Canto 84, the last Pisan Canto, nonetheless, this Taoist/Chan-Buddhist landscape sticking in Pound's mind for more than thirty years finally returns in its prototypical form:

> where one walks into Spagna
> that T'ao Ch'ien heard the old Dynasty's music
>   as it might be at the Peach-blossom Fountain
> where are smooth lawns with the clear stream
> between them, silver, dividing. . . .
> (552)

So far, we haven't given a name to the style of concrete presentation, conflation, ellipsis, discontinuity, allusion, and juxtaposition that characterizes Pound's refashioned cantos from Ur-Canto 4 onward. The procedure, according to Bush, remained nameless until 1927, when Pound began to speak of it as the "ideogrammic method" (*Genesis* 10). We have reason to believe now that the seed of this method was nourished between 1917 and 1919 through Pound's study of Fenollosa's essay on "The Chinese Written Character" and the work of Wang Wei, de Gourmont, Laforgue, Eliot, and Joyce.[19]

In discussing Pound's development of the "ideogrammic method," critics tend to pay more attention to the source that provided its name and aesthetic framework than to the factors that contributed the substance. The fact is that Pound was in search of a theory promoting the kind of poetry he was constructing, and Fenollosa's essay on "The Chinese Written Character" appeared to serve the purpose ideally. Yes, we must understand that the essay's admiration for the alleged pictorial qualities of the Chinese written language is absurd and misleading.[20] But, as Bush has observed, Pound's interest was in "the spirit of Fenollosa's remarks about oriental logic," and not in "their letter" (*Genesis* 10). A proof for this, he points out, exists in one of Pound's 1919 notes to the essay: "These precautions should be broadly conceived. It is not so much their letter, as the underlying feeling of objectification and activity, that matters" (qtd. in Bush 179). So, for the Pound of 1919 Fenollosa's big essay was valuable principally because it offered him a way to account for the spirit underlying the poetry he was incorporating into his modern epic. In other words, in Pound's effort of 1917–19 to modernize the style of his Ur-Cantos, Fenollosa's essay on "The Chinese Written Character" served at most as a postulate that supported his spiritual sentiment, whereas the examples of Wang Wei, de Gourmont, Laforgue, Lewis, Eliot, Joyce, Cubist collage, and so on combined to supply the material and technique for the mode of presentation that gradually grew to be known as the "ideogrammic method."

To sum up, we see that what characterized Pound's transitional phase—the phase that witnessed the births of "Homage to Sextus Propertius" (1917) and his first refashioned Ur-Cantos—was his conscious effort to link past with present, and Eastern culture with Western culture. If, prior to 1917, he had in the main submitted himself to one influence at a time, starting from 1917 he began consciously to bring all the influences together. Pound's Modernist style for *The Cantos* is thus a style of superposition, superposing not just imagery upon emotion, but Wang Wei upon de Gourmont/Laforgue; Kung upon Malatesta/Adams—in short, past upon present and Eastern culture upon Western culture.

I will return to Pound in the Epilogue. The discussion of Williams' early encounter with the Chinese that follows in Part Two will show that the Orient bulked as large in Williams' move toward Modernism as in Pound's, though there is a difference between his and Pound's sense of China, and there is a difference between their ways of borrowing.

II

WILLIAMS'

EARLY

ENCOUNTER

WITH THE

CHINESE

7 "GIVE ME YOUR FACE,

YANG KUE FEI!"

I n "Portrait of the Author," first published in *Contact* in the spring of 1921, William Carlos Williams, who would some forty years later collaborate with David Rafael Wang (1931–1977) in translating and adapting thirty-eight Chinese poems including Li Bo's "Song of Chang-gan" (Pound's "The River-Merchant's Wife"),[1] alludes to a figure in Chinese history and literature. The allusion occurs in the fourth stanza of the poem Marianne Moore is willing to hail as "a super-achievement" (60):[2]

> In the spring I would drink! In the spring
> I would be drunk and lie forgetting all things.
> Your face! Give me your face, Yang Kue Fei!
> your hands, your lips to drink!
> Give me your wrists to drink—
> I drag you, I am drowned in you, you
> overwhelm me! Drink!
> Save me! The shad bush is in the edge
> of the clearing. The yards in a fury
> of lilac blossoms are driving me mad with terror.
> Drink and lie forgetting the world.
> (*CP* 1: 173)

Interestingly, in the oft-cited "Prologue to *Kora in Hell*," which Williams wrote in the summer of 1918, there is an allusion to the same figure:

My dear Miss Monroe:-
              No, I dont like "The
Growing Year" better would be "The In-Growing
year" but let me see now - what shall we call
these five ?
    "Fingers" might do, or "Relics" or "At last!"
    No.
    Call them : "Polemon" which according to a
small friend of ours is a new kind of Heaven.
    No.
    Call them: "Root Buds" There!

    Inclosed please find check for renewal of
my subscription.
    Best wishes to "Poetry" though I haven't
relished it as much recently as in the past -
for no reason that I can see either. Pound's
translation from the Chinese is something
of great worth well handled. Superb! I suppose
you've see his "Cathay" the Chinese things
are perhaps a few of the greatest poems written.
The first part of the Anglo Saxon thing shows
splendidly in contrast with the oriental stuff.

              Sincerely yours

              W. Williams

April 13, 1915

23. William Carlos Williams, letter to Harriet Monroe. The Joseph Regenstein
Library, The University of Chicago.

But some have the power to free, say a young matron pursuing her infant,
from her own possessions, making her kin to Yang Kuei-fei because of a
haunting loveliness that clings about her knees, impeding her progress as
she takes up her matronly pursuit. (SE 17)

Who was Yang Guifei? Where did Williams dig up her story? Did he
learn it from an English version of Bo Juyi's (Po Chü-i) narrative poem,
Chang hen ge ("The Everlasting Wrong"),[3] that is largely responsible for

the lady's fame in China? If this is true, what relation may his interest in Bo Juyi's long poem bear to the recently discovered short lyric "To the Shade of Po Chü-i" (CP 1: 133)? Is it possible that Williams, who called Pound's *Cathay* "something of great worth well handled" and "a few of the greatest poems written" in his 13 April 1915 letter to Harriet Monroe (fig. 23),⁴ was inspired to engage in an extended dialogue with the Tang poet Bo Juyi (772–846) shortly afterward? An examination of these questions will not only add a new dimension to our comprehension of relevant poems by Williams, but shed light on the enigma of his early enthusiasm for Chinese poetry.

As is vaguely suggested in Williams' allusions, Yang Guifei (719–56) was a famous enchantress in Chinese history. She lived in an era designated by historians as "high Tang,"⁵ and was the favorite concubine of Ming Huang, the Brilliant Emperor (also known as Xuanzong) (685–762), whose reign (712–56) produced such gifted poets as Meng Haoran (689–740), Wang Wei (699–759), Li Bo (701–62), and Du Fu (712–70). By her extraordinary beauty and talent for music and dance, she won from the Tang monarch the affection he had previously given to the three thousand courtesans in his harem. After her advent in the palace, the Emperor spent all of his days and nights with her indulging in revelry and dissipation. As both lovers were fond of art, they surrounded themselves with musicians and dancers from the "Pear Garden," an imperial college of performing arts set up by Ming Huang for the purpose of training young entertainers. Li Bo, the foremost poet of the country, then holding a post at the Hanlin Academy (for distinguished scholars), was sometimes called in to compose verse to be sung for happy occasions.⁶ Indeed, Ming Huang and Yang Guifei were not only enthusiastic patrons of literature, but poets themselves. Ming Huang's best-known work, "To Confucius," written on his journey through the ancient sage's birth-place, is collected in the *Three Hundred Poems of the Tang* (*Tang shi san bai shou*, 1852).⁷

Yang Geifei's poems are mostly about inner court life. One of them, called "Dancing," has been rendered into English:

> Wide sleeves sway.
> Scents,

Sweet scents
Incessantly coming.

It is red lilies,
Lotus lilies,
Floating up,
And up,
Out of Autumn mist.

Thin clouds
Puffed,
Fluttered,
Blown on a rippling wind
Through a mountain pass.

Young willow shoots
Touching,
Brushing,
The water
Of the garden pool.
(Ayscough and Lowell 144)[8]

The version is included in *Fir-Flower Tablets*, a Chinese poetry anthology by Amy Lowell and Florence Ayscough, intended "to knock a hole" in Ezra Pound's *Cathay* (MacNair 43). It appeared in print no more than nine months after Williams brought out his "Portrait of the Author" in *Contact*.[9]

As the Brilliant Emperor spent too much time with Yang Guifei and favored her so much that he appointed her first cousin Yang Guozhong prime minister, discontent grew in his court. In the winter of 755, An Lushan, a powerful general competing for imperial favor with Yang Guozhong, rose in rebellion against the throne. When the capital Chang'an was taken by the rebellious army, Ming Huang and his court fled in haste southwest toward the mountain province of Shu (present-day Sichuan). On arrival at the foot of a hill called Mawei, however, the imperial soldiers refused to move on until Yang Guozhong was executed and Yang Guifei was forced to strangle herself with her own silk sash right in front

24. Qian Xuan (ca. 1235–1301), *Yang Guifei Mounting a Horse*. The Freer Gallery of Art, Washington, D.C.

of the dethroned monarch, who "cover[ed] his face / powerless to save" (Giles, *History* 171).

Yang Guifei's story, enriched by legend, has been the subject of numerous Chinese poems, dramas, novels, history books, and artworks. In the Freer Gallery of Art in Washington, D.C., is a short handscroll, *Yang Guifei Mounting a Horse* (fig. 24), in which the thirteenth-century traditionalist artist Qian Xuan delineates a dramatic scene from Yang Guifei's court life.[10] As the art critic James Cahill notes, in the painting, both of Ming Huang's "two greatest loves, beautiful women and fine horses," are embodied (*Chinese Painting* 100). Hanging in the Museum of Penn, where Pound and Williams were once students, is a large painting in the Tang "blue and green" style, *Ming Huang's Journey to Shu* (fig. 25). The piece was accessioned into the collection in 1916. For many years it was simply identified as "Travellers in the Mountains." In the late 1960s (several years after Williams' death) this painting was finally recognized as a copy of a Tang masterpiece, one of the three extant versions of *Ming Huang's Journey to Shu* (the other two are in the Palace Museum, Taiwan) (Lyons 22).

Of literary works portraying Ming Huang and Yang Guifei, the most

25. Anonymous (fifteenth-century copy of a ninth-century composition?), *Ming Huang's Journey to Shu*. The University of Pennsylvania Museum, Philadelphia.

26. Edith Emerson, "Yang Guifei as a Spirit at Peace." Reproduced in *Asia* magazine, October 1921.

brilliant is indisputably *Chang hen ge,* a 120-line poem by the mid-Tang poet Bo Juyi. The classic was composed in 806, exactly half a century after the death of Yang Guifei. Bo Juyi, then serving at a county some fifty miles west of Chang'an, was visiting a monastery in the suburb with two friends. The three of them talked about the love tragedy of Ming Huang and Yang Guifei with lots of sighs. At the suggestion of the two friends, Bo Juyi, who enjoyed a national fame as a poetic genius, made the immortal song. In it he boldly blended history with imagination, letting the enchantress first die a tragic death and then appear as an immortal making an avowal of eternal love for the Emperor. This anticlimactic ending is inexpertly represented by an illustration for "The Loveliest Lady of China," an October 1921 *Asia* magazine adaptation of the classic (fig. 26).

With its unique combination of romance and tragedy, lyricism and narrative, Bo Juyi's masterpiece has an appeal for both Chinese readers of various ages and Western sinologists of modern times. In the past hundred years or so, it has been repeatedly translated into English, French, German, and other languages.[11] At the time when Williams wrote "Prologue to *Kora in Hell*" and "Portrait of the Author," as far as I know, there were two English versions available: one by H. A. Giles in *A History of Chinese Literature* and one by L. Cranmer-Byng in *A Lute of Jade* (1909). Of the two books, Giles' *History* was by far the more influential. Indeed, it supplied Pound material for making his pre-Fenollosan adaptations from the Chinese. There is no indication of Williams' use of Cranmer-Byng's *A Lute of Jade.* But we know from the Williams Collection at Fairleigh Dickinson University that he owned a copy of Giles' book (the 1914 printing). A note in his hand on the front endpaper shows that he gave the book to his mother in 1916, knowing that she, too, would appreciate "the gentleness of the ancient Chinese poets" (see fig. 27).[12]

Most probably Williams purchased the volume shortly after reading Pound's *Cathay.* In "Prologue to *Kora in Hell,*" it may be noted, Williams alludes not only to Yang Guifei, but also to Li Bo, a poet Pound had translated in *Cathay* and Williams himself would much later recreate in "The Cassia Tree" (published posthumously in 1966). Speaking of the effect of alcohol on artistic creation, Williams refers to the high Tang poet as a genius who "is reported to have written his best verse supported

1916.

*For Mammie,
from her son
Billie

for the gentleness
of the ancient
Chinese poets –
knowing how you
love all gentle
things.*

27. William Carlos Williams, autograph note on front endpaper of H. A. Giles'
A History of Chinese Literature. The Florham-Madison Campus Library, Fairleigh
Dickinson University.

in the arms of the Emperor's attendants and with a dancing girl to hold
his tablet" (SE 25–26). Apparently, this story is taken from Giles' *History,*
for it is Giles who tells us that Li Bo wrote in drunkenness some of his
best lines for the Emperor. On one occasion, he did this with "a lady of
the seraglio to hold his ink-slab." On another occasion, he was brought
to the palace "supported between two eunuchs" (see fig. 28). Thereupon
two dancing girls "held up in front of him a pink silk screen," and he
dashed off some of his best-known poems (152).

Internal evidence thus indicates that Williams studied Giles' *History* no
later than 1916.[13] The story of Yang Guifei told in a form that well
matches Bo Juyi's original made such an impression on Williams that he

28. Su Liupeng (nineteenth century), *Li Bo in Drunkenness*, 1844. The Shanghai Museum, Shanghai.

first alluded to the figure in passing in "Prologue to *Kora in Hell*" (1918), and then, in "Portrait of the Author" (1921), he not only called up the charming image of the courtesan, but borrowed scenes and a theme from the Chinese classic.

The poem in Giles' rendering indeed begins with a depiction of Yang Guifei's outstanding beauty, followed by an account of how, on a chilly spring day after bathing in the warm water of an imperial pool, the enchantress captivates the Tang monarch's heart by her flower-like face and graceful movements, and of how she spends the spring nights with the Emperor finding the nights too short and the mornings coming too soon. This spring scene, with images such as "flowers," "face," "wine," "apartments," "chills," "darkness," and so on, is echoed in Williams' "Portrait of the Author." As far as the theme and the mood are concerned, however, the latter part of the poem shows a distinct resemblance to Williams' self-portrait. In this section, the speaker emphasizes the Tang emperor's extraordinary grief over the loss of Yang Guifei when he eventually returns to his palace in Chang'an. Gazing at the familiar objects and people, we are told, the heart-broken monarch wishes to forget everything in the present and have his beloved lady back. However, he never even has the good fortune to see her spirit in his dreams. This section of the Chinese classic is well presented in Giles' version:

> There is the pool and there are the flowers,
> > as of old.
> There is the hibiscus of the pavilion,
> > there are the willows of the palace.
> In the hibiscus he sees her face,
> > in the willow he sees her eyebrows:
> How in the presence of these
> > should tears not flow,—
> In spring amid the flowers
> > of the peach and plum,
> In autumn rains when the leaves
> > of the *wu t'ung* fall?
> To the south of the western palace
> > are many trees,
> And when their leaves cover the steps,
> > no one now sweeps them away.
> The hair of the Pear-Garden musicians
> > is white as though with age;
> The guardians of the Pepper Chamber
> > seem to him no longer young.
> Where fireflies flit through the hall,
> > he sits in silent grief;
> Alone, the lamp-wick burnt out,
> > he is still unable to sleep.

Slowly pass the watches,
          for the nights are now too long,
And brightly shine the constellations,
          as though dawn would never come.
Cold settles upon the duck-and-drake tiles,
          and thick hoar-frost,
The kingfisher coverlet is chill,
          with none to share its warmth.
Parted by life and death,
          time still goes on,
But never once does her spirit come back
          to visit him in dreams.
(172)

If we compare the passage above with lines in "Portrait of the Author" such as

My rooms will receive me. But my rooms
are no longer sweet spaces where comfort
is ready to wait on me with its crumbs.
A darkness has brushed them. The mass
of yellow tulips in the bowl is shrunken.
Every familiar object is changed and dwarfed.
I am shaken, broken against a might
that splits comfort, blows apart
my careful partitions, crushes my house
and leaves me—with shrinking heart
and startled, empty eyes—peering out
into a cold world.

and

In the spring I would drink! In the spring
I would be drunk and lie forgetting all things.
Your face! Give me your face, Yang Kue Fei!
your hands, your lips to drink!
(CP 1: 173)

we are immediately struck by a likeness in imagery, diction, and mood. One discerns that both poems reveal a bleak emptiness of the heart, and that both use the technique of juxtaposing associations with feelings to convey the theme. Though nothing has been said by Williams, the resemblance we find here should convince us that in "Portrait of the Author," Williams is alluding to this particular scene in Bo Juyi's masterpiece. Whereas the scene in the Chinese classic is imbued with the Tang emperor's sad feelings, the parallel setting in Williams' poem is filled with the poet's own sense of depression (hence the title "Portrait of the Author"). By calling forth the charming face of Yang Guifei, Williams, indeed, makes us feel the miraculous beauty and terror of spring as the Tang monarch experienced it in the eighth century and as Williams himself passed through it in his Rutherford home some twelve centuries later.[14]

Williams most probably rendered his self-portrait in the opening months of 1921.[15] Before spring has actually arrived, he already perceives the renewal of life in nature accompanied by a terrible violence. Thus the poem begins:

> The birches are mad with green points
> the wood's edge is burning with their green,
> burning, seething—No, no, no.
> The birches are opening their leaves one
> by one. Their delicate leaves unfold cold
> and separate, one by one.
> (CP 1:172)

For Williams, at this moment, the burning of natural energy is connected with the turbulence of human emotions. "[W]rapped by this flame" like the birches and flowers, he feels an urge to express the self in relation to the outside world, but finds his native art form inadequate, thus exclaiming, "Oh, I cannot say it. There is no word." He laments, "The world is gone, torn into shreds / with this blessing. What have I left undone / that I should have undertaken?" (CP 1: 172) Then, in the second stanza of the poem, he turns with a dramatic abruptness to his countrymen for an answer. By repeating the word "face" six times in seventeen lines ("O my

29. Henri Matisse, *The Blue Nude* ("Souvenir de Biskra"), 1907. The Baltimore
Museum of Art, The Cone Collection.

brother, you redfaced, living man," "We are alone in this terror, alone, /
face to face on this road," "But that face of yours—!" "I will poke my face /
into your face"), he articulates his disgust with the old face he and his
countrymen have to wear for so long[16] and his desire to get a new face, a
face that is expressive of the infusion of sense and sight and of the
metamorphosis of subject and object.

That face Williams discovered in modern French art, for example in
Henri Matisse's 1907 shock piece *The Blue Nude* ("Souvenir de Biskra") (fig.
29), which in a review ("A Matisse," SE 30–31) for *Contact* he urged his
countrymen to view as it was being displayed in the De Zayas Gallery in
New York City (Mariani 175).[17] That face he discovered also in classic
Chinese poetry, notably Bo Juyi's portrayal of Yang Guifei in *Chang hen ge*.
Thus he calls out:

Your face! Give me your face, Yang Kue Fei!
your hands, your lips to drink!
Give me your wrists to drink—
I drag you, I am drowned in you, you
overwhelm me! Drink!
(CP 1: 173)

What Williams will drink is, in fact, the art form of the Chinese poet. Given this understanding, here Williams is speaking directly to Bo Juyi himself and imploring the Chinese master to lend him his power of creating the charming face of Yang Guifei, which combines sense and sight, romance and tragedy. The self-portrait Williams makes shows how he labors to absorb the Chinese art form and how he succeeds in adapting it to his domestic need.

8 IN THE SHADOW

OF BO JUYI: *SOUR GRAPES*

I f in "Portrait of the Author" Williams' parleying with Bo Juyi is masked and ambiguous, in "To the Shade of Po Chü-i" we hear an unveiled dialogue between the modern American poet and the eighth- and ninth-century Chinese master:

> The work is heavy. I see
> bare branches laden with snow.
> I try to comfort myself
> with thought of your old age.
> A girl passes, in a red tam,
> the coat above her quick ankles
> snow smeared from running and falling-
> Of what shall I think now
> save of death the bright dancer?
> (*CP* 1: 133)

According to Dennis M. Read, who discovered the typed manuscript of "To the Shade of Po Chü-i" (see fig. 30) among five other poems in the *Little Review* files at the Golda Meir Library, University of Wisconsin-Milwaukee, Williams submitted these poems in a sequence to *The Little Review* no later than 1920. While three of them, namely "Winter Trees," "Complaint," and "The Cold Night," got published elsewhere in 1921,

To the Shade of **Po Chü-i**

The work is heavy . I see

bare branches laden with snow

I try to comfort myself

with thought of your old age .

A girl passes, in a red tam.

the coat above her quick ankles

snow smeared from running and falling

Of what shall I think now

save of death the bright dancer ?

30. William Carlos Williams, typescript of "To the Shade of Po Chü-i." The Golda
Meir Library, University of Wisconsin-Milwaukee.

"To the Shade of Po Chü-i" and the other two poems, namely "The Cats'
Month" and "Daybreak," were "either discarded or forgotten" (Read 424).
Read has ruled out the possibility of *Cathay* being a direct source of
inspiration for "To the Shade of Po Chü-i." As he points out, "nothing of
Po Chü-i is in that collection" (425). On the other hand, he suggests that
Arthur Waley's *A Hundred and Seventy Chinese Poems* (1919)[1] and *More Trans-
lations from the Chinese* (1919) deserve our close examination because they
contain a large number of Bo Juyi's poems—fifty-nine in his first volume
and another fifty-two in his second (425).

We now know that Williams kept in his personal library both of
Waley's books with inscriptions (see fig. 31).[2] After his death in 1963,
Flossie donated a large portion of his collection—"some 600 volumes as
well as a few original manuscripts and a number of little magazines"—to
Fairleigh Dickinson University (Heal 21). Among these are not only
Waley's two volumes and Giles' *History of Chinese Literature* (1914), but
Walter Brooks Brouner and Fung Yuet Mow's *Chinese Made Easy* (a hand-

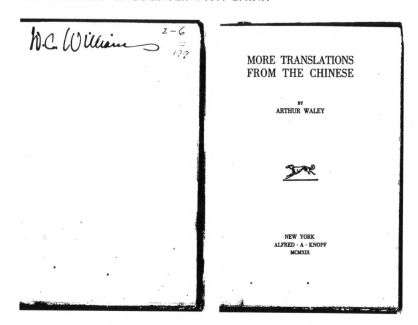

31. William Carlos Williams, inscription on front endpaper of Arthur Waley's *More Translations from the Chinese*. The Florham-Madison Campus Library, Fairleigh Dickinson University.

book of Chinese language introduced by H. A. Giles) (1904), Lafcadio Hearn's *Japanese Lyrics* (1915), and Ezra Pound's *Lustra* (with *Cathay*) (1916), *Instigations* (with Fenollosa's essay on "The Chinese Written Character") (1920), and *Confucius: The Great Digest and Unwobbling Pivot* (1951) (Berrien et al.).[3] Furthermore, an inspection of the 1918–20 issues of half a dozen magazines reveals an extraordinary amount of attention given to Waley's translations. Harriet Monroe's *Poetry*, for instance, featured ten of Waley's Chinese poems, including one by Bo Juyi ("On Barbarous Modern Instruments"), in February 1918 and two reviews of his books—one by John Gould Fletcher and one by Harriet Monroe herself—in February 1919 and March 1920, respectively. *Future* carried perhaps the earliest review of Waley's first book by Pound in November 1918. *The Dial* advertised *A Hundred and Seventy Chinese Poems* in May 1919:

Mr. Waley has here produced what should be for our generation, at least, the standard anthology of Chinese poems in English. In addition to the translations themselves, the volume contains a valuable introduction by Mr. Waley addressed especially to the general reader, a note on "The Method of Translation" and a Bibliography. $2.00 net.

And it printed John Gould Fletcher's review of Waley's second book in February 1920 and Babette Deutsch's review of a Mr. Mathers' book of Chinese poems with favorable references to Waley in March 1920.[4] Williams was associated with all these periodicals. He must have been impressed by the enthusiasm with which his peers had responded to Waley's books. Indeed, Miss Monroe calls Bo Juyi a "very modern poet" ("Waley's Translations" 339). Fletcher claims that Waley's skill at translation is "above suspicion" ("Perfume of Cathay" 273). And Pound, while considering *A Hundred and Seventy Chinese Poems* "somewhat heavy going," frankly admits that "Mr Waley has an excellent eye for subject matter . . ." (*EPPP* 3: 216).

Looking into Waley's two volumes of Chinese poems, we find that the English translator (1889–1966), who taught himself Chinese and Japanese while working with Binyon in the Sub-department of Oriental Prints and Drawings of the British Museum, has a modern sensibility and taste. (Like Pound he was a regular diner at the Vienna Café near the British Museum before it shut down in 1914. And in June 1915, a matter of weeks after the publication of *Cathay*, he visited Pound "to see Fenollosa mss."[5]) In introducing Bo Juyi, for example, his predecessor Giles translates two of the Chinese master's narrative poems, *Chang hen ge* ("The Everlasting Wrong") and *Pipa xing* ("Song of a Lute Girl"), both ranking high in his oeuvre but revealing little of his personal life and feelings. Waley, by contrast, omits both the classics[6] and offers a large number of Bo Juyi's lighter poems, many "inspired by some momentary sensation or passing event" (Waley, *Chinese Poems* 167). In doing so, Waley had in fact introduced to English readers an important form of Chinese poetry, which is now called the "occasional poem." According to Liu Wu-chi, this form of poetry inaugurated by Tao Qian (365–427) and perfected in the hands of Bo Juyi and other Tang poets is "not only an inspired comment on life, but also a faithful record of the author's everyday feelings and thoughts, and of his contacts with the people surrounding him." It came to be called an "occasional poem" precisely because it was "written on any occasion, about any subject, at any time whenever the poet's spirit moves him" (89). Evidently the concept embodied in this form of poetry corresponds to Williams' own notion of poetic composition formulated in *Kora in Hell: Improvisations*. One can thus imagine without any difficulty how Williams would respond to the hundred or more poems of Bo Juyi available in Waley's two volumes.

It is in these poems rather than in the narrative classics offered by Giles that we catch glimpses of Bo Juyi's personal life and inner thoughts. There we hear the mid-Tang statesman-poet speak of his domestic happiness and sorrow in terms of natural objects. The things he presents always have a visual clarity. The emotions conveyed often have a power of touching one's heart. In some dozen poems, Po Juyi, whose career was full of ups and downs (being the emperor's adviser at one time and the subprefect of a remote town in the South at another), writes about aging or old age. His tone in dealing with such topics is serene rather than bitter. In "On Being Sixty," for example, one actually perceives a cheerfulness:

> Strength of limb I still possess to seek the
> rivers and hills;
> Still my heart has spirit enough to listen to
> flutes and strings.
> At leisure I open new wine and taste several cups;
> Drunken I recall old poems and sing a whole volume.
> (Waley, *Chinese Poems* 233)

Another poem, "On His Baldness," opens with a regretful note:

> At dawn I sighed to see my hairs fall;
> At dusk I sighed to see my hairs fall.

But this is swiftly overcome by a stronger note of acceptance and optimism:

> They are all gone and I do not mind at all!
> I have done with that cumbrous washing and getting dry;
> My tiresome comb for ever is laid aside.

> Best of all, when the weather is hot and wet,
> To have no top-knot weighing down on one's head!
> (Waley, *More Translations* 84)

The poem that best illustrates Bo Juyi's Taoist serenity, however, is "Going to the Mountains with a Little Dancing Girl, Aged Fifteen: Written when the poet was about sixty-five," where, as we can perceive, the speaker identifies his old age with youth and nature:

> Two top-knots not yet plaited into one.
> Of thirty years—just beyond half.
> You who are really a lady of silks and satins
> Are now become my hill and stream companion!
> At the spring fountains together we splash and play:
> On the lovely trees together we climb and sport.
> (Waley, *Chinese Poems* 236)

As for why the Chinese poet can enjoy such a serene state of mind with regard to all things in the world, Bo Juyi himself gives an answer in a poem called "At the End of Spring (To Yuan Chen)," which he wrote at the age of thirty-eight. The poem opens with his typical equation of the cycles of vegetable life and animal life with the cycle of the seasons:

> The flower of the pear-tree gathers and turns to fruit;
> The swallows' eggs have hatched into young birds.

followed by his statement of the truth:

> When the Seasons' changes thus confront the mind
> What comfort can the Doctrine of Tao give?
> It will teach me to watch the days and months fly
> Without grieving that Youth slips away;
> If the Fleeting World is but a long dream,
> It does not matter whether one is young or old.
> (Waley, *More Translations* 45)

Williams' "To the Shade of Po Chü-i" seems inspired by these poems by the Chinese poet that bear a distinct Taoist tendency in outlook and method of composition. It is easy to recognize the bearings of the above-quoted passages on Williams' homage to Bo Juyi. As the Chinese poet in "At the End of Spring" tries to derive comfort from the Taoist principles of nondiscrimination and universal emptiness,[7] Williams, confronting the sight of "bare branches laden with snow," attempts to ease his mind with the memory of the older poet's tranquility at the change of the seasons in nature and in man. (The parallel becomes even more striking when one realizes that the two poets composed their respective chance poems at approximately the same prime age.) Williams' reference to Bo Juyi's "old age" is in actuality to the Chinese poet's capacity for carrying old age with equanimity, or, more plainly, to his capacity for ignoring the difference between age and youth. This capacity makes it possible for Bo Juyi at the age of about sixty-five to equate his declining years with the energy and sexuality of a fifteen-year-old dancing girl. This same capacity now transferred to Williams has made it possible for him to see against the somber sight of "bare branches" the image of a girl "in a red tam." The snow on her coat "smeared from running and falling" signifies the same kind of flamboyance as is seen in Bo Juyi's teenage dancing companion.

While the unexpected equation in "To the Shade of Po Chü-i" is reminiscent of Bo Juyi, it is also characteristic of the Williams of *Kora in Hell*. Surprisingly enough, in the *Improvisations*, which Williams wrote shortly before he began his dialogue with Bo Juyi, one can find examples of equation that bear a close resemblance to the Chinese master. Thus in the first improvisation of Chapter XII, Williams writes: "The browned trees are singing for my thirty-fourth birthday. Leaves are beginning to fall upon the long grass. Their cold perfume raises the anticipation of sensational revolutions in my unsettled life" (*I* 52). The equation of the seasonal cycle with the cycle of his own life present here seems almost taken from Bo Juyi's "At the End of Spring." In the third improvisation of Chapter XV, moreover, Williams juxtaposes landscape ("April clouds" and "dry snow") with female sexuality ("a Scotch lady" who "weighs 118 pounds" and whose "lips are turned and . . . calf also") (*I* 58–59) in virtually the same manner as Bo Juyi does in "Going to the Mountains" and as he himself later echoes in "To the Shade of Po Chü-i."

In his discussion of the various "influences" manifest in *Kora in Hell*, Rod Townley makes an attempt to distinguish between likeness and influence (105–14). In our examination of Williams' complex dialogue with Bo Juyi, we, too, need to make such a distinction. Williams, indeed, resembles the Chinese poet in talent and impulse. His improvisations, moreover, happened to be written in essentially the same circumstances as the composition of Bo Juyi's occasional poems. These facts not only account for the striking parallels between *Kora in Hell* and Bo Juyi's chance poems, but explain why Williams should respond to the Chinese poet so enthusiastically once he discovered him. As Williams told us much later, in the course of writing his improvisations, he "envisaged a new form of poetic composition, a form for the future" (*IWWP* 30). He was eager "to push on with the freedom he had found in *Kora*" (*I* xiii). Waley's translations of Bo Juyi came to him at an opportune moment. In the mid-Tang poet, Williams saw an ideal model. Earlier, he had learned from the French Symbolists how "to force a connection between objects most intimate and most remote" (Taupin 240). Now he was amazed to find that the Chinese poet was able to unite contrasting objects and moods with effortlessness. Bo Juyi, of course, acquired this capacity for freely moving between opposed images and feelings from his Taoist vision of the world as one of perfect harmony. For Williams, who knew little about Taoist assumptions, however, Bo Juyi's tranquil manner simply embodied a great freedom of the imagination. In pursuit of his own freedom of the imagination, Williams was certainly eager to embrace the Chinese poet as a master.

Thus "To the Shade of Po Chü-i" represents not only Williams' tribute to the Chinese poet but also his effort to pursue his spirit and art form. The poem opens with the equation of a somber feeling (human suffering) with a somber landscape (nature's suffering) very much in the manner of *Kora in Hell*, but with the "thought of [Bo Juyi's] old age," it abruptly switches to the Tang poet's harmonious world, where the same cheerless scene is juxtaposed with the image of the flamboyant girl. Here Williams is obviously seeing and imagining at the same moment. While the "bare branches" is an object in reality, the girl in a red tam seems but a visionary projection of what is craved after. (She "passes" Williams' mind rather than the street.) The juxtaposition of the two—the bleak with the cheer-ful—really marks a triumph in Williams' dance of the imagination.

Admittedly, Williams was capable of violent juxtaposition in *Kora in Hell*. Until "To the Shade of Po Chü-i," he was not in the habit of weav-ing contrasting scenes and moods. What is more, the image of "bare branches" may allude to Shakespeare's Sonnet 73 ("That time of year thou mayst in me behold, / When yellow leaves, or none, or few, do hang / Upon those boughs . . . "), thus suggesting not only old age but also impending death. Only by shaking off the Shakespearean influence and entering Bo Juyi's Taoist world will Williams be able to see spring in winter, youth in old age, life in death. Williams is apparently thrilled by the wholeness he has achieved through the fusion of opposites. In tran-quility, he ends the poem asking: "Of what shall I think now / save of death the bright dancer?" The coupling of "death" with "the bright dancer" is only possible in Taoist philosophy. But here Williams is also thinking of the Tang poet in history. The title of "the bright dancer" is fitting for Bo Juyi not only because bright dancers—such as Yang Guifei and the fifteen-year-old dancing girl—happen to be his favorite per-sonae, but because by giving the world some of the most imaginative poetic works, he himself has proven to be a bright dancer.

By his dialogue with Bo Juyi, Williams of course benefited more than by just producing the two beautiful poems above with Chinese tones. The mid-Tang poet had not been Williams' only model in his early devel-opment, but he had been his chief master in *Sour Grapes* (1921). Indeed, Williams originally called the book *Picture Poems*,[8] which only too obvi-ously reveals his admiration for the pictorial manner of his Chinese mod-els. In his description of the volume in 1956, Williams actually remarked:

This is definitely a mood book, all of it impromptu. When the mood pos-sessed me, I wrote. Whether it was a tree or a woman or a bird, the mood had to be translated into form. . . . To me, at that time, a poem was an image, the picture was the important thing. (*IWWP* 34–35)

Notice the key terms: impromptu, image, and translation of the mood into form—all essential elements in Bo Juyi's occasional poems. If Williams had not taken these ideas directly from the Chinese master, he had at least been encouraged by this example in his effort to create the "mood book."

The Chinese influence in *Sour Grapes* hasn't escaped the eyes of critics. In his 1922 review of the book, Yvor Winters notes "a certain serenity of manner," which he "associates with Mr. Pound's Chinese translations" (15). Later critics like Rod Townley have called attention to signs of Eastern approaches to art visible in Williams' "impromptus" (119). Without evidence, however, they have not been able to identify the actual source of the influence. It is Dennis Read who first tells us that Williams owes to Bo Juyi his "striking combination of sorrow and happiness, of regret and joy" in many poems in *Sour Grapes* (425). By pointing out the parallel, he has helped to lay the question of the Chinese influence in *Sour Grapes* to rest.

Bo Juyi gave Williams the technique of achieving wholeness by means of uniting opposing elements. The immediate effect of using the strategy is a tangible harmony in *Sour Grapes* poems—the dark is balanced with the light, the cold with the warm, the dead with the living, and the sour with the sweet. Thus, in "Winter Trees" the trees are not "straining / against the bitter horizontals of / a north wind" as in "Trees" of *Al Que Quiere!* (CP 1: 98), but basking in tranquil beauty: "A liquid moon / moves gently among / the long branches" (CP 1: 153). Their sleep "in the cold" has the promise of awakening and renewal of life rather than of decay and death. In "Complaint," the house at which the doctor calls is filled with cold as well as warmth, sickness as well as health, misery as well as happiness. The poem reminds one of "Portrait of a Woman in Bed" in *Al Que Quiere!*— a 1916 treatment of a house call.[9] By contrast, there one confronts nothing but impoverishment and bitterness. The difference in tone and attitude between the two verses dealing with similar situations indicates that what Williams has gained from Bo Juyi is not merely a method of expression, but a vision, an approach, and a philosophy.

With the affirmative approach that is characteristic of Bo Juyi, Williams in *Sour Grapes* deals with a number of topics that have been dealt with by Bo Juyi. In "Spring," for example, he treats the subject of aging:

> O my grey hairs!
> You are truly white as plum blossoms.
> (CP 1: 158)

The first thing that strikes one here is the *haiku*-like form in which Williams juxtaposes "grey hairs" with "plum blossoms." Even though Bo Juyi does not write in the *haiku* form, the visual clarity and the sensual precision one finds here are clearly reminiscent of the Chinese master's art. Furthermore, the sharp turn from the regretful mood in the first line to the playful mood in the second line is most probably borrowed from Bo Juyi's poems such as "On His Baldness."

Williams' "To Waken an Old Lady" deals with the topic of old age. The poem opens with a conceit:

> Old age is
> a flight of small
> cheeping birds
> skimming
> bare trees
> above a snow glaze.
> (CP 1: 152)

It is evident that the image of "small / cheeping birds" here is used by Williams as an objective equivalent of a blend of moods associated with old age—frustration, futility, yearning, and so on. Surprisingly enough, the same image as an equivalent of the same set of feelings is to be seen in these lines from Bo Juyi's "Being Visited by a Friend During Illness":

> Sadly chirping in the grasses under my eaves
> The winter sparrows morning and evening sing.

As is typical of Bo Juyi, the sad emotion evoked by the saddening image is compensated for in the second half of the poem by the happiness of the visit of a friend:

> Tranquil talk was better than any medicine;
> Gradually the feelings came back to my numbed heart.
> (Waley, *Chinese Poems* 223)

Likewise, in Williams' poem one is struck by the abrupt shift from a mood of frustration to one of rejoicing:

> On harsh weedstalks
> the flock has rested,
> the snow
> is covered with broken
> seedhusks
> and the wind tempered
> by a shrill
> piping of plenty.
> (CPI 1: 152–53)

Thus the poem can be seen as an attempt by Williams to cheer up his mother, who was deeply depressed because of old age and the loss of her husband on Christmas Day of 1918.

The same fusion of moods and the same harmony is to be found in Williams' "The Widow's Lament in Springtime," also written especially for his grieving mother. The poem indeed begins in the widow's own voice of deep sorrow:

> Sorrow is my own yard
> where the new grass
> flames as it has flamed
> often before but not
> with the cold fire
> that closes round me this year.
> (CP 1: 171)

The grief, however, doesn't turn to complete despair. Instead, it changes to an attitude of quiet acceptance, so familiar to readers of Bo Juyi. When the speaker's son tells her about the trees in white blossom in the meadows, she says that she "would like / to go there / and fall into those flowers / and sink into the marsh near them." By concluding the poem in this manner, Williams has perhaps unconsciously signaled a vision in Taoist terms, that is, the promise of harmony and perfection in one's attempt to merge with nature.

Williams' effort to create a wholeness by fusing contrasting moods is also reflected in the poem "Waiting," where the happy mood of the speaker in the first stanza ("When I am alone I am happy") is unexpectedly turned to sadness in the second stanza ("It seems much as if Sorrow / had tripped up my heels") (CP 1: 163–64). Probably Williams owes to Bo Juyi, too, his ability to envisage sorrow in joy, for the Chinese poet exhibits the same capacity in such poems as "The Beginning of Summer" (Waley, *More Translations* 59) and "Parting from the Winter Stove" (77). In *Sour Grapes*, there are certainly poems of joy without sorrow and poems of sorrow without joy. The two examples that immediately come to mind are "Light Hearted William" and "Portrait of the Author." It is not by accident that Williams arranges these two poems of opposed moods in a pair. His purpose of bringing them together is evidently to reach a wholeness that is missing in them when separated.

Sour Grapes, therefore, to a certain extent embodies Williams' effort to see life as whole, as Bo Juyi did in his time. Since the title often gave readers the wrong impression about the book, Williams found it necessary to make the following statement thirty-five years after its publication:

Everyone knows the meaning of sour grapes, but it had a special meaning for me. I've always thought of a poet as *not* a successful man except in his own mind, which is devoted to something entirely different than what the world thinks of as success. The poet puts his soul in his work and if he writes a good poem he *is* successful. When I decided on the title I was playing a game, sticking my fingers up to my nose at the world. All the poems are poems of disappointment, sorrow. I felt rejected by the world. But secretly I had my own idea. Sour grapes are just as beautiful as any other grapes. The shape, round, perfect, beautiful. I knew it—*my* sour grape—to be just as typical of beauty as *any* grape, sweet or sour. But the world undoubtedly read a sour meaning into my title. (*IWWP* 32–33)

The real emphasis of the book is thus on the wholeness of his sour grapes—their being at once sour and beautiful and their likelihood of turning from sour to sweet or vice versa. Amusingly enough, in a poem called "Children," Bo Juyi not only employs the same metaphor, but employs it to illustrate precisely the same truth about the world:

The sweetest vintage at last turns sour;
The full moon in the end begins to wane.
And so with men the bonds of love and affection
Soon may change to a load of sorrow and care.
But all the world is bound by love's ties;
Why did I think that I alone should escape?
(Waley, *Chinese Poems* 221)

It is certainly possible that Williams took both the image and the idea from the Chinese poet.[10] If this is true, we shall have more reason to claim that Bo Juyi is Williams' chief master in *Sour Grapes*.

To sum up, I will say that like other poets who came under the impact of Pound's *Cathay*, Williams became involved in a serious exploration of Chinese literature and culture between 1916 and 1921. Whereas Pound was fascinated by Li Bo in his initial Chinese studies, Williams was charmed by Bo Juyi in his exploration of Chinese poetry around 1920. That Williams should choose Bo Juyi (772–846) over his predecessor Li Bo (701–62) is no surprise. The mid-Tang poet happened to be his forerunner Arthur Waley's favorite. Besides, Williams himself must have found, after examining both Tang poets, that the younger one was China's "bread" (his mirror image) whereas the older was her "caviar" (Pound's mirror image).[11] Indeed, in Chinese literary history, Bo Juyi's name, along with that of his closest literary ally Yuan Zhen (779–831), is associated with a poetic movement in the early ninth century called *Xin yue fu* or "New Music Bureau Poetry," which strove for a break from mannered artificiality and an emphasis on contact with common objects and common people.[12] The shared beliefs and sensibilities must have encouraged Williams to imitate Bo Juyi's approach and technique. The immediate result of the encounter was a transmission of ideas and methods that took place in Williams' poetry. Without the dialogue with Bo Juyi, Williams could not have attained such a wholeness in many of his *Sour Grapes* poems.

9 ESCAPING THE OLD MODE

IN *SPRING AND ALL*

If *Cathay* paved the way for Pound's transition toward Modernism between 1917 and 1919, when he made the first refashioned Ur-Cantos, then *Sour Grapes* to a certain extent laid the groundwork for Williams' transition toward Modernism around 1923, when he brought out *Spring and All*. Interestingly, "the two halves of . . . a fairly decent poet" (L 225) followed a very similar pattern in their respective modernizing processes: first absorption and imitation, then dissatisfaction with mere imitation, and then a leap to the capacity for blending past and current influences and for bold invention. The transmission of a poetic power rooted in a non-Western culture really took place in the last phase of this process, a phase characterized by the spirit of "Making It New."

There is, of course, a marked difference in attitude between these two experimenters who turned to the Chinese for Modernist inspiration in the 1910s and early 1920s. Whereas Pound never shrank from acknowledging his debt to his Far Eastern masters, Williams was curiously silent about his early enthusiasm for Chinese culture. About foreign studies, Pound once offered this advice: "Be influenced by as many great artists as you can, but have the decency either to acknowledge the debt outright, or to try to conceal it" (LE 5). Apparently, Williams had taken his college pal's advice to absorb as many things foreign as possible, but as for his debt he chose to hide it rather than to acknowledge it freely.

Williams' reluctance to announce his indebtedness to China may have been due to his pride in reliance on native sources for the development of an individual style. In fact, as Peter Schmidt has noted, Williams is silent on his debt to Guillaume Apollinaire's Cubist poems and essay ("Les Peintres cubistes") for probably the same reason (62). In "Prologue to *Kora in Hell,*" one may note, he attacks Pound and Eliot for copying the poetry of the past and of Europe. It is hardly thinkable that shortly after he made the protest, he should be compelled to declare himself a copier of a foreign poetry just like his two rivals residing in Europe. There may be a second reason, though, for Williams' silence on his imitation of the Chinese. Unlike Pound, who considers imitation a part of creative work, Williams seems to think of it as mere exercise. When asked about the publication of his imitative "Portrait of the Author," therefore, he offers this answer: "Bob McAlmon, my co-editor on *Contact,* rescued it from the wastebasket. I threw it away because I thought it was sentimental and I was afraid I was imitating Pound. I hated to imitate. But Bob said it was good so I let it survive" (*IWWP* 35–36).[1] Here it is worth pointing out that Williams has told us only part of the truth. "Portrait of the Author" is an imitation, but the one he imitates is the Chinese poet Bo Juyi (or, to be more exact, Giles' version of Bo Juyi) rather than Pound.

As Paul Mariani has noted, Williams in fact became dissatisfied with *Sour Grapes,* which reprints "Portrait of the Author" and other imitative works of the period, even before it was published in December 1921 (184). In his letter to Kenneth Burke, dated 21 October 1921, he discloses that "Of the few books I have spewed, this is the one in which I have been least interested" (*SL* 53). This feeling of dissatisfaction apparently grew to be tremendously intense and burdensome in the following year, when Williams witnessed the appearances of Pound's Ur-Canto 8 (now incorporated into Canto 2) and Eliot's *The Waste Land* on the literary scene.[2] *The Waste Land,* he complained a quarter of a century later in his *Autobiography,* "wiped out our world as if an atom bomb had been dropped upon it . . ." (174). It was Williams, it must be remembered, who took the initiative to challenge Pound and Eliot to the rivalry. Now that Eliot had stolen a march on him, how was he to take the defeat? Tenacious as he was, Dr. Williams was to fight back with his old conviction but using a new tactic. And the book he turned out under these circumstances was *Spring and All* (1923).

It is now commonly agreed that *Spring and All* is the work that marked Williams' completion of modernization in the early 1920s. Indeed, some critics consider the volume "in its integral form . . . perhaps the most important single work by Williams" (Miller, "Williams' *Spring and All*" 415). And many more are willing to place it among the half-dozen or so books of verse that signified the coming of age of Modernist poetry in English. In discussing the strengths of this important work, few will overlook such marked Modernist features as the fusion of verse with prose theorizing on the craft of verse, the fusion of verbal art with European avant-garde visual art (Cubism, Dadaism, and Surrealism), and the fusion of spontaneous writing with studied work. While I agree that these traits constitute the modernity of Williams' *Spring and All*, I will also argue that the fusions were possible only because each and every segment had been used and tested separately, if not in combination, in earlier works such as *Kora in Hell* (1920) and *Sour Grapes* (1921). And in addition, I will claim that central to the basis of all these fusions is a fusion that has been slighted: the fusion of the Eastern poetic tradition and the Western poetic tradition.

It is important to note here that all three technical fusions that give *Spring and All* the Modernist appearance have origins in the Chinese poetic heritage. First, the fusion of poetry with prose (or *fu* as the Chinese call it[3]) is a genre frequently practiced by the fourth- and fifth-century poet Tao Qian (A.D. 365–427). The great Taoist recluse's best-known poems, such as "The Unmoving Cloud" (*Ting yun*), "Drinking Wine" (*Yin jiu*), and "The Return" (*Gui qu lai xi ci*), are all prefaced by exquisite prose, whereas his prose classic "Peach-blossom Fountain" (*Tao hua yuan ji*) is followed by a fine lyric. This tradition of matching poetry with prose was handed down and perfected by Tang poets such as Han Yu (768–824) and Bo Juyi. Arthur Waley, in *More Translations from the Chinese*, provides two specimens of this genre by the latter: "Prose Letter to Yuan Chen" and "Song of Past Feelings." The two pieces, actually prose improvisations—like Williams' own in *Kora in Hell*—mingled with short lyrics, may have inspired Williams to experiment with the form in

Spring and All. (Indeed, this form of prose surrounding complementary verse is made more conspicuous in Waley's book by his interposing the pieces between other poems by the mid-Tang poet.)

Second, the fusion of poetry with painting is a characteristic shared by virtually all Chinese lyrics. Williams, whose very first poem, "A black, black cloud" (*IWWP* 4), shows a likeness to a simple Chinese landscape painting, must have found himself quite at home in producing the picture poems of *Sour Grapes.* When he evolved to *Spring and All,* he just had to fuse into his painterly poems more techniques borrowed from European avant-garde art. As for the fusion of spontaneity and study, it belongs to a tradition that has its underpinnings in Taoism/Chan-Buddhism. Chinese Taoist/Chan-Buddhist artists, whether painters, calligraphers, or poets (sometimes all three in one person), believe in "a fundamental correspondence . . . between the patterns (*wen*) and workings of the universe and those of human culture" (Yu, *The Poetry of Wang Wei* 2). For them "improvisation means concentration-in-motion, one-pointedness moving infallibly and swiftly across a page, turning into lines that reveal the inner qualities of the flower, bird, or other object that the artist[s have] chosen" (Townley 119). Williams, who admired Bo Juyi's Chan-like impromptus, pursued this art in *Sour Grapes.* If "The Great Figure" of *Sour Grapes* is not Chan-like impromptu in the strict sense,[4] it paved the way for the birth of "The Red Wheelbarrow" of *Spring and All* that is.[5]

So, Williams' *Spring and All,* like Pound's first revised Ur-Cantos, is a success not only in Modernism, but also in the marriage of Eastern and Western poetic concepts and forms. Theoretically speaking, it is not rigorous to examine the union of forms out of the context of the union of concepts. For the convenience of exposition, however, I will deal with matters of concept alone here and leave matters of form for the next chapter.

Of the Chinese notions Williams has fused into *Spring and All,* the most striking is perhaps that of nondiscrimination. This view of regarding all things in the universe—humanity and nature, spring and fall, life and death, joy and woe, and so on—as the same is derived from Taoism and Chan-Buddhism. H. A. Giles, who was among the first to introduce

Taoist thinking to the West,[6] devotes a whole chapter of his *History* to Laozi and Zhuangzi, the legendary founder and the principal exponent, respectively, of Taoism. His version of Zhuangzi's parable about how he dreamed of being a butterfly (63) may well have appealed to Williams as it had appealed to Pound. Years later, in a letter to Pound of 19 October 1929, Williams observes: "The Chinese ancients seem to have known more of life than we." Quite probably, the reference here is to Pound's admiration in "Ancient Wisdom, Rather Cosmic" for the Chinese sage's refusal to make distinctions among worldly things.

It was, nevertheless, in Arthur Waley's translations of Bo Juyi rather than in Giles' elaborations of the Taoist philosophers that Williams may have found a way to fuse this ancient idea into his own poetry. In *Sour Grapes*, he strove to achieve a wholeness characteristic of the mid-Tang poet by combining contrasting images and moods. When he progressed to *Spring and All*, he was able to work in that vein with an effortlessness that was evident in Bo Juyi's own verse. Thus, in the fourteenth poem of the volume, now titled "Death the Barber," one witnesses Williams' fusion of the Taoist notion of nondiscrimination into a typical American conversation. The poem opens with the town barber's casual remark equating life with death,

> It's just
> a moment
> he said, we die
> every night—
> (CP 1: 212)

followed by citizen Williams' witty comment that unites old age with vitality. He tells the barber

> of an old man
> who said
> at the door—
> Sunshine today!
> (CP 1: 213)

The voices we hear are characteristically Williams', but the attitude revealed is strongly reminiscent of Bo Juyi.

In Bo Juyi's Taoist capacity for seeing everything in the world as alike, Williams may have found a possibility to make his verse opaque and Modernist. In the fifteenth poem, now called "Light Becomes Darkness," he uses the method to view the contrasting scenes in a modern city. From this perspective, he is able to see through "The decay of cathedrals" and "the phenomenal / growth of movie houses" the simultaneity of "destruction and creation" (CP 1: 213). According to J. Hillis Miller, here Williams is also speaking of literary imagination. For Williams, imagination must be at once destructive and creative ("Williams' *Spring and All*" 419–20). Only by denying light can one see light, and only by destroying novelty can one create novelty.

Indeed, it is the power of imagination that has enabled Williams to see light in darkness, youth in old age, and oasis in wasteland. If in "To the Shade of Po Chü-i" he still has to borrow imagery and idea from the mid-Tang poet to ease his depression in a somber season, in *Spring and All* he himself has become a "bright dancer" in the ever-changing world. In the prose passage preceding the opening poem, Williams gives us the key to his newly acquired outlook:

Now at last that process of miraculous verisimilitude, that great copying which evolution has followed, repeating move for move every move that it made in the past—is approaching the end.

Suddenly it is at an end. THE WORLD IS NEW.
(CP 1: 182)

Apparently, it was equipped with this cyclical view of the world articulated by Bo Juyi in "At the End of Spring" that Williams gave birth to the first poem of the volume, "Spring and All." Like Eliot's *The Waste Land*, Williams' famous Modernist lyric presents a concrete depiction of a modern desert:

All along the road the reddish
purplish, forked, upstanding, twiggy
stuff of bushes and small trees
with dead, brown leaves under them
leafless vines—
(CP 1: 183)

Unlike Eliot's modern desert that is filled with despair, however, Williams' waste fields are "not dead but teeming with promise" (Mariani 198). Through the "leafless vines," the imaginative speaker indeed sees young lives

> . . . enter the new world naked,
> cold, uncertain of all
> save that they enter. All about them
> the cold, familiar wind—
>
> Now the grass, tomorrow
> the stiff curl of wildcarrot leaf
>
> One by one objects are defined—
> It quickens: clarity, outline of leaf. . . . [7]
> (CP 1: 183)

As one reads the lines, one is sure to perceive a miraculous force erupting from the jostling of words representing contrasting elements. If a major part of the modernity in Williams' verse arises from his setting words that embody antagonistic objects side by side, it is possibly the Chinese concept of sameness that ensures him the capacity for making such arrangements.

John Gould Fletcher, in discussing the Chinese influence on modern American poetry, observes that like Pound, Amy Lowell, and himself, who persistently looked to the Chinese for methods, the three New York poets—William Carlos Williams, Wallace Stevens, and Marianne Moore—also "displayed an objective approach akin to the Chinese" (Selected Essays 79). His remark brings us to a second Chinese notion that Williams appears to have fused into Spring and All: the "spirit of intense observation, of patient surrender to truth, of complete identification with the object" (79).

It is true that Williams' pre-Waleyan prose and poetry (Kora in Hell and Al Que Quiere!) already showed a strong tendency toward objectivism. His theory of immediacy and spontaneity, formulated shortly before he turned his attention to the Chinese, actually shared much in common with the ideas underlying Bo Juyi's poetry. Through his encounter with the mid-Tang poet, however, Williams probably discovered not only a crystallizing example of his own objectivism, but a sophisticated doctrine for perfecting his poetic ideals.

In *Spring and All,* Williams renames his theory of contact the theory of imagination, which he elaborates in a series of prose passages surrounded by illustrative poems. Miller is very much to the point in stating that "The key to Williams' theory of imagination is the idea that the imagination is a natural force" ("Williams' *Spring and All*" 423), but it is far-fetched to trace the origin of this notion to Aristotle's theory of mimesis (427). Quite contrary to this forced connection, Williams' theory of imagination clearly indicates a departure from the Western concept of imitation, which is based on the Greek assumption of "a dichotomy between this world and another transcendent one" (Yu, *The Poetry of Wang Wei* 2). In the prose section titled "Samuel Butler," one notes, Williams straightforwardly questions the validity of this ancient tradition:

—they ask us to return to the proven truths of tradition, even to the twice proven, the substantiality of which is known. Demuth and a few others do their best to point out the error, telling us that design is a function of the IMAGINATION, describing its movements, its colors—but it is a hard battle. (CP 1: 186)

And in the ensuing sections, he goes on to challenge Shakespeare's concept of imitation on the one hand (208), and the Symbolists' crude association of emotions with natural things on the other (188). For the Williams of *Spring and All,* imagination is not imitation of reality, but rather "reality itself" (204). This view of artistic creation deviates from the dualism of Western thought. Only in the Eastern heritage is one likely to find a theoretical foundation for this monistic outlook.

Did I say that Williams was silent about his debt to the Chinese? His silence was not complete after all. In the fifth poem, now titled "The Black Winds," he alludes to Chinese poems as possessing the same rhythmical beauty and power as "boxing matches" and Miss Wirth's equestrian arts (190).[8] Sensing that his reader will be puzzled by this analogy, he elaborates:

Now I run my hand over you feeling
the play of your body—the quiver
of its strength—

The grief of the bowmen of Shu
moves nearer—There is
an approach with difficulty from
the dead—the winter casing of grief

How easy to slip
into the old mode, how hard to
cling firmly to the advance—
(191)

The "old mode" Williams speaks of here is obviously the Aristotelian tradition, and the "advance" the Chinese. He alludes to Chinese poetry not only by a *Cathay* title ("Song of the Bowmen of Shu"), but by "cling . . . to," a picturesque verb Pound repeats in two of his pre-Fenollosan Chinese adaptations ("Liu Ch'e" and "Ts'ai Chi'h"). The doctrine he refers to as associated with rhythm (or "quiver"), however, is obscure to most present-day readers. The reference, I think, is to the first of the "Six Canons" (*Liu fa*) set forth in the sixth century by the Chinese art critic Xie He (Hsieh Ho). Giles calls it "Rhythmic vitality." And Laurence Binyon, in *The Flight of the Dragon* (1911), retranslates it as "The fusion of the rhythm of the spirit with the movement of living things."[9] "At any rate," Binyon elaborates, "what is certainly meant is that the artist must pierce beneath the mere aspect of the world to seize and himself to be possessed by that great cosmic rhythm of the spirit which sets the currents of life in motion" (13).

It is worth noting that Binyon's *The Flight of the Dragon* is a book that Pound had helped to promote by reviewing it for Lewis' *Blast* 2 (July 1915). Indeed, in Pound's review Xie He's Canon of "Rhythmic vitality" is emphasized in bold print: "P. 21. **FOR INDEED IT IS NOT ESSENTIAL THAT THE SUBJECT-MATTER SHOULD REPRESENT OR BE LIKE ANYTHING IN NATURE; ONLY IT MUST BE ALIVE WITH A RHYTHMIC VATALITY OF ITS OWN**" (EPPP 2: 99). By

January 1922, Binyon's publisher John Murray had brought out a third printing of the book. Quite probably, I think, Williams was reading the volume early that year while he was making *Spring and All*. In explaining the power of the rhythm, one may note, Binyon speaks of the surpassing energy and beauty produced by "the rhythmical movements of the body, as *in games* or *in the dance*" (emphasis added) (15). For the Chinese, Binyon goes on to observe, poetry is "not an adjunct to existence, a reduplication of the actual; it is a hint and a promise of that perfect rhythm, of that ideal life" (19). It is quite likely that these statements made by Binyon about the "First Canon" had incited Williams to equate the rhythmical beauty and vitality of Chinese poetry with those of "boxing matches" and Miss Wirth's equestrian arts.

At any rate, Williams seems to have discovered a key to success in artistic creation. For him at this moment, the beauty and power of the "Song of the Bowmen of Shu" are derived from its fusion of spirit (imagination) with material (object) by catching the rhythm. The success of Matisse's *Blue Nude* (fig. 29), it may have occurred to him, rests also on its fusion of spirit with material by means of rhythms. To accomplish a similar effect in his own work, he just had to "cling firmly to the advance" and not "to slip / into the old mode"; or, in Townley's words, try "to 'become' the objects he describes" and "fuse the imagination with the things he [is] contemplating . . ." (141).

In *Spring and All*, Williams does succeed in bringing about a complete union of imagination and object. In poems like "The Pot of Flowers," "The Rose" ("The rose is obsolete"), and "The Red Wheelbarrow," the speaker appears to be both the viewer of the object and the object itself. His seeing, imagining, and being all miraculously fuse into one process. Similarly, in "Spring and All," the speaker identifies so closely with the approaching spring plants that one feels that he is possessed by the quiver or rhythm of the awakening life in them. Fletcher, in speaking of Williams' resemblance to the Chinese in approach, names his 1932 lyric "The Red Lily" as a telling example (*Selected Essays* 79). The objective approach one finds in "The Red Lily" is actually visible in many of the *Spring and All* poems. Williams indeed began as an objectivist writer, but with repeated exposure to Chinese influence between 1916 and 1921, his objectivism took on a noticeable Taoist color in *Spring and All*. The Chinese appears to have given him not only a basis for sharpening his theory, but examples for perfecting his poetry.

As has been noted, Chinese objectivism is based on the Taoist/Chan-Buddhist conviction of a correlative harmony between humanity and nature, spirit and material, self and cosmos. Typically, a Taoist/Chan-Buddhist artist adopts a passive attitude toward the world and sees being as evolved from nonbeing and form as evolved from formlessness. This paradoxical view leads to a third Chinese notion Williams has fused into *Spring and All*: the reliance on nonbeing for being and on formlessness for form.

This is, of course, no place to explain at length the Taoist concept of *wu* (nonbeing/being) and the Buddhist concept of *śūnyatā* (emptiness / fullness).[10] Briefly speaking, just as a Taoist sees nothing in all and all in nothing, a Buddhist finds emptiness in form and form in emptiness. Giles, in dealing with Taoism, refers to Laozi's doctrine of Inaction (*History* 58–59) and in discussing Buddhism cites the famous saying from *The Diamond Sutra*: " . . . every external phenomenon is like a dream, like a vision, like a bubble, like shadow, like dew, like lightning, and should be regarded as such" (115). Moreover, in his *History*, he offers poems by masters of different periods that exemplify this notion, among which the most illustrative is perhaps Wang Wei's quatrain "The Bamboo Grove House"[11]:

> Beneath the bamboo grove, alone,
>   I seize my lute and sit and croon;
> No ear to hear me, save mine own:
>   No eye to see me—save the moon.
> (150)

Although it was possibly from Giles that Williams first learned about the notion of nonbeing/being or emptiness/form, I think more probably it was in Waley's versions of Bo Juyi that he finally discovered its true value. Like Wang Wei's poetry, Bo Juyi's work often appears simple but contains profound philosophical undercurrents. One theme frequently treated by him is the world's empty/full nature. In a quatrain, which Waley calls "Passing T'ien-men Street in Ch'ang-an and Seeing a Distant

View of Chung-nan Mountain," for example, he contrasts the "fullness" of the city with the "emptiness" of the mountains:

> The snow has gone from Chung-nan; spring is almost come.
> Lovely in the distance its blue colours, against the brown of the streets.
> A thousand coaches, ten thousand horsemen pass down the Nine Roads;
> Turns his head and looks at the mountains,—not one man!
> (*Chinese Poems* 173)

Like Wang Wei's "The Bamboo Grove House," Bo Juyi's quatrain shows its philosophical depth in the surprise ending that brings to light the paradoxical theme of the fullness of a void nature versus the emptiness of a busy society.

Owing to Williams' silence, we are still not certain how he actually responded to these poems. But in *Sour Grapes* we do find striking parallels to the Chinese themes of emptiness/fullness. The concluding lines of "The Late Singer" ("A moon hangs in the blue / in the early afternoons over the marshes. / I am late at my singing" [*CP* 1: 137]), for example, seem to echo Wang Wei's "The Bamboo Grove House." And the speaker of "Waiting," on the other hand, shares with that of Bo Juyi's "Children" (*Chinese Poems* 221) the feelings of fullness when alone and of emptiness when with his children.

One is on surer ground in speaking of Williams' interest in the Chinese notion of nonbeing/being in *Spring and All*, for there he has actually made this idea a predominant theme. "The Red Wheelbarrow," Williams' best-known lyric, is said to be an attempt at showing how nothing is something extraordinary and less is more. This same attempt is repeated in a considerable number of other poems in the volume. If in most cases Williams has tried to avoid an identifiable Chinese tone, in the sixth poem, now called "To Have Done Nothing," he appears to speak in an unmasked Taoist-like voice:

> No that is not it
> nothing that I have done
> nothing
> I have done

                    is made up of
                    nothing
                     . . . .

And when the poem draws to its close, one hears almost an aping of
Laozi's teaching, "Do nothing, and all things will be done" (Giles, *History*
59):

                    for everything
                    and nothing
                    are synonymous
                    when

                    energy *in vacuo*
                    has the power
                    of confusion

                    which only to
                    have done nothing
                    can make
                    perfect
                    (*CP* 1: 191–92)

    The notion that nothing becomes something extraordinary in con-
centration seems explored in greater vividness in the eleventh poem,
"The Right of Way," where the speaker driving along a road is continu-
ously seeing something remarkable in "nothing":

                    an elderly man who
                    smiled and looked away

                    to the north past a house—
                    a woman in blue

                    who was laughing and
                    leaning forward to look up

                    into the man's half
                    averted face

and a boy of eight who was
looking at the middle of

the man's belly
at a watchchain—

The poem finally ends in a Bo Juyi-like surprise manner,

Why bother where I went?
for I went spinning on the

four wheels of my car
along the wet road until

I saw a girl with one leg
over the rail of a balcony
(CP 1: 205–06)

which really stresses "The supreme importance / of this nameless spectacle" (206). Looking back on the title, "The Right of Way," one wonders whether Williams is punning here on the likeliness of "Way" meaning road and "Way" meaning the Tao. In any case, Williams' aim in *Spring and All* is to demonstrate the power of human imagination. In accomplishing this goal, he benefits most from the Taoist/Chan-Buddhist paradox that all is nothing/nothing is all.

10 IN PURSUIT OF

MINIMAL, AGRAMMATICAL FORM

In considering Williams' possible borrowings of Chinese forms, we confront a more difficult task. Williams didn't know the Chinese language. How could he learn about Chinese poetic forms in translations? True, original Chinese forms are largely sacrificed even in excellent translations. But Giles and Waley, the authors of Williams' Chinese source materials, happened to be students of Chinese poetry who had set themselves the task of not only translating masterpieces of China but describing vital aspects of Chinese prosody lost in their versions. Giles, in *A History*, for example, explains how the alternate tones of "flats" (*ping*) and "sharps" (*ze*) work in Chinese versification. He even takes the trouble to illustrate the tonal arrangement of a verse form called *jueju* by giving a paradigm:

Sharp	sharp	flat	flat	sharp
Flat	flat	sharp	sharp	flat
Flat	flat	flat	sharp	sharp
Sharp	sharp	sharp	flat	flat.

Waley, in *A Hundred and Seventy Chinese Poems*, likewise devotes a whole long section of his introduction to "Technique" (22–26) covering such essential expedients as "Rhyme," "Length of line," "Tone-arrangement," and "Verbal parallelism in the couplet."[1] Both writers emphasize that Chinese poetry is noted for its compression and pithiness. Giles, in particular, remarks that "Brevity is . . . the soul of a Chinese poem" and that "The ideal length is twelve lines" (145). It may be remembered that the statement so impressed Pound that, at least on two separate occasions, he refers to it commenting that the Chinese hold "if a man can't say what he wants to in 12 lines, he'd better leave it unsaid" (ED 267; GB 88).

The concise nature of Chinese poetry must have appealed to Williams, who was at that point constructing a verse that is distinguished by minimalism. According to Giles, Chinese poems are short in both number of lines and length of lines. The two most frequently practiced verse forms, *jueju* and *lushi*, are, respectively, a five- or seven-syllable quatrain and a five- or seven-syllable double quatrain (*History* 144–45). Giles calls *jueju* "stop-short." In his description, "according to the measure employed," this minimal verse form "is just long enough for the poet to introduce, to develop, to embellish, and to conclude his theme in accordance with certain established laws of composition." "The third line," he particularizes, "is considered the most troublesome to produce, some poets even writing it first; the last line should contain a 'surprise' or *dénouement*" (146). Two *jueju* poems we referred to earlier, Li Bo's *Jing ye si* ("Calm Night Thought") and Wang Wei's *Tian yuan le: qi liu* (no. 6 of "Farm Field Pleasure"), will serve as fine illustrations.

Quatrains in English were a familiar form to Williams. Between 1909 and 1917, he composed a good many poems made up of quatrains of trochaic tetrameter or iambic pentameter. His 1909 "Love," for example, opens,

> Love is twain, it is not single,
> Gold and silver mixed in one,
> Passion 'tis and pain which mingle
> Glist'ring then for aye undone.
> (CP 1: 21)

His 1910 "Martin and Katherine" commences,

> Alone today I mounted that steep hill
> On which the Wartburg stands. Here Luther dwelt
> In a small room one year through, here he spelt
> The German Bible out by God's good will.
> (CP 1: 23)

And in his 1912 "In San Marco, Venezia" we read,

> Around me here are arching walls gold-decked,
> Of her grey children breathing forth their praise,
> I am an outcast, too strange to but raise
> One least harmonious whisper of respect.
> (CP 1: 26)

The idea that the Chinese were capable of doing a lot of things in quatrains of shorter lines may have fascinated Williams and, moreover, encouraged him to reform quatrains in English by cutting their line length. In *Sour Grapes*, one may notice, he produces a *jueju*-like single quatrain, "The Gentle Man," and two *lushi*-like double quatrains, "Complete Destruction" and "The Nightingales." A glance from Li Bo's celebrated *lushi* Song you ren (Pound's "Taking Leave of a Friend") to Williams' "Complete Destruction" and "The Nightingales" will make clear how closely they correspond to each other in line length:

Song you ren

> qing shan heng bei guo
> bai shui rao dong cheng
> ci di yi wei bie
> gu peng wan li zheng

> fu yun you zi yi
> luo ri gu ren qing
> hui shou zi zi qu
> xiao xiao ban ma ming

Complete Destruction

> It was an icy day.
> We buried the cat,
> then took her box
> and set match to it

> in the back yard.
> Those fleas that escaped

earth and fire
died by the cold.
(CP 1: 159)

The Nightingales

My shoes as I lean
unlacing them
stand out upon
flat worsted flowers.

Nimbly the shadows
of my fingers play
unlacing
over shoes and flowers.
(169)

As Thomas Whitaker has observed, the two *lushi*-like little poems by Williams both "focus on the fullness and the emptiness of the world" (38), which paradox, as we can see, is frequently manifest in specimens of Chinese *jueju* and *lushi*.

In *Spring and All*, Williams has sought to bring out an individualized minimal style. No poem in the volume, it seems, shows a clear sign of imitation of any particular Chinese or Japanese verse forms. A scrutiny of Williams' most-anthologized lyric, "The Red Wheelbarrow," however, reveals that it resembles a Chinese *jueju* in several essential ways.[2] First, the poem contains twenty-two syllables. This corresponds almost exactly to the number of syllables a Chinese *jueju* has. (A Chinese *jueju* can have twenty, twenty-four, or twenty-eight syllables.) Second, the eight lines of the poem,

so much depends
upon

a red wheel
barrow

glazed with rain
water

> beside the white
> chickens
> (CP 1: 224)

can be seen as four lines, each having a tag of a two-syllable word. (The typographic device is used by Pound in "Taking Leave of a Friend," a rendering of a *lushi*, for foregrounding.) Third, seen in this manner, each line of the poem constitutes a self-contained image as in a Chinese *jueju*. Put together, they form a unified picture. Fourth, as in a Chinese *jueju*, each line (containing five to seven syllables) is just long enough to play a fixed role: the first line ("so much depends / upon") introduces, the second line ("a red wheel / barrow") develops, the third line ("glazed with rain / water") embellishes, and the fourth line ("beside the white / chickens") concludes the theme with a surprise. Giles considers the third line of a Chinese *jueju* the most difficult to compose because it has to perform an extra role of showing relations between the preceding and following parts. Williams' third line, "glazed with rain / water," precisely fulfills this purpose. With a picturesque verb phrase ("glazed with") plus a noun phrase indicating a shimmering image ("rain / water"), this pivotal line at once glues the disconnected parts together and sharpens the contrast between them.

It is interesting to remark that Williams' single most successful short lyric resembles Wang Wei's famous *jueju*, *Tian yuan le: qi liu* (no. 6 of "Farm Field Pleasure" or Pound's "Dawn on the Mountain"), in both spirit and form. Wang Wei's "untranslatable poem," one will recollect, is a brilliant example of an effort to demonstrate the abundance and vividness of an "empty world." Like Williams' "The Red Wheelbarrow," it depends on color contrast (pink peach blossoms versus green willows) sharpened by the image of "rain water" to emphasize the paradoxical theme, "nothing is something extraordinary." Here one may recall that Wang Wei, in *Song Yuan er shi Anxi* (Pound's epigraph to "Four Poems of Departure") ("Light rain is on the light dust / The willows of the inn-yard / Will be going greener and greener / . . . "), and Williams, in "The Great Figure" ("Among the rain / and lights / I saw the figure 5 / . . . "), also use the image of "rain water" to stress color difference.

Williams' "The Red Wheelbarrow" is not an imitation of Wang Wei's "Farm Field Pleasure." But surprisingly, it succeeds almost effortlessly in bringing out the sort of beauty Pound takes pains to reproduce from Wang Wei's minimal classic. This fact eloquently testifies to a truth: while a certain charm in Chinese poetry is untranslatable, it can be recaptured by transmission of the general approach. Williams shares with Chinese poets such as Wang Wei and Bo Juyi a gift for writing minimal, painterly poems. This talent has, to a considerable degree, ensured his triumph in transferring a power from short, pithy Chinese lyrics.

According to Giles, Chinese poetry is characterized not only by its compact size, but also by its relational quality. A Chinese poem, he observes in *A History*, has no "inflection, agglutination, or grammatical indication of any kind, the connection between which has to be inferred by the reader from the logic, from the context, and least perhaps of all from the syntactical arrangement of the words" (144). In his early contact with Chinese poetry, Pound was rather obsessed by this agrammatical quality. Though deeply aware of its potential energy, he seemed hesitant about imitating it in his *Cathay* translations. Thus, in "Taking Leave of a Friend," instead of giving

> Floating clouds, a wanderer's mood
> Sunset, an old friends' feeling,

he offers

> Mind like a floating wide cloud,
> Sunset like the parting of old acquaintances
> . . . . . .
> (p 141)

By adding the connective "like" in both lines, he has gained clarity but sacrificed the ambiguity and simultaneity in the original. Similarly, the third line of Li Bo's original text for "The Jewel Stairs' Grievance" has no subject. According to Yip, it has the power of inviting the reader to guess "Who lets down the blind and watches the autumn moon." The answer will be either the "specific lady or all other ladies of the same fate" (68).

By introducing "I" into the line, Pound has certainly deprived the poem of this puzzle, thus also depriving readers of their interpretation of a possible universal theme.

In translating Chinese poetry, especially in the early decades of the twentieth century when Western audiences were still unfamiliar with the "elliptical method," I think it was well-advised to insert missing pronouns, connectives, noun forms, and verb forms where necessary. Insofar as I know, Pound has dealt with such details only with regard to an improvised Japanese *haiku*. After citing his version in the 1914 essay on "Vorticism," he explains, "The words 'are like' would not occur in the original, but I add them for clarity" (GB 89). So, in his early translations of Chinese and Japanese verse, Pound gives priority to clarity. Once he starts to compose his own monumental work, he adopts the elliptical technique without reserve. In arguing for this vital point, Yip has cited the most effective examples: in Canto 21, Pound gives us

> Moon on the palm-leaf,
>> confusion;

in Canto 52,

> Orion at sunrise.
>> Horses now with black manes.
> Eat dog meat.

and in Canto 64,

> Prayer: hands uplifted
> Solitude: a person, a NURSE.
> (CA 100, 260, 355; qtd. in Yip 69)

Williams' case is slightly different from Pound's. He began his Chinese exploration perhaps also with Giles' *History*. But to the best of our knowledge, he made no attempt to rework his precursor's translations. True, he imitated versions of Bo Juyi in *Sour Grapes*. But it seems that it took him less time to leap from the stage of imitation to that of "Making It New." At any rate, in *Spring and All*, he has already built up his own relational poetry without the word "like." In the prose passage between the fourth and fifth poems, he explicitly announces his disapproval of the use of "like" in verse. "It is typified by use of the word 'like' or that 'evocation' of the 'image' which served us for a time," says he. "Its abuse is apparent. The insignificant 'image' may be 'evoked' never so ably and still mean nothing" (CP 1: 188). One has to admit that Williams drew the inspiration first from European avant-garde painting to strip his verse of almost all words of logic. The verbal model that supported his experiment, however, was from China.

Chinese poetry is distinguished by its reliance on simply naming things after things after things to stir up the imagination. An extended example of this art is Qu Yuan's "The Genius of the Mountain." Giles' version gives one a sufficient idea of what it is like: "Methinks there is a Genius of the hills, clad in wistaria, girdled with ivy, with smiling lips, of witching mien, riding on the red pard, wild cats galloping in the rear, reclining in a chariot, with banners of cassia . . ." (History 52).

According to Mariani, between 1921 and 1923 Williams' poetry underwent a fundamental change (196). The direction he took is most clearly shown in the thirteenth poem of Spring and All, "The Agonized Spires," which Williams himself considers "fairly representative . . . of the sort of thing I am working on now" (qtd. in Mariani 196). The opening stanza of the piece reads:

> Crustaceous
> wedge
> of sweaty kitchens
> on rock
> overtopping
> thrusts of the sea

Mariani is perceptive in pointing out that the poem is "like a dadaist collage" (196). But I think the way it twists syntax to "paint with words" is also reminiscent of Chinese lyrics. Indeed, when one moves on to the third stanza, one witnesses more distinctly the sort of elusive Chinese effect produced by the method of piling things upon things without indicating their logical connection:

> Lights
> speckle
> El Greco
> lakes
> in renaissance
> twilight
> with triphammers
> (CP 1: 211)

Notice the line arrangement on the page. It anticipates Williams' 1935 version of "The Locust Tree in Flower," which Henry W. Wells associates with Chinese poetry that is written in a vertical line (4):

> Among
> of
> green
>
> stiff
> old
> bright
>
> broken
> branch
> come
>
> white
> sweet
> May
>
> again
> (CP 1: 379–80)

The influence is traceable to a 1904 Chinese-language handbook (*Chinese Made Easy*) that Williams kept in his personal library. In it the popular Chinese primer *San zi jing* or *Three Character Classic* is printed out along with transliteration and translation precisely in this manner:

yun (Men)	人
gee (Arrive)	之
chaw (Begin- ning)	初
sun (Nature)	性
boon (Root)	本
seen (Good)	善

(Brouner and Fung 94)

In the spire-shaped third stanza of "The Agonized Spires," Mariani has noted the ambiguity. He points out that the lines set us wondering whether we should read them as "Lights speckle like El Greco lakes with the flickering engine rapidity of triphammers in this renaissance twilight?" or as "Lights speckle on the El Greco–like lakes of the Hudson and East rivers, as in that artist's late Renaissance handling of light on dark, with the modern *Mechanique Ballet* sounds of triphammers for accompaniment?" or as something else (197). In accounting for the making of the puzzle, Mariani remarks that "Williams had learned—master that he was—how to bend syntax to his own ends to let the images flood over the reader's sensibility simultaneously with their multifoliate possibilities, as in the reading of a scene or a painting" (197). Without evidence, however, he will not claim, as I will, that Williams actually had specific Chinese examples in mind to back up his revolutionary attempt to transfer Cubist and Dadaist techniques to his verse.

EPILOGUE:

THE BEGINNING OF A LITERARY ERA

Thus we see that between 1921 and 1923 Williams was moving in very much the same direction that Pound had moved between 1917 and 1919. The conscious and unconscious fusion of influences from the East and from the West had greatly accelerated his modernizing process as the same sort of fusion had accelerated Pound's a few years earlier.

By 1923 Pound had composed the tremendously important Malatesta Cantos, the Confucius Canto, and the Hell Cantos, and was ready to launch *A Draft of XVI. Cantos* (1925).[1] Meanwhile, he had gotten William Bird at the Three Mountains Press to print the prose series that includes his own *Indiscretions* (1923), Ford's *Women & Men* (1923), Williams' *The Great American Novel* (1923), and Hemingway's *In Our Time* (1924).[2] Williams was to travel to Europe with Flossie in January 1924, where he was to meet Ford and Joyce for the first time. Soon he was to write his long-planned *In the American Grain* (1925), a book to be selected by Pound along with Fenollosa's seminal essay and his own *Ta Hio* (a version of Confucius' *The Great Learning*) (1928) to form the 1936 "Ideogrammic Series" (Kenner 447). There was every indication, then, that by the end of 1923 "the two halves of . . . a fairly decent poet" had joined forces in helping to usher in a new era in American literary history, the Pound Era, or more aptly, the Pound-Williams Era.

Williams certainly deserves to be recognized as a cofounder of this

literary tradition, for when the next generation of American poets—
Louis Zukofsky, George Oppen, Kenneth Rexroth, David Ignatow, Rob-
ert Lowell, Charles Olson, Robert Creeley, Denise Levertov, James
Dickey, A. R. Ammons, Allen Ginsberg, Gary Snyder, and many more—
began struggling to form their individual styles and to carry on the
poetic revolution, they really benefited as much—or more[3]—from him as
from his Penn classmate for the Modernist influence.

In receiving this heritage from the two pioneers, most of the younger
poets perhaps were unaware of the Chinese influence they received
along with many other things.[4] When Olson utters a line like "in! in! the
bow-sprit, bird, the beak" in one of his Maximum poems ("I, Maximus of
Gloucester, to You") (8), he is actually imitating his masters' imitation of
the Chinese elliptical style. When Ginsberg endlessly piles image upon
image in "Howl" or "Kaddish," he is really stretching to the extreme a
mode of expression that his literary fathers had introduced from a fourth-
century B.C. Chinese Imagist.

Things non-Western can, therefore, be converted into part of a West-
ern literary heritage. It is in this light that we see the importance of
Pound's and Williams' remarkable exploration in Chinese poetry and
culture during the crucial decade extending from the making of *Des
Imagistes* to the births of such high Modernist masterpieces as Pound's
Early Cantos and Williams' *Spring and All.*

APPENDIX I: A TRANSCRIPT OF FENOLLOSA'S

NOTES FOR "TAKING LEAVE OF A FRIEND"

	So	Yu	Jin	

Taking leave of a friend

Sei	zan	o	hoku	kaku
Blue	mt.	lie	North	side of walled city.
		horizontally		

Where blue mt. peaks are visible toward the Northern suburb

Haku	sui	gio	to	jo
White	water	encircle	East	castled town

And white water flows encircling the East of the city.

Shi	chi	ichi	i	betsu
This	place	once	make	separation
	ground			

At this place we have for once to separate.

Ko	ho	ban	ri	sei
Solitary	rootless	10000	miles	go away
	plant			
	dead grass			

Like solitary dead grass (blown by northern wind) the departing
one goes through 1000 miles

<u>Fu</u>	wun	yu	shi	i
Floating	cloud	wanderer		mind

His (or your) mind may be that of a floating cloudlike wanderer.

<u>Raku</u>	jitsu	<u>ko</u>	jin	<u>jo</u>
Falling	sun	old	acquaintance	emotion
setting				

(As for me) the sorrow of parting with an old acquaintance is
   comparable to the setting of the sun.

<u>Ki</u>	shu	<u>ji</u>	<u>ji</u>	<u>kio</u>
Shaking	hands	from	this	away
Brandishing			place	

Wringing hands in despairing resolution.
   from this place it is away! (We have decided to separate)

"<u>Sho</u>	<u>sho</u>"	<u>ham</u>	<u>ba</u>	<u>mei</u>
onomatopoeia for a		separating	horse	neigh
solitary horse neighing				

(We men have so decided) and yet our very horses
   separating, neigh <u>sho sho</u>.

APPENDIX II: A TYPESCRIPT OF POUND'S

DRAFTS FOR EIGHT POEMS OF

WANG WEI[1]

[1.]

WHITE PARROT. (On the boredom of a lady in waiting)
The name comes from the West,
the tribe from the southern seas,
It speaks with the Red-beak's eas[e],
a clear tone comes from its mouth.
It turns its green feathers white
Admi[ss]ion being its delight,
And whiteness, being as we know, the
    true note of beauty.
       This evinces,
true tas[t]e in those who would become the toys of princes
    ~~(perception)~~
    (cea[s]ing from being themselves.)
They permit you to
Be considered exotic,
you are given the run of the orchid chamber,
among magically beautiful women,
      a little faded, blas[é] and ghostly, perhaps,
      orchids and ghosts go together,

You have left the ivies, and the incommodity
    of alternate cloud and sun,
    which you had to bear in their forest.
Changing the [the] high-bending branch
      for gauzy sleeves,
     (perch not on branch
        wind bent, but on [on]
      diaphanous sleeves.
    Leaving the lofty nest
      perillous high, now knowing the jeweled room
      room of bibelots,
Considering you[r] own kind, naturally distant,
You will end fast in human hands, certainly,
      certainly,
You can speak . . . . when the words have been said
    in your presence.
Yet the words in your mouth are but shadows,
You move in the jeweled grating,
Bob up through the gilded ~~ring~~
         (hoop)
No other parrot is near you.
Your shadow alone can match you,
Two white pheasants stalk by the pond's edge,
The white storks rest in the cranies.
You regret ~~that they have the same colour~~,
   ~~that whiteness is not only yours~~,
      ~~life~~
     ~~does not distinguish you from them~~.
    This democratization of whiteness.
You weep at not being unique
You see ~~the thing only too clearly~~,
   you[r] own transparence of vision is
     equal to the distress,
Your thought moves out without bridle or bound[a]ry.
on this topic, mind you.
Your thoughts are cut off from the fragrant tree

You preen your wing on carved rafters,
      only on rafters exquisitely carved.
~~Biting the fine flower, but speechless~~,
(One putting a flower in your mount, and silent,
      you only perched on a wrist, merely resting
      ready for flight.
Your intelligence was yours only,
            (your thought[s] were your own private
            amusement)
Your graceful form unadorned,
                  southern,
      you had the five graces,
            clear light,
You are covered with the gilt dust of the west,
      filmy white powder,
As to the sea swallow bringing good omen,
            you have had the food from the jewel box,
Mountain cock learning dancing,
                  (cock danced before mirror,
try dance down reflection, died of exhaustion)
Facing tr[e]asure mirror, keep dancing till death.
You have all the talents and graces of all these
      bright feathered birds
Raised up for (reverenceing) the sun and moonlight,
      How pitiful this bird
so small, so far from home,
Its colour rivals white silk,
            the robe and flesh fade *blend*
                  when they meet
their edges, one can not see ~~the lines of~~
                  ~~demarcation~~.
The big cage is long closed.
She has not flown to a tree since her capture,
If she could borr[o]w wing feathers (of cock and swallow)
      it would fly with wild flying night[i]ngale.?
(? like poor singing girl. ??? with author)

Omakitsu   3.

Poor dwelling near valley mouth
High tree belts rough village
Palanquin twists about stone road
Who comes to gate of mountain abode?
Freezing bay glues fishing boat
Hunters fire burns in cold field
Only white cloud overhead
Temple bell and monkey cry rarely heard.

4.

Sitting in mystic bamboo grove, back unseen
Press stops of long whistle
Deep forest unpierced by man
Moon and I face each other.

5.

       turn
Peach flowers ~~hold up~~ the dew ~~that shows~~ crimson
~~The~~ green willows belt in the ~~smoke~~-mist,
    will ~~making lines in its denseness~~.
The Servant ~~has~~ not swept up the fallen petals,   *The guest is*
The guest of this mountain,   *not yet up.*
  sleeps through the night[i]ngales noise.   *The nightingales*
                                        are still
                                        crying

6.

"When you come to the gates of Go." vide Cathay.
        it
Someone said to Gengi when he was going to Arisei as
    messenger, still sung at parting in Japan.

7.

Red sun fills heaven and earth
Fiery clouds are heaped up like mountain on mountain

Grasses and trees are parched, twisted,
River and marsh are baked dry.
The light gauze weighs heavy upon me
The thick tree shade is worn thin,
~~(forest, tangled forest shade is worn thin)~~
Bamboo mats are to[o] hot to touch
~~Rattan mats and bamboo etc.~~
We must wash our summer net dress over and over
I send my though[t] out from the world
I give it space in the open
Long wind from 10,000 miles
a sea wind clears off the dust.
Then I reflect that the boredom comes from body
I know[n] that I am not fully enlightened
What pleas[u]re have in ~~heavens~~
like that of going into the gates drenched with dew
detachment

8.

The mountain is empty and empty
Dark trees crowd thicker and thicker
Pompous officers stuff up the court,
How are you in your vacant valley?

Letters little harmony, think deep.
you walk alone, breaking an[d] unknown path.
(tree-c[ir]cling)
Rest glad on a stone, drink of the shadweed free
flowing stream
Your gate is of pine boughs, your house a grass thatch
reed thatch
You feed your cocks in the clouds
Have you lugged that calf up in your arms?
God makes your Natsume like melons,
a tame   (dates)
Does ~~your~~ tiger yet sell your apricots,
and get in your autumn corn.

(Story of sages tame tiger who used to keep stall
for his master. [P]eople took fruit and left money.)

I am ashamed of my stupidity, interrupting your
                              meditation
I dislike being so old, so dependent on a salary
     that I have to get through six rows of ~~officials~~ *officers*
     pawed over by sixteen officials.
I promise you I will give up my office
                         and follow you.
What need of asking *old* In Sen, for a judgement in
                    augury

                    2.d ode on same topic.
                              (go toward)
The mountain dweller wishes to return to the mountain
The black cloud ~~grows~~ blacker
                    goes ~~darker~~ spilling out torrents of rain
The water ripples out from the stream bed
                    flushing the green dark grass
          (~~and sweeps it o[ve]r~~
                    bends it ~~low~~ with the current
                    aslant
A white heron fall like white paper
rough,   (? ~~attracted by surprise of somethin[g]~~
rough is the way!   ~~loose in the stream)~~
This way is too rough, do not go. (????)

A thousand dusks gather into one cloud
You can not tell the sky from the mountain
The mist is interwoven with darkness
               ~~close woven~~
The monkeys themselves can not see.
                    (~~nor hear themselves shrie[k]ing~~
                    ~~in the open)~~
                    ////

Evening sun strikes over the mountain
The far eastern village stands out as if near
   the fields in betw[e]en are all hazy
    and invisible
   ~~(green intervening fields do no[t] show)~~
    ~~But~~
I am sad at your going. ~~I am~~ full of envy,
   my friend.

    [9.]

The playing in Goshinje

In that gold-coloured country
They have an open field of white jade,
They have upset the mount[ain] getting out their big stones
The[y] can conjure spring on the mountain peak
   ~~(make spring come flying)~~
The rough tigers mount into paradisal meditation
 thought-burdened
The ~~sadly thinking~~ monkeys learn the four stages
~~they~~ buy incense and burn green Katsura
ask fire, to step into crimson lotus.
  ~~(i.e. incantations)~~
The grass colour mounts through the mist
The pine-sound drifts up ~~through the moon light~~
    ~~visibly~~ (beside the moon)
The mountain river spreads out to the hundred
    castles beneath us,
~~World limit fills the three thousand.~~
  ~~(rotten b[uddh]ism,)~~
   ~~idiotic references.~~
In the midst is the little brahmin temple,
The far castle is at last seen distinctly.
Ha Rio juts out through the trees,
The river fades into the sky line,

the far town lie cut out on a map,
Smoke goes up from an orphan village
   expect to see
I think I see the Lord in the clouds.
      [Mr H. thinks emperor not Budd[h]a]
Breaking the fog I think of a crowd of officials,
???   ????? saints,

BREAKING THE VISION.

I am ashamed as a small officer in a dead office,
End body res[em]bles respectable black
Until life ends reverend dark mystery
Who knows the guest now in AN temple
ever in harmony oak rafter essay (Zen meditation)
(rafter thinks what it was, oak slow growth.)

APPENDIX III: A DESCRIPTIVE LIST OF WORKS

ON ORIENTAL SUBJECTS FROM WILLIAMS'

LIBRARY NOW AT FAIRLEIGH DICKINSON

UNIVERSITY AND ELSEWHERE[1]

Brounder, Walter Brooks & Fung Yuet Mow, *Chinese Made Easy*, Intro. H. A. Giles, Inscribed to "my friend John with the compliments of the author Walter Brooks Brouner, Oct. 26/04," New York & London: Macmillan, 1904

**Bynner, Witter, trans., *The Way of Life According to Laotzu*, (A version of *Dao de jing*), Inscribed to Florence Williams by Bynner, 1955, New York: John Day, 1955

Chin P'ing Mei, *The Adventurous History of Hsi Men and His Six Wives*, Intro. Arthur Waley, Inscribed to Dr. & Mrs. Williams in English & Chinese by David Rafael Wang, spring 1960, New York: Capricorn, 1960

*Dawson, Miles M., ed., *The Wisdom of Confucius: A Collection of the Ethical Sayings of Confucius and His Disciples*, Boston: International Pocket Library, 1932

Giles, Herbert A., *A History of Chinese Literature*, Autograph note from WCW to his mother, 1916, New York: D. Appleton, 1914

Hearn, Lafcadio, trans., *Japanese Lyrics*, Japanese and English on opposite pages, Boston & New York: Houghton Mifflin, 1915

Ibara, Saikaku, *Quaint Stories of Samurais*, Trans. Ken Sato, Inscribed by WCW, Paris: Private printing, 1928

*Ibara, Saikaku, *Quaint Stories of Samurais*, Trans. Ken Sato, Paris: Private printing, 1928

Kagawa, Toyohiko, *A Grain of Wheat*, Trans. Marion R. Draper & Ed. Glenn Clark, Inscribed by WCW, New York: Harper & Brothers, 1936

Lin Yutang, *The Gay Genius: The Life and Times of Su Tungpo*, New York: John Day, 1947

Michaux, Henri, *A Barbarian in Asia*, Trans. Sylvia Beach, New York: New Directions, 1949

Mishima, Yukio, *Confessions of a Mask*, Trans. Meredith Weatherby, New York: New Directions, 1958

Mishima, Yukio, *Five Modern No Plays*, Trans. Donald Keene, New York: Alfred A. Knopf, 1957

On the Delights of Japanese Novels, (Extracts from reviews of Japanese novels published by Knopf) New York: Alfred A. Knopf, 1957

Pound, Ezra, intro. & trans., *Confucius, The Great Digest and Unwobbling Pivot*, New York: New Directions, 1951

Reps, Paul, *Gold/Fish Signatures*, Bound & printed on rice paper, San Francisco: Auerhahn Press, 1962

*Rexroth, Kenneth,[2] *One Hundred Poems from the Japanese*, New York: New Directions, 1955

Ricci, Matthew, *China in the 16th Century: The Journals of Matthew Ricci*, Trans. Louis J. Gallagher, New York: Random House, 1953

Rowe, David N., *Modern China*, Princeton, N.J.: Van Nostrand, 1959

Tsiang, H. T., *China Red*, Inscribed to WCW by author, New York: Private printing, 1933

Tsing, H. T., *The Hanging on Union Square*, Inscribed to WCW by author, New York: Private printing, 1935

Waley, Arthur, *A Hundred and Seventy Chinese Poems*, Inscribed by WCW, New York: Alfred A. Knopf, 1919

Waley, Arthur, *More Translations from the Chinese*, Inscribed by WCW, New York: Alfred A. Knopf, 1919

NOTES

Abbreviations

WORKS BY EZRA POUND

CA   *The Cantos.* 11th printing. New York: New Directions, 1989.

DI   *Des Imagistes: An Anthology.* New York: Albert and Charles Boni, 1914.

ED   *Ezra Pound and Dorothy Shakespear: Their Letters 1909–1914.* Ed. Omar Pound and A. Walton Litz. New York: New Directions, 1984.

EPPP   *Ezra Pound's Poetry and Prose Contributions to Periodicals.* Ed. Lea Baechler, A. Walton Litz, and James Longenbach. New York: Garland, 1991.

GB   *Gaudier-Brzeska: A Memoir.* New York: New Directions, 1970.

L   *The Letters of Ezra Pound 1907–1941.* Ed. D. D. Paige. New York: Haskell, 1974.

LE   *Literary Essays.* Ed. T. S. Eliot. New York: New Directions, 1968.

MN   *Make It New.* New Haven: Yale UP, 1935.

P   *Personae: The Shorter Poems.* Ed. Lea Baechler and A. Walton Litz. New York: New Directions, 1990.

PJ   *Pound/Joyce: The Letters of Ezra Pound to James Joyce, with Pound's Essays on Joyce.* Ed. Forrest Read. New York: New Directions, 1967.

SR   *The Spirit of Romance.* New York: New Directions, 1968.

YCAL   Unpublished Pound/Fenollosa manuscripts. Collection of American Literature, the Beinecke Rare Book and Manuscript Library, Yale University.

WORKS BY WILLIAM CARLOS WILLIAMS

CP 1   *The Collected Poems.* Vol. 1, 1909–1939. Ed. A. Walton Litz and Christopher MacGowan. New York: New Directions, 1986.

CP 2   *The Collected Poems.* Vol. 2, 1939–1962. Ed. Christopher MacGowan. New York: New Directions, 1988.

I   *Imaginations.* Ed. Webster Schott. New York: New Directions, 1970.

IWWP   *I Wanted to Write a Poem: The Autobiography of the Works of a Poet.* Ed. Edith Heal. Boston: Beacon Press, 1958.

SE   *Selected Essays.* New York: Random House, 1954.

SL   *Selected Letters.* Ed. John C. Thirlwall. New York: New Directions, 1984.

PROLOGUE: THE PLACE OF THE
ORIENT IN THE MODERNIST MOVEMENT

1. Chan is the Chinese equivalent of the Japanese term Zen. As Daisetz Suzuki notes in *Zen and Japanese Culture,* "Zen is one of the products of the Chinese mind after its contact with Indian thought, which was introduced into China in the first century A.D. through the medium of Buddhist teachings." In the same passage Suzuki also remarks, "While the Chinese mind was profoundly stimulated by the Indian way of thinking, it never lost its touch with the plurality of things, it never neglected the practical side of our daily life. This national or racial psychological idiosyncrasy brought about the transformation of Indian Buddhism into Zen Buddhism" (3). For a more recent treatment of the topic, see Robert E. Buswell, Jr., *The Formation of Ch'an Ideology in China and Korea.*

1 "GETTING ORIENT FROM ALL QUARTERS":
BINYON, UPWARD, FENOLLOSA

1. Pound was introduced to Laurence Binyon by his London publisher Elkin Mathews (1851–1921) in early February 1909. In his correspondence to his parents during that period, Pound refers to Binyon first as "the Wordsworth-Mathew Arnold of today," and then as "one of the best loved men in London," a man with "a sort of pervading slow charm in him & in his work." And he mentions on several occasions that he had been "seeing a fair bit of Binyon" and that they were lunching together (YCAL).

2. According to Pound's letter of 15 March 1909 to his mother, Binyon sent him "a ticket for his lectures on Oriental & European Art." Pound found the first one "intensely interesting" (YCAL). As Woon-Ping Chin Holaday has suggested, the

substance of Binyon's 1909 lectures is likely to have been taken from his work of the previous year, *Painting in the Far East*, whose "main concern was to explain the aesthetic value and significance of Eastern paintings to the Western viewer" (29). See Holaday, "Pound and Binyon: China via the British Museum."

3. Laurence Binyon, who entered the British Museum in 1893, was appointed Assistant-Keeper of the Department of Prints and Drawings in 1909. In November 1912 an Oriental Sub-department was established to house its growing collection of Chinese and Japanese paintings and color prints. Binyon was put in charge of this Sub-department (1912–32), out of which grew the British Museum's Department of Oriental Antiquities that now includes more than eleven hundred Chinese paintings (Farrer 7).

4. Dorothy Pound's early interest in drawing Chinese pictures is documented by Ezra Pound. In a letter to his father, 3 December 1912, he remarks, "This being Tuesday. And D' [Dorothy] goes on painting chinese pictures" (YCAL). Omar Pound, in response to my query about his mother's enthusiasm for Chinese art, confirms that there are "several examples of 'Chinese style'" among his collection of Dorothy's drawings and paintings. Samples of these, "An Imperial Palace Tower" (fig. 3), "A Dragon" (fig. 1), and "The God of Longevity," are published in Omar Pound's own volume of verse, *The Dying Sorcerer* (Nova Scotia: Antigonish, 1985). The influences may be traced to various early Chinese art holdings of the British Museum, among which are *The Forbidden City* by Zhu Bang (fig. 4) (Reg. No. 1881.12-10.87.144) and *A Dragon* by Tao Yi (fig. 3) (Reg. No. 1910.2-12.134).

5. No. 1 in the British Museum's 1910–12 Exhibition of Chinese and Japanese Paintings (Binyon, *Guide* 14–15). See my discussion in Chapter Two, 43–45.

6. In 1907 the British archaeologist and geographer Sir (Mark) Aurel Stein (1862–1943) recovered from the "Cave of the Thousand Buddhas" near Dunhuang, northwest China, a considerable number of banners and rolls of silk painted with Buddhist subjects, dated A.D. 600–900, which he brought to England in 1909. The reports of the event caused a great sensation in London. In the British Museum's 1910–12 Exhibition of Chinese and Japanese Paintings, twenty-five specimens of this material were therefore included to show their extraordinary value. Among these were *Standing Guanyin* (fig. 7) (no. 21) and four other scrolls (nos. 13, 23, 25, and 26) representing the Bodhisattva of Compassion Guanyin (Binyon, *Guide* 18–20). In addition, on display in the 1910–12 Exhibition were two Yuan (thirteenth to fourteenth centuries) copies of the figure: no. 39, *Guanyin, the Goddess of Mercy*, and no. 44, *The Unsurpassable Guanyin*. For the latter Binyon offers a detailed caption:

Kwanyin (Avalokitésvara in Sanskrit, Kwannon in Japanese), originally conceived of as a male impersonation of the Buddha, became transformed in course of time into the Goddess of Mercy and Lovingkindness. Sometimes she is represented seated by a waterfall, illustrating a passage of Buddhist scripture, which tells how the sinner, even if he be plunged into a pit of fire, by earnest prayer to Kwanyin, may see the flames turned into living water. Here, as often, she is seated solitary on a wave-beaten rock, with a spray of leaves in a little vase beside her. (*Guide* 23)

The *Guide* prepared by Binyon with the caption above was sold threepence a copy during the 1910–12 Exhibition. Ezra and Dorothy may have obtained one. About Guanyin, see also *Painting in the Far East* 65, 124, and 162.

7. To the best of my knowledge, Pound's earliest reference to Guanyin occurs in the first of his 1917 "Three Cantos": "Kwannon / Footing a boat that's but one lotus petal, / . . ." (P 233). The image seems to match *Bodhisattva* (Guanyin) (fig. 7), no. 25 in the British Museum's 1910–12 Exhibition, in which the Bodhisattva of Compassion is depicted as "standing on lotus with two lotus flowers rising from diadem" (Binyon, *Guide* 20).

8. Nos. 128–34 in the British Museum's 1910–12 Exhibition of Chinese and Japanese Paintings (Binyon, *Guide* 37–38). See fig. 8, Scene 2 from the Japanese artist Sesson's set of *The Eight Views*. Also on display in the 1910–12 Exhibition were the set by the Japanese artist Kano Tōun (nos. 153–56; *Guide* 40) and two Ming (fourteenth to seventeenth centuries) copies of the subjects (no. 91, "Snowy Evening," and no. 92, "Rainy Evening") (29). In the *Guide*, Binyon indicates that these copies "form a traditional series of landscape subjects, the Eight Famous Views or Scenes originally associated with the scenery of Lake Tung-Ting in China, and afterwards transferred to the scenery of Lake Biwa in Japan and to that of other localities" (37). About *The Eight Views*, see also *Painting in the Far East* 133–35. For a more recent treatment, see "Eight Views of the Hsiao and Hsiang Rivers by Wang Hung," in Wen C. Fong et al., *Images of the Mind* 213–35.

9. Pound's incredible memory of Binyon is further revealed in a dream he had a little over two months before his death. Olga Rudge, on 26 August 1972, entered an account of the curious dream in her notebook titled "I Ching: Apr 72—Nov 72":

he dreamt:
"of Mrs Binyon . . . it was said that Queen Victoria had helped her with the twins" "it was only sending clothing or something." Later in conversation E. said that their birth was announced in London papers as "To Mr & Mrs Laurence Binyon, twins, prematurely." (They were born when E. just got to London). (YCAL)

10. The Exhibition of Chinese and Japanese Paintings in 1910 was opened in June 1910 in the Prints and Drawings Gallery situated in the Museum's White Wing. It remained open until April 1912, when it was replaced by an exhibition of the principal drawings of the various European Schools acquired since 1905. I

am grateful to Christopher Date, Assistant Archivist of the British Museum, who provided the information above along with transcriptions of relevant minute entries from the Meetings of the Trustees of the British Museum together with two reports, the first from Sidney Colvin, Keeper of the Department of Prints and Drawings, and the second from Laurence Binyon, at that time an Assistant Keeper.

11. An earlier "Exhibition of Chinese and Japanese Paintings" was held in the British Museum's Prints and Drawings Gallery in 1888. Among its 237 exhibits, only thirteen were of probable Chinese origins (*Guide to the Exhibition of Chinese and Japanese Paintings,* 1888). It was the 1910–12 Exhibition of 108 Chinese paintings and 126 Japanese paintings that provided the English public with their first opportunity to examine a large collection of both Chinese and Japanese paintings. For a complete catalog of the 1910–12 Exhibition, see Binyon, *Guide to an Exhibition of Chinese and Japanese Paintings* (London: British Museum, 1910).

12. On his return from the U.S., Binyon lamented in the presence of Pound that "England will never have a collection comparable to the 'Fuller' lot in the U.S." See Pound's letter of 4 January 1913 to Dorothy (*ED* 177).

13. Pound's earliest reference to Fenollosa's *Epochs,* so far as I know, is in a letter to his father written on 5 December 1913. The remark seems to suggest an earlier familiarity with the work: "If you get Fenollosa's 'Epochs of Chinese & Japanese Art', you'll get some idea of what his work means, & of his unique opportunity." I am indebted to Donald Gallup, who called my attention to this letter.

14. Mary Fenollosa had, by 1913, published a volume of verse (*Out of the Nest: A Flight of Verses*) and several books of fiction (notably *Truth Dexter* and *The Dragon Painter*).

15. Pound gives the credit of this point of view to Ford Madox Hueffer (Ford). He contributes a footnote (dated January 1937) in Harriet Monroe's autobiography *A Poet's Life: Seventy Years in a Changing World* (1938):

It should be realized that Ford Madox Ford had been hammering this point of view into me from the time I first met him (1908 or 1909) and that I owe him anything that I don't owe myself for having saved me from the academic influences then raging in London. (267)

16. The essay was published in the *New Age,* in seven installments, from 4 September to 16 October 1913 (*EPPP* 1: 153, 154–55, 156–59, 159–61, 180–83, 183–85, and 191–93).

17. One finds such pieces as "L'éscalier de jade" (Pound's "The Jewel Stairs' Grievance") and "Le départ d'un ami" (Pound's "Taking Leave of a Friend") in Judith Gautier's version, and "En bateau" (the first part of Pound's "The River Song") in Marquis d'Hervey-Saint-Denys' version. Marquis d'Hervey-Saint-

Denys' book begins with a one-hundred-page introduction on "L'art poétique et la prosodie chez les Chinois."

18. Among the Chinese titles of the "Wisdom of the East" series are L. Cranmer-Byng's *A Lute of Jade* and *The Book of Odes*, Lionel Giles' *Sayings of Confucius*, and Laurence Binyon's *The Flight of the Dragon*.

19. Pound reviewed *The New Word* for the *New Age* (23 April 1914). See "Allen Upward Serious" in EPPP 1: 233–34.

20. Note that both Upward and Pound call Confucius "K'ung Fu-tsze" or "K'ung the Master."

21. "A Song of the Degrees" and "Further Instructions," first published in the November 1913 *Poetry* (Gallup C109). Since both poems show a desire for "Chinese colours" but no trace of concrete knowledge of Chinese poetry, it is highly probable that they were composed between mid-September and early October 1913 when Pound had read Upward's "Scented Leaves" but had not yet taken up Chinese studies.

2 VIA GILES: QU YUAN, LIU CHE, LADY BAN

1. Chisolm informs us that "This account follows Mrs. Fenollosa's MS, 'Ezra Pound,' which, despite several lapses in recollection, seems reliable on the point of Fenollosa's papers" (222 n).

2. Pound wrote of that visit on 13 October 1913 to his mother: "You'll find Giles 'History of Chinese Literature' a very interesting book. Upward has sort of started me off in that direction. I have also embarked on a french translation of Confucius and Mencius" (YCAL).

3. Pound is inaccurate about China having no long poems. To give two quick examples, the original text of Qu Yuan's *Li sao* has 373 lines (see Hawkes' version in *The Songs of the South* 68–78), and that of the *Yue fu* ballad *Southeast the Peacock Flies* has 353 lines (see Watson's version in *The Columbia Book of Chinese Poetry* 82–92). Pound's remark is, of course, based on Giles, who observes:

Brevity is indeed the soul of a Chinese poem, which is valued not so much for what it says as for what it suggests. As in painting, so in poetry suggestion is the end and aim of the artist, who in each case may be styled an impressionist. The ideal length is twelve lines, and this is the limit set to candidates at the great public examinations at the present day, the Chinese holding that if a poet cannot say within such compass what he has to say it may very well be left unsaid. (*History* 145)

4. John Gould Fletcher recalled in 1945 that he was introduced to Chinese literature around 1910 by H. A. Giles' *History of Chinese Literature* (*Selected Essays* 58).

5. In *Gems of Chinese Literature*, one will find earlier versions of Qu Yuan's "The

Genius of the Mountain" (35), Tao Qian's "The Peach-blossom Fountain" (104), Mei Sheng's "Neglected" ("The Beautiful Toilet") (302), and Lady Ban's "The Autumn Fan" (305).

6. *The Songs of Chu* (*Chu ci*), consisting of sixteen books of poems by Qu Yuan, Song Yu, and others, was supposedly put together by the Western Han bibliographer Liu Xiang (77–6 B.C.). The earliest extant edition of the anthology, however, was made by the Eastern Han scholar Wang Yi (fl. 110–20), who added one book by himself to the original sixteen.

7. For an account of Qu Yuan's life, see David Hawkes, *The Songs of the South: An Ancient Chinese Anthology of Poems by Qu Yuan and Other Poets* 51–66.

8. For discussions of the ancient *wu* culture, see Hawkes, *The Songs of the South* 42–51, and Arthur Waley, *The Nine Songs: A Study of Shamanism in Ancient China* 9–19.

9. For a description of the prosodic structure of *Li sao* and other Chu songs, see Hawkes, *The Songs of the South* 39–41.

10. *The Nine Songs* actually consists of eleven songs, to which Hawkes has given these titles: (1) The Great Unity, God of the Eastern Sky (*Dong huang tai yi*); (2) The Lord within the Clouds (*Yun-zhong jun*); (3) The Goddess of the Xiang (*Xiang jun*); (4) The Lady of the Xiang (*Xiang fu-ren*); (5) The Greater Master of Fate (*Da si ming*); (6) The Lesser Master of Fate (*Shao si ming*); (7) The Lord of the East (*Dong jun*); (8) The River Earl (*He bo*); (9) The Mountain Spirit (*Shan gui*); (10) Hymn to the Fallen (*Guo shang*); and (11) Honouring the Dead (*Li hun*) (*The Songs of the South* 95–118).

11. Qu Yuan's original poem consists of only twenty-seven lines. See Waley's version ("The Mountain Spirit") in *The Nine Songs* 53–54; Hawkes' version ("The Mountain Spirit") in *The Songs of the South* 115–16; and Watson's version ("The Mountain Spirit") in *The Columbia Book of Chinese Poetry* 51–52.

12. According to Arthur Evans, the chorus singers are "wild, unkempt foreigners." They have "followed [Dionysus] to Thebes from Asia Minor in the East" (203).

13. The subject of Qu Yuan's "The Mountain Spirit" is taken to be a female deity by Hawkes (*The Songs of the South* 115–16), Watson (*Chinese Poetry* 51–52), and Liu Wu-chi (26–27). Waley alone interprets it to be a male god (*The Nine Songs* 55). His view is close to Su Xuelin's, published more recently.

14. Su Xuelin's *Qu Yuan yu Jiu ge* (Qu Yuan and *The Nine Songs*) was first printed in 1973 under the auspices of the Sun Yat-sen Foundation for Learning and Culture in Taipei. The 1992 "first edition" is in fact a facsimile reprint of the 1973 limited edition. See Su's "1992 Preface" (i–ii).

15. In his version for *An Introduction to Chinese Literature* (26–27), Liu Wu-chi renders *bili* (Giles' "wistaria") as "creeping vine." Thus, in his opening passage, all the four natural things sacred to Dionysus—the vine, the ivy, the leopard, and the lynx—are literally represented.

16. According to Su Xuelin, the first wave of immigration from Western Asia occurred prior to the Shang period, i.e., before the seventeenth century B.C. (91–97).

17. "Vorticism," first published in *Fortnightly Review* (1 September 1914) (Gallup C158).

18. "The Renaissance," first published in *Poetry* (February, March, and May 1915) (Gallup C175, C186, C189).

19. As Joseph R. Allen has noted, Li Bo's *Yu jie yuan* (Pound's "The Jewel Stairs' Grievance") is a *Yue fu* ballad. It "'imitates' poems of the same title by Xie Tiao (464–499) and Yu Yan (fl. 500)" (169).

20. One previous discussion of Pound's "Liu Ch'e" (with reference to the Chinese original as well as versions by Giles, Waley, and Amy Lowell) is that of A. C. Graham in his introduction to *Poems of the Late T'ang*.

21. I.e., the Church of San Francesco in Rimini. According to certain Romantic writers, the Tempio was erected under the personal order of Sigismondo Malatesta (1417–68) to honor his favorite mistress and later third wife, Isotta degli Atti (ca. 1433–74). In an early draft for Canto 8, Pound "admires the Tempio as 'a song caught in the stone'" (Rainey, *Monument of Culture* 184). Interestingly, while Malatesta is said to have written a *capitolo ternario* in praise of Isotta (Rainey 180), Liu Che is believed to have had a stone statue erected to honor Lady Li (Jing Wang 82).

22. The attribution of *The Admonitions of the Instructress to Court Ladies* to Gu Kaizhi has been questioned by Chinese art historians, who believe it to be a Tang copy of the original. See, for example, Wang Bomin et al., *Zhongguo meishu tongshi* (A History of Chinese Art) 60.

23. C. W. Luh remarks, "A *jue ju* [a five-syllable or seven-syllable quatrain] . . . is composed of twenty or twenty-eight syllables. The Japanese took it over in the Tang Dynasty and later made it the *haiku*, composed of seventeen syllables" (106).

3 CHINA CONTRA GREECE IN *DES IMAGISTES*

1. My inspection of the Beinecke set of *The Glebe* (1.1, 1.2, 1.3, 1.4, 1.6, 2.4) confirms Charles Norman's description. No internal evidence exists to designate whether the series was started by Alfred Kreymborg, Man Ray, Sam Halpert, or any other people. The first number (vol. 1, no. 1, September 1913), consisting of Adolf Wolff's *Songs, Sighs and Curses*, is indicated as "Published by The Glebe at Ridgefield New Jersey," "Copyright 1913 by Adolf Wolff." The volume was dedicated to a Mr. Leonard D. Abbott. On the inside back cover there is an announcement: "The October issue of The Glebe will present 'The Azure Adder,'

a one-act comedy by Charles Demuth." There isn't an October 1913 issue of *The Glebe*, however. The second number (vol. 1, no. 2, November 1913) is adorned by *Diary of a Suicide* by Wallace E. Baker. (*The Azure Adder* by Charles Demuth appeared in the third number in December 1913.) On the inside front cover of that number, Alfred Kreymborg was for the first time named as Editor, Leonard D. Abbott, Albert Boni, Alanson Hartpence, Adolf Wolff as Associate Editors, and Charles Boni, Jr., as Business Manager. From that issue on, the series was published by "New York Albert & Charles Boni: 96 Fifth Ave" and "Copyright 1913 [or 1914], By The Glebe."

2. Cournos set sail for the United States most probably in January 1914, as Pound wrote his mother on an unspecified date in that month: "Cournos is sailing for America in a few days. He will call on dad" (YCAL).

3. Two possible dates have been given for H. D. and Aldington's wedding: 18 October 1913 or 28 October 1913 (Doyle 330 n). James Wilhelm, in *Ezra Pound: London and Paris 1908–1925*, eludes the controversy by loosely dating it "after the 18th" of October 1913 (132).

4. I am grateful to Donald Gallup for calling my attention to this letter. He points out to me that "In that same letter Pound goes on to say that 'Williams' book [*The Tempers*] in final proofs arrived yesterday' (the book was, according to Emily Wallace, published only five days later—on 13 Sept. 1913), and 'Have only 1½ more articles [of the series 'The Approach to Paris'] to do for N. A.' These references would seem to establish beyond any doubt that the date of the letter is 6 September 1913" (letter to ZQ).

5. "Δώρια" was first published in *Poetry Review* (February 1912); "The Return" was first published in *English Review* (June 1912) (Gallup C39 and C47).

6. Omar Pound informs me that he keeps a 1901 notebook of his mother showing that she was learning Chinese around that time (letters to ZQ).

7. See Chapter One, note 4.

8. "Heather," first published in *Poetry and Drama*, March 1914 (Gallup C132); "Epitaphs (Fu I; Li Po)" and "Meditatio," first published in *Blast* 1, June 1914 (C148); and "The Seeing Eye," first published in *Poetry*, August 1914 (C154).

4 THE POUND-FENOLLOSA VENTURE: AN OVERVIEW

1. I am indebted to Donald Gallup for bringing this letter to my attention.

2. I did notice one inaccuracy in Kenner's account, though. Fenollosa had five, instead of three, sessions with Hirai—on 5, 9, 10, 22, and 25 September 1896. See Fenollosa Notebook 7, kept in the Beinecke Rare Book and Manuscript Library.

3. Bush states "Pound records a 121 which corresponds to no poem" ("Pound

and Li Po" 57). Pound's 121 in fact corresponds to the second half of Li Bo's *Shu dao nan* ("The Szechwan Road," in Waley, *Li Po* 38–40), whereas his 120 corresponds to the first half of the same poem.

4. Pound mistakenly assigned seventeen numbers to three poems translated by Fenollosa in the first "Rihaku" notebook. No. 87 corresponds to a poem not by Li Bo; 88–98 correspond to parts of a poem by Li Bo (*Gufeng*, no. 1); and 99–103 correspond to parts of another poem by Li Bo (*Gufeng*, no. 3).

5. Kenner reports that in 1900 "Fenollosa was also working at early and Taoist poems with another teacher" (198). This unnamed teacher was Kakuzo, whose sessions covered eight poems, among which no. 30 is the source of the "wind poem" of Canto 4, 31 that of "A Ballad of the Mulberry Road," and 36 that of "Sennin Poem by Kakuhaku."

6. The "Fenollosa Papers" kept in the Beinecke Rare Book and Manuscript Library of Yale University are filed in sixty-two folders (Folders 3370–3431) that are stored in Boxes 89–94 of Ezra Pound Papers YCAL MSS 43, Series V. As these sixty-two folders are also marked by a number starting from 1 through 58 (with split numbers for 42 and 48), investigators, for convenience sake, often choose it over the four-digit number to refer to the notebooks and sheaves of leaves kept in the folders. I follow this practice despite my awareness of its probable confusion. First, a number of the folders—for example, nos. (9), (10), (12), (13), (15), (18), and (19)—contain sheaves of leaves rather than notebooks. Second, a number of the folders—nos. (9), (10), (15), (18), and (19)—are composed of material contributed by Pound rather than by Fenollosa.

The following provides the listing of the first twenty-one folders that contain "Fenollosa Papers." In the list that follows the box number and the folder number is the reference number I use in parentheses followed by the title. The forty-one folders unlisted here contain notes and manuscripts on the Chinese Written Character (92 3391–92 3401), Landscape Poetry and Painting in Medieval China (92 3402–93 3407), and Japanese Noh Play (93 3408–94 3431).

89 3370 (1) Certain Noble Plays: [printed] proofs
    3371 (2) Chinese Course I
    3372 (3) Chinese Course IV
    3373 (4) Chinese Ideals
90 3374 (5) Chinese Intercourse, 2 Vols.
    3375 (6) Chinese & Japanese Poetry: Synopsis of Lectures, 3 Vols.
    3376 (7) Chinese Poetry, Hirai & Shida
    3377 (8) Early Chinese Poetry: Kutsugen (Ka-Gi): tr. by Ariga
    3378 (9) Chinese Poetry: Mori [E. P.'s notes for editions of lectures, ca. 1935]
    3379 (10) Chinese Poetry: Mori [E. P.'s notes for editions of lectures, 1958–59; in part reworked from 1935]

91 3380 (11) Chinese Poetry: Prof. Mori's Lectures [on the History of Chinese Poetry], 3 Vols.

3381 (12) Chinese Poetry: Notes

3382 (13) Chinese Poetry: Notes and translations

3383 (14) Chinese Poetry: Notes and translations

3384 (15) Chinese Poetry: Notes by Pound, including translations

3385 (16) Chinese Poetry: Notes (from outside sources)

3386 (17) Chinese Poetry: Okakura, Sogioku and others

3387 (18) Chinese Poetry: Sai-bi: Short Introduction

3388 (19) Translations from Chinese Poetry [in E. P.'s hand]

3389 (20) Chinese Poetry: Translations: Rihaku (Mori & Ariga), Vol. 1

91 3390 (21) Chinese Poetry: Translations: Rihaku (Mori & Ariga), Vol. 2

7. There are actually twelve poems in the original *Cathay* sequence. Bush has overlooked the epigraph to "Four Poems of Departure," a version of Wang Wei's *Song Yuan er shi Anxi* ("Farewell to Yuan the Second on His Mission to Anxi," in Yu 176–77); "Seeing Yuan Off on His Official Trip to Anxi," in Barnstone, Barnstone, and Xu 65).

8. See Pound's letter to Thomas Bird Mosher, 3 December 1914, kept in the Mosher Collection of the Houghton Library, Harvard University.

9. According to Mori, who drew on Chinese sources, the ancient song ("Song of the Bowmen of Shu") was written by "Bun No" (King Wen) and edited by Confucius. The attribution of Song 167, *Cai wei*, to King Wen, however, has proven invalid.

10. Giles is mistaken about Li Bo's dates of birth and death. The high Tang poet was born in 701 and died in 762.

11. In *Noh or Accomplishment* (1917), the four plays "Kumasaka," "Nishikigi," "Hagoromo," and "Kagekiyo" are reprinted from *Certain Noble Plays of Japan* (1916) along with a new introduction by Pound to replace Yeats' written in 1916. On Pound and the *Noh* drama, see Nobuko Tsukui, *Ezra Pound and Japanese Noh Plays*.

5   VIA FENOLLOSA: TAOISM VERSUS VORTICISM IN *CATHAY*

1. To give a typical example, Ford Madox Ford remarks in " 'From China to Peru,' *Outlook*," "The poems in *Cathay* are things of a supreme beauty" (Homberger 108).

2. In the 1960s, Yip was able to inspect reproductions of Fenollosa's notes for only a few *Cathay* poems: those for "Song of the Bowmen of Shu" provided by Lawrence Chisolm, those for "The Beautiful Toilet" and "South-Folk in Cold

Country" provided by Hugh Kenner, and those for "Lament of the Frontier Guard" provided by Dorothy Pound. See Yip 169–79.

3. For a transcript of Fenollosa's notes for "The City of Choan," see Kodama 73–74.

4. For a full description of these qualities in the Chinese syntax, see Yip 21–23.

5. For a discussion of the "poetics of silence," see Zhang Longxi, *The Tao and the Logos* 119–29. Zhang alludes to Mad Crank, a figure in *The Complete Works of Zhuangzi*, "who mumbles, when asked about the meaning of *tao*, 'Ah, I know it and will tell you.' But at the moment when he wants to say it, he forgets what word it is that he wants to say." For Zhuangzi, the Taoist philosopher, Zhang remarks, "Mad Crank's forgetting signals his true knowledge of the *tao*, since *tao* is unsayable" (125). From this Zhang proceeds to show Tao Qian's awareness of the "inadequacy of language." In the fourth-century A.D. recluse's poetry, Zhang asserts, there is often "a moment that at once indicates the difficulty of articulation and the poet's skillful use of silence to overcome that difficulty." In "Taking Leave of a Friend," we may add, one also experiences such a climactic moment when "silence can be more expressive than words" (128).

6. The line is from Song 179, *Che gong* ("Our Chariots Were Strong"). For the Chinese text and English translation, see Legge 290 or Karlgren 124.

7. Cf. the closing lines of the "Exile's Letter" (P 139).

8. Cf. Pound's retranslation of the poem ("Ode 167") in *The Classic Anthology, Defined by Confucius* (Cambridge: Harvard UP, 1954). The opening stanza reads:

> Pick a fern, pick a fern, ferns are high,
> "Home," I'll say: home, the year's gone by,
> no house, no roof, these huns on the hoof.
> Work, work, work, that's how it runs,
> We are here because of these huns.
> (86)

9. Gao Heng notes in his 1980 edition of the *Shi jing*, "This poem must be composed during the reign of King Xuan of the West Zhou [827–781 B.C.]. In King Xuan's time, the northern tribe Xianyun invaded the Zhou. King Xuan sent expeditions to drive out the Xianyun. The frontier guards then sang this song. (Expeditions against the Xianyun were formed also in King Yi's time [?–841 B.C.]. The poem could be written then.)" (227). See also Waley, who writes of *Cai wei* and three related poems:

The next four poems deal with or mention the campaigns of the Chou people against the fierce Hsien-yün tribes. The two Chinese generals, Nan-chung, in No. 132, and Chi-fu, in No. 133, are both traditionally placed in King Hsün's reign (827–782 B.C.). Of the Hsien-yün we know very little. All that we can be certain of is that they were a dreaded foe who invaded Shensi, the home-country of the Chou, and were driven back in a series of campaigns some of which took place round about 800 B.C. (*The Book of Songs* 122)

10.   Quoted, for example, in Jiang Jianyuan and Cheng Junying, *Shi jing zhu xi* 463.

11.   See, for example, Jiang Jianyuan and Cheng Junying, *Shi jing zhu xi;* Zhu Shouliang, *Shi jing ping she* (Taipei, 1984); Yuan Mei, *Shi jing yi zhu* (Jinan, 1981); Gao Heng, *Shi jing jin zhu* (Shanghai, 1980); and Wang Jingzhi, *Shi jing tong she* (Taipei, 1968). In addition, Xia Zhuancai et al.'s *Zhongguo gudai mingpian xuandu* (Anthology of Chinese Masterpieces) (Beijing, 1985) and Liu Yialing et al.'s *Zhongguo lidai shige jianshang cidian* (A Companion to Classical Chinese Poetry) (Beijing, 1988) also treat *Cai wei* as a song of complaint.

12.   For a transcript of Fenollosa's notes for the "Song of the Bowmen of Shu," see Kodama 64–68.

13.   In a note appended to the *New Age* text of "The Seafarer," Pound speaks of a possible addition to the original and explains why he has left it out of his translation:

The text of this poem is rather confused, I have rejected half of line 76 [77], read "Angles" for angels in line 78 [79], and stopped translating before the passage about the soul and the longer lines beginning, "Mickle is the fear of the Almighty" [*Micel biþ se Meotudes egsa*], and ending in a dignified but platitudinous address to the Deity: "World's elder, eminent creator, in all ages, amen" [*wuldres Ealdor, / ece Dryhten, in ealle tid. / Amen*]. There are many conjectures as to how the text came into its present form. It seems most likely that a fragment of the original poem, clear through about the first thirty lines, and thereafter increasingly illegible, fell into the hands of a monk with literary ambitions, who filled in the gaps with his own guesses and "improvements." The groundwork may have been a longer narrative poem, but the "lyric," as I have accepted it, divides fairly well into "The Trials of the Sea," its Lure and the Lament for Age. (qtd. in Ruthven 213–14)

14.   In fact, no. 1 of the two poems of *Chang-gan xing*.

15.   For a transcript of Fenollosa's notes for "The River-Merchant's Wife: A Letter," see Kodama 80–84.

16.   Bush offers a perceptive analysis of Pound's intensification of the complaint theme, though I have reservations about his conclusion that "Pound, maintaining the beautiful indirection of the poem, transformed its subject" ("Pound and Li Po" 40–42).

17.   The translation is mine. For the Chinese text, see Li 132.

18.   The translation is mine. For the Chinese text, see Li 111.

19.   "Song of Chang-gan" ("The River-Merchant's Wife"), "Wretched Me, Flimsy Fate," and "Rebellious Yang" are among Li Bo's *Yue fu* ballads noted for imitation of a folk style.

20. The translation is mine. For the Chinese text, see Li 572.

21. A more literal rendering of the line is: "Always have the faith of 'holding to the pillar'" (the name Weisheng is absent). The phrase alludes to a legend narrated in *The Complete Works of Zhuangzi*. It goes like this in Watson's version: "Wei Sheng made an engagement to meet a girl under a bridge. The girl failed to appear and the water began to rise, but, instead of leaving, he wrapped his arms around the pillar of the bridge and died" (329–30).

22. See note 1 above.

23. Comparing Pound's "The River-Merchant's Wife: A Letter" to Waley's re-translation of the poem, Yip notes that "Pound has crossed the border of textual translation into cultural translation and Waley has not, though he is close enough to the original" (90).

24. For "A Transcript of Fenollosa's Notes for the 'Exile's Letter,' not Including Transliterations," see Bush, "Pound and Li Po" 48–56.

25. Yip makes this remark with regard to Pound's "Lament of the Frontier Guard."

26. Yip's literal translation for this line is: "Among cloud-riding worthies and heroes all over the world" (204). Waley has it: "Among us were the wisest and bravest within the Four Seas, with thoughts high as the clouds" (*Li Po* 12).

27. Fenollosa glosses lines 4 and 5 thus:

> yellow gold white jewel buy songs laughter
> one drink successive months disdain kings (+) princes

and lines 7 and 9 thus:

> Take middle with lord mind not ran counter
> to make Mt. to make sea not make hard
> roll   turn   consider

28. See Yip (88–89), who cites Achilles Fang, who reports that Waley "read a paper on 'The Poet Li Po, A.D. 701–762' before the China Society at the School of Oriental Studies, London, on November 21, 1918 (published by East and West, Ltd., London, 1919), in which he gives his translation of Poems No. 3, 4, 8, and 14 of *Cathay*. . . ." Fang speculates that this was "a shot meant for Pound" (221 n).

29. For lines 4, 5, 7, 9, and 10, Waley gives:

> And we were drunk month after month,
>   scorning princes and rulers.
> Among us were the wisest and bravest within
>   the Four Seas, with thoughts high as
>   the clouds.
>
> . . . . . .

> Going round mountains, skirting lakes
> > was as nothing to them,
> All their feelings, all their thoughts were ours
> > to share; they held nothing back.
> (*Li Po* 12–13)

30. Yip elaborates in a footnote: "Again we do not know if Pound was actually following an already improvised crib by Fenollosa" (83).

31. See note 2 above.

32. It is true that there are many deviations in *Cathay*. One notorious example is Pound's conflation of two separate poems by Li Bo into "The River Song." In Kenner's description,

> this came about because Fenollosa kept the left-hand pages of the 'Rihaku' notebooks for comments by Professor Mori. Three right-hand pages of 'River Song' face three left-hand pages of comment; then a blank left-hand page faces the long title of a new poem about Li Po in the garden full of spring softness. Pound mistook this for more of "The River Song," and the blank left-hand page, which signals a new poem, for absence of comment by Mori. (204)

My inspection of Fenollosa's notes for the two poems confirms Kenner's account. The title of the "new poem" can easily be mistaken for more of "The River Song" not only because it is extremely long (filling an entire right-hand page) but because on the page it is written out and glossed line by line in exactly the same manner as the poetry of "The River Song" on the previous pages. Kodama claims that "At the end of the first poem, Fenollosa comments, 'having come to conclusion,' suggesting that it is the end of the poem" (85). In my repeated examinations of the notes in question, I have failed to locate the phrase, "having come to conclusion." However, Kodama is probably right in assuming that "Pound, at his first hasty reading . . . confused the two poems" and that "By the time he got to serious work on them, he . . . was trying deliberately to make one poem out of two in the form of superposition" (85). For transcripts of Fenollosa's notes for the two poems, see Kodama 86–91.

6   IMITATING WANG WEI: TOWARD *THE CANTOS*

1. For Pound's draft version of the poem, see Ann Chapple 21 n.

2. Pound's draft of the poem is in Fenollosa Notebook 15. The typescript at Yale shows that it has been crossed out in the middle in black pencil.

3. It is a fair guess that Pound had read Giles' version of the parable from *The Complete Works of Zhuangzi*:

Once upon a time, I, Chuang Tzu, dreamt I was a butterfly fluttering hither and thither, to all intents and purposes a butterfly. I was conscious only of following my fancies as a butterfly, and was unconscious of my individuality as a man. Suddenly, I awaked, and there I lay, myself again. Now I do not know whether I was then a man dreaming I was a butterfly, or whether I am now a butterfly dreaming I am a man. (*History* 63)

See also Watson's version (*Chinese Poetry* 49).

4. "So Shu" was changed to "Chuang-tzu" in the late 1960s New Directions printings of *Personae*, according to A. Walton Litz, by "well-meaning experts" (letter to ZQ). In the 1990 revised *Personae*, Pound's original form is restored. See Baechler and Litz' note (*P* 275).

5. According to Pauline Yu, Wang Wei and the Symbolists share (1) the notion of "a non-representational, suggestive poetry"; (2) "the preference for embodiment over assertion, the intuitively apprehended image over logically structured, propositional discourse"; (3) the "reliance on the image or symbol to convey meaning impersonally, rather than direct description or personal expression"; and (4) the notion of "poetry as the manifestation of a unitary principle" (*The Poetry of Wang Wei* 22–28).

6. See "Poem of Peach Blossom Spring," in Levy 12–14, and "Song of Peach Tree Spring," in Barnstone, Barnstone, and Xu 101–02.

7. See "Preface to the Poem on the Peach Blossom Spring," in Watson, *The Columbia Book of Chinese Poetry* 142–43.

8. The painting was accessioned into the Art Institute of Chicago in 1951. The attribution of it to Qui Ying in Kei Suzuki's *Comprehensive Illustrated Catalog of Chinese Paintings* (1: 425) has proven to be incorrect.

9. For a comparative study of the two paintings, see Richard Edwards 134–39.

10. No. 27 and no. 37 in the British Museum's 1910–12 Exhibition of Chinese and Japanese Paintings (Binyon, *Guide* 20 and 22). The attribution of no. 27 to Wang Wei is outdated. James Cahill, in *An Index of Early Chinese Painters and Paintings: T'ang, Sung, and Yuan*, records sixteen paintings that have been attributed to Wang Wei. Whereas the Chishakuin scroll (*A Waterfall*) is included among these, the British Museum piece (*Landscape in Blue and Green Style*) is not.

11. In fact, no. 6 of a suite of seven *jueju* poems titled "Farm Field Pleasure" (*Tian yuan le*). The suite is believed to have been composed after Wang Wei acquired the Wang River estate miles east of the Tang capital Chang'an. See fig. 19, detail of *Landscape of the Wang River* by the Yuan artist Zhao Mengfu after Wang Wei.

12. Pound may well have reworked all of Fenollosa's versions of Wang Wei. However, despite my repeated searches through the "Fenollosa Papers" and Pound's drafts for the Ur-Cantos, I have not been successful in locating his draft for no. 2, "Peach Source Song."

13. In the same sheaf of leaves Pound was also drafting new translations for Qu Yuan, Li Bo, and Tao Qian. Attached to the typed manuscript is an unused ticket for Pound's lecture of March 18 with Pound's autograph on the back:

	Kung
5 peak essay	Kutsugen [Qu Yuan]
	Toenmei [Tao Qian]
	R. [Li Bo] ? O.
	O. [Wang Wei] R

Next to it is a slip of paper with a short list, also in Pound's hand: Kutsugen, Omakitsu, Rihaku, Toenmei. Was Pound preparing a "5 peak essay" or a "4 peak essay," for which he was drafting illustrative versions? At any rate, if there was such an attempt, Wang Wei claimed most of Pound's attention.

14. For an account of Wang Wei's life and career, see Owen 27–51, or Barnstone, Barnstone, and Xu xxvi–lxii.

15. In June 1916 Pound wrote Iris Barry, advising her to "see Fenollosa's big essay on verbs, mostly on verbs." In that same letter, he lamented, "Heaven knows when I shall get it printed" (L 131). It was after two more years' negotiation that he finally arranged to have the essay published in installments in the September–December 1919 Little Review (EPPP 3: 326–28, 331–36, 346–51, and 361–64).

16. I.e., The Chinese Language and How to Learn It: A Manual for Beginners by Sir Walter Caine Hillier (1907–09; 2d edition, 1910) (ED 298 n).

17. For a discussion of de Gourmont's impact on Pound, see also Schwartz 79–84.

18. Dasenbrock, in The Literary Vorticism of Ezra Pound and Wyndham Lewis, notes that The Pisan Cantos indicates a return to the Taoist poetic "developed at the time of Pound's first immersion in Oriental material" (226).

19. It was during the same summer of 1916 that Pound advised Iris Barry to read "Fenollosa's big essay on verbs" (L 131) and informed her that he had "spent the day with Wang Wei, eighth century Jules Laforgue Chinois" (144). In fact, Pound's effort to publish Fenollosa's essay and his experiments with Wang Wei persisted concomitantly from 1916 through 1919.

20. For criticism of Fenollosa's admiration for the alleged pictorial qualities of Chinese characters, see, in particular, James Liu 3–6.

7 "GIVE ME YOUR FACE, YANG KUE FEI!"

1. See "The Cassia Tree: A Collection of Translations and Adaptations from the Chinese in Collaboration with David Rafael Wang" (CP 2: 359–76) and Christopher MacGowan's note (500–502). The sequence presents thirteen poems of

Li Bo, including "Long Banister Lane," a version of the "Song of Chang-gan" (Pound's "The River-Merchant's Wife").

2. In her review of *Kora in Hell* (*Contact* 4 [January–March 1921]), Moore refers to Williams' "Portrait of the Author" as "a super-achievement." "It preserves the atmosphere of a moment," she wrote, "into which the impertinences of life cannot intrude. In the sense conveyed, of remoteness from what is detestable, in the effect of balanced strength, in the flavor of newness in presentation, it is unique" (60).

3. See "The Everlasting Wrong," in Giles, *History* 169–75; "The Never-Ending Wrong," in Cranmer-Byng 79–89; and "Song of Everlasting Sorrow," in Levy 129–33.

4. The manuscript of the letter is kept at the Joseph Regenstein Library, the University of Chicago. It has been quoted from by Paul Mariani (122) and others.

5. The Tang dynasty (618–906) is subdivided into four periods by historians: "early Tang," "high Tang," "mid-Tang," and "late Tang."

6. One classic example of Li Bo's lyrics composed to be sung at Ming Huang's court is the "Three Songs to the *Qing ping* Melody," written in honor of Yang Guifei and the peony-rose planted in the imperial garden. Stephen Owen's version of the first song reads:

> Clouds call to mind her robes,
>   the flowers recall her face.
> Spring breezes brush the railing,
>   dew full on the blossoms.
> If you don't see her in gods' abode,
>   on the mountain Hoard of Jade,
> You can surely meet her in moonlight,
>   there on the Terrace of Jasper.
> (116)

The scene is echoed in Bo Juyi's *Chang hen ge*.

7. See Witter Bynner and Kiang Kang-hu's version in *The Jade Mountain: A Chinese Anthology: Being Three Hundred Poems of the T'ang Dynasty 618–906* 39.

8. The version corresponds to Yang Guifei's *Zeng Zhang Yunrong wu* ("For Zhang Yunrong in Appreciation of Her Dancing"), a song in five irregular lines, collected in *Quan tang shi* (The Complete Poems of the Tang) (Shanghai: Guji, 1986) 1: 34. The breaking of the five lines in the original into nineteen short ones in four stanzas is Amy Lowell's invention.

9. *Fir-Flower Tablets* was published by Houghton Mifflin on 14 December 1921 (MacNair 166 n).

10. The handscroll *Yang Guifei Mounting a Horse* by Qian Xuan (ca. 1235–1301) was accessioned into the Freer collection in 1957.

11. Eight English versions, four French versions, and one German version are

NOTES TO CHAPTER 8   199

listed in Martha Davidson, *A List of Published Translations from Chinese into English, French, and German* 2: 344–53. For a listing of more recent English versions of *Chang hen ge*, see Kai-chee Wong, Pung Ho, and Shu-leung Dang, *A Research Guide to English Translation of Chinese Verse (Han Dynasty to T'ang Dynasty)*.

12. The William Carlos Williams Collection, originally housed in the Rutherford Campus Library of Fairleigh Dickinson University, was in 1994 turned over to the Florham-Madison Campus Library of the University. The material was described by Edith Heal Berrien, Barbara Perkins, and George Perkins in 1964 (published in 1984) and by myself in 1995.

13. In XXIII.1 of *Kora in Hell*, Williams contends that writing poetry for the "poets of the T'ang dynasty or of the golden age in Greece or even the Elizabethans" was "a kind of alchemy of form, a deft bottling of a fermenting language" (75). The high tribute he pays to the Tang poets here reinforces our surmise that he read Giles' *History* no later than 1916.

14. I am grateful to Paul Mariani, who has suggested to me this idea. Mariani also tells me that Williams was having an affair with the writer Evelyn Scott about the time he wrote "Portrait of the Author." "As a doctor and husband with two sons," he says, "Williams knew that he must get over his infatuation" (letter to ZQ). This state of feeling is probably embedded in his creation of the poem.

15. Williams told us that he discarded the poem because he found it imitative of Pound but that Bob McAlmon retrieved it from a wastebasket and called it one of his best (*IWWP* 35–36; *CP* 1: 499). Since Bob McAlmon left with Bryher (Winifred Ellerman) for Europe either on 14 February 1921 (Mariani 178) or on 26 February 1921 (Smoller 46), we can safely assume that Williams wrote "Portrait of the Author" no later than late February 1921.

16. Williams articulated this feeling of disgust also in his letter to Alva N. Turner, 27 October 1920:

Disgust is my most moving emotion. Sometimes I wish it were otherwise, but it is not, so an end of it.

Particularly this morning I feel that the best thing that could happen to me would be for me to drown myself. Stupidity is powerful here as elsewhere. . . . I am drowned in triviality, stupidity, my own heaviness, everything. (*SL* 46)

17. See Terence Diggory, "The Blue Nude and Mrs. Pappadopoulos," in *William Carlos Williams Review* 18.2 (1992): 24–34.

8   IN THE SHADOW OF BO JUYI: *SOUR GRAPES*

1. Arthur Waley's *A Hundred and Seventy Chinese Poems* was published first by Constable and Company in London in 1918 and then by Alfred A. Knopf in New York in 1919.

2. According to James Fraser, director of the Florham-Madison Campus Library, Fairleigh Dickinson University, Williams' copy of *A Hundred and Seventy Chinese Poems* by Arthur Waley has been missing since about 1980. We know from Berrien et al.'s "Descriptive List," available with the Collection, that the missing volume bears "insc. by WCW."

3. In addition to the books already cited in Chapter Eight there are a dozen more in the Collection showing Williams as a follower of Far Eastern culture: Saikaku Ibara, *Quaint Stories of Samurais* (1928); H. T. Tsiang, *China Red* (1933) and *The Hanging on Union Square* (1935); Toyohiko Kagawa, *A Grain of Wheat* (1936); Lin Yutang, *The Gay Genius: The Life and Times of Su Tungpo* (1947); Henri Michaux, *A Barbarian in Asia* (1949); Matthew Ricci, *China in the 16th Century: The Journals of Matthew Ricci* (1953); Yukio Mishima, *Five Modern No Plays* (1957) and *Confessions of a Mask* (1958); David N. Rowe, *Modern China* (1959); Arthur Waley, introd., *Chin P'ing Mei: The Adventurous History of Hsi Men and His Six Wives* (1960); and Paul Reps, *Gold/Fish Signatures* (1962). The last item (Reps) in the "Descriptive List" compiled by Edith Heal Berrien, Barbara Perkins, and George Perkins in 1964 is left out in the 1984 published version. See Appendix III.

4. Babette Deutsch published a poem called "And Again to Po Chü-i" in the September 1921 *Dial*:

> In exile, forlorn,
> Plucking the solitary lute,
> Drinking alone,
> Feeding on the remembrance
> Of festivals at the Court:
> The crimson pagodas
> Ringing with song, the feasts,
> The dancing-girls;
> The prizes
> From august imperial hands;
> And friends of rich autumns. . . .
> Now earth is shaken
> With war and civil wars.
> Men lie in exile
> Gnawing the crust of hunger
> Till they die.
> Yet in this wilderness of gaping graves
> We open our hearts
> To the knock
> > of a thousand-year-old sorrow.

I searched the 1918–21 issues of a dozen magazines kept at the Poetry/Rare Books Collection, SUNY-Buffalo, in the summer of 1990 with the remarkable assistance of Robert Bertholf and his staff. Not a poem called "To Po Chü-i" or anything to that effect was found. Nor did I find Deutsch's "And Again to Po Chü-i" reprinted in any of her volumes of verse published before 1969, not even in her *Collected Poems: 1919–1962* (1963). Nevertheless, in *The Collected Poems of Babette Deutsch* (1969), I did find a poem titled "To Po Chü-i" listed as one of her ten "new poems." A comparison reveals that it is no more than a revision of "And Again to Po Chü-i." Since Williams and Deutsch were both associated with *The Little Review* around 1920 (Williams' "Prologue II" and Deutsch's "Two First Books" both appeared in the May 1919 issue of the magazine), we have reason to suspect that Deutsch had either seen or heard about Williams' "To the Shade of Po Chü-i." Thus, "And Again to Po Chü-i" was probably her response to both Waley's translations of Bo Juyi and Williams' homage to the Chinese poet. Since "To the Shade of Po Chü-i" never appeared in print during Williams' lifetime, Deutsch couldn't possibly include her poem in her books either under the original title (readers would ask "Why 'And Again'?") or under the new one (Williams would say that it was his title). The difficulty, however, was removed after the death of Williams in 1963; hence the inclusion of the poem under the title "To Po Chü-i" in Deutsch's 1969 collection.

5. See Pound's letter of 30 June 1915 to his father, kept in the Beinecke Rare Book and Manuscript Library.

6. Arthur Waley observes that he doesn't think much of Bo Juyi's narrative classics because they "are in the old style of versification" (*Chinese Poems* 168).

7. According to Pauline Yu, the four doctrines shared by Taoism and Buddhism are "nondiscrimination; universal *śūnyatā* or emptiness; the simultaneous transcendence and immanence of the absolute; and the ultimate inadequacy of language" (*The Poetry of Wang Wei* 114).

8. In his letter to Williams, 28 February 1921, Edmund Brown of the Four Seas Publishing Company writes: "I received the manuscript, 'Picture Poems,' safely. I have not had time to read it entire but there is some great stuff in it" (qtd. in Townley 115).

9. "Portrait of a Woman in Bed," first published in *Others* 3.4 (December 1916) (Wallace C15).

10. Also, Williams may have borrowed the title "Portrait of the Author" from Waley, who, in reference to the autobiographical nature of Bo Juyi's poetry, observes, "If 'With a Portrait of the Author' had been the rule in the Chinese book-market, it is in such occupations as these that he would be shown; a neat and tranquil figure compared with our lurid frontispieces" (*Chinese Poems* 19).

11. In his letter to Robert Lowell, 26 September 1947, Williams remarks that "Li Po cannot be imitated not with the synthetic moons we have about us nowadays" (*SL* 262).

12. The movement, called *Xin yue fu* or "New Music Bureau Poetry," was initiated by Bo Juyi and his friend Yuan Zhen (779–831). Among their followers

were Li Shen (772–846), Wang Jian (ca. 766–ca. 830), and Zhang Jie (ca. 766–ca. 830). The poems that exemplify their literary ideal are collected in *Xin yue fu* (New Music Bureau Poetry) prefaced by Bo Juyi. For a study of Bo Juyi's life and career, see Arthur Waley's *The Life and Times of Po Chü-i*.

9 ESCAPING THE OLD MODE IN *SPRING AND ALL*

1. Williams said more or less the same thing to John C. Thirlwall while assisting him in annotating *The Collected Earlier Poems* in the late 1950s. See CP 1: 499.

2. Pound brought out Ur-Canto 8 in *The Dial* in May 1922 (Gallup C640), and Eliot brought out *The Waste Land* quasi-simultaneously in *The Criterion* and *The Dial* in October 1922 (Rainey, "The Price of Modernism" 92).

3. Arthur Waley, in *A Hundred and Seventy Chinese Poems*, defines *fu* as "descriptive prose-poems" that "resemble the *vers libres* of modern France . . . " (32). His definition is not precise, however, for a lot of *fu* writings are at once descriptive and argumentative.

4. "The Great Figure" went through at least three revisions. See Townley 124–25.

5. According to Thomas Whitaker, "Williams claims to have written 'The Red Wheelbarrow' in two minutes' time" (46).

6. See Giles, *Chuang Tzu: Mystic, Moralist, and Social Reformer* (London, 1889).

7. These two lines are absent in Williams' early draft of the poem kept in the Poetry/Rare Books Collection, SUNY-Buffalo. The addendum has apparently intensified the theme of promise.

8. The reference is to Marsden Hartley's praise of the equestrienne May Wirth, whose art "gives the body a chance to show its exquisite rhythmic beauty . . . " (*Adventures in the Arts* 178). See CP 1: 502.

9. Aside from Binyon—who elaborates on the "Six Canons" in both *Painting in the Far East* (66) and *The Flight of the Dragon* (11–21)—H. A. Giles, in *An Introduction to the History of Chinese Pictorial Art* (24, 29), Kakuzo Okakura, in *The Ideals of the East* (51), and Friedrich Hirth, in *Scraps from a Collector's Note Book* (58), also deal with the concept.

10. For a discussion of the concepts of *wu* and *śūnyatā*, see Yu, *The Poetry of Wang Wei* 114–15.

11. See Pound's draft version (no. 4) of the same poem in Appendix II.

10 IN PURSUIT OF MINIMAL, AGRAMMATICAL FORM

1. Waley, in discussing "The Method of Translation," notes, "I have . . . tried to produce regular rhythmic effects similar to those of the original. Each character

in the Chinese is represented by a stress in the English; but between the stresses unstressed syllables are of course interposed" (*Chinese Poems* 33).

2. Williams may have acquired a concrete knowledge of the *jueju* form from Giles' illustration of the tonal arrangement of a *jueju* (see *History* 144).

EPILOGUE: THE BEGINNING OF A LITERARY ERA

1. In a letter to Kate Buss, dated 12 May 1923, Pound writes, "The Three Mts. is following this prose series by a dee looks edtn of my Cantos (about 16 of 'em, I think) of UNRIVALLED magnificence" (*L* 187).

2. In planning the series in 1922, Pound was also thinking of including Eliot and Lewis. He observed to Williams on 1 August 1922: "The series is open: Though I don't at the moment see much more than half a dozen names: Hueffer, you, Eliot, Lewis, Windeler, Hemingway, et moi meme. (That's seven.)" (*L* 184). William Bird eventually brought out six volumes of similar format: the four mentioned, *Elimus* by B. C. Windeler (1923), and *England* by B. M. G. Adams (1923) (Gallup 34).

3. For this point of view, see James E. B. Breslin, "Introduction: The Presence of William Carlos Williams in Contemporary Poetry," in *Something to Say: William Carlos Williams on Younger Poets* (5–37).

4. Kenneth Roxroth and Gary Snyder are two obvious exceptions. Both poets later developed a keen interest in Chinese and Japanese literature.

APPENDIX II.

1. The eight draft versions correspond to the following texts in Wang Wei, *Wang Youcheng ji jianzhu*: (1) *Bai yingwu fu* (283–84); (3) *Chou yu bu su yuan wai guo lan tian bie ye bu jian liu zhi zuo* (118) ("Answering the Poem Su Left in My Blue Field Mountain Country House, on Visiting and Finding Me Not Home," in Barnstone, Barnstone, and Xu 23); (4) *Zhu li guan* (249) ("Bamboo Lodge," in Yu 204); (5) *Tian yuan le: qi liu* (258) (no. 6 of "Joys of Fields and Gardens," in Yu 199); (6) *Song Yuan er shi Anxi* (263) ("Farewell to Yuan the Second on His Mission to Anxi," in Yu 176–77); (7) *Ku re* (68) ("Suffering from Heat," in Yu 133); (8) *Song you ren gui shan ge er shou* (5–6) ("Saying Goodbye to a Friend Returning to the Mountains," in Barnstone, Barnstone, and Xu 52); and (9) *You wu zhen si* (229).

APPENDIX III.

1. The items with a single asterisk (*) are in the Beinecke Collection (see YCAL, "List of Works from the Library of William Carlos Williams"). The item with two

asterisks (**) is in the collection purchased from the Williams family by the William Reese Company of New Haven in 1987 (see Halladay, "A Descriptive List of Books from the Library of William Carlos Williams Purchased by the William Reese Company, 1987"). The remaining items are in the Fairleigh Dickinson University Collection (see Berrien et al., "Descriptive List of Works from Williams' Library Now at Fairleigh Dickinson University"). I will be grateful for any information regarding unlisted works on Oriental subjects from Williams' library.

2. Williams is supposed to have kept a copy of Kenneth Rexroth's *One Hundred Poems from the Chinese* (New York: New Directions, 1956). He reviewed that book in *Poetry* 90.3 (1957). See *Something to Say: William Carlos Williams on Younger Poets*, introd. James E. B. Breslin, 236–46.

WORKS CITED

Allen, Joseph R. *In the Voice of Others: Chinese Music Bureau Poetry*. Ann Arbor: U of Michigan Center for Chinese Studies, 1992.

Athanassakis, Apostolos N., trans. *The Homeric Hymns*. Baltimore: Johns Hopkins UP, 1976.

Ayscough, Florence, and Amy Lowell, trans. *Fir-Flower Tablets*. New York: Houghton Mifflin, 1921.

Barnstone, Tony, Willis Barnstone, and Xu Haixin, trans. *Laughing Lost in the Mountains: Poems of Wang Wei*. Hanover: UP of New England, 1991.

Berrien, Edith Heal, Barbara Perkins, and George Perkins. "Descriptive List of Works from Williams' Library Now at Fairleigh Dickinson University." Ed. Peter Schmidt. *William Carlos Williams Review* 10.2 (1984): 30–53.

Binyon, Laurence. *The Flight of the Dragon: An Essay on the Theory and Practice of Art in China and Japan Based on Original Sources*. London: John Murray, 1911.

———. *Guide to an Exhibition of Chinese and Japanese Paintings*. London: British Museum, 1910.

———. *Painting in the Far East*. London: Edward Arnold, 1908.

Breslin, James E. B. Introduction. *Something to Say: William Carlos Williams on Younger Poets*. New York: New Directions, 1985.

Bridson, D. G. "An Interview with Ezra Pound." *New Directions in Prose and Poetry* 17. Ed. James Laughlin. New York: New Directions, 1961. 159–84.

Brouner, Walter Brooks, and Fung Yuet Mow. *Chinese Made Easy*. Introd. H. A. Giles. New York: Macmillan, 1904.

Bush, Ronald. *The Genesis of Ezra Pound*. Princeton: Princeton UP, 1976.

———. "Pound and Li Po: What Becomes a Man." *Ezra Pound Among the Poets*. Ed. George Bornstein. Chicago: U of Chicago P, 1985. 35–62.

Buswell, Robert E. Jr. *The Formation of Ch'an Ideology in China and Korea*. Princeton: Princeton UP, 1989.

Bynner, Witter, and Kiang Kang-hu, trans. *The Jade Mountain: A Chinese Anthology: Being Three Hundred Poems of the Tang Dynasty 618–906*. New York: Alfred A. Knopf, 1929.

Cahill, James. *An Index of Early Chinese Painters and Paintings: T'ang, Sung, and Yuan*. Berkeley: U of California P, 1980.

———. *Chinese Painting*. New York: Rizzoli International Publications, 1977.

Carpenter, Thomas H. *Dionysian Imagery in Archaic Greek Art*. Oxford: Clarendon Press, 1986.

Chang, K. C. *Art, Myth, and Ritual: The Path to Political Authority in Ancient China*. Cambridge: Harvard UP, 1983.

Chapple, Anne S. "Ezra Pound's *Cathay*: Compilation from the Fenollosa Notebooks." *Paideuma* 17.2 and 3 (1988): 9–42.

Chisolm, Lawrence W. *Fenollosa: The Far East and American Culture*. New Haven: Yale UP, 1963.

Cournos, John. *Autobiography*. New York: G. P. Putnam's Sons, 1935.

Cranmer-Byng, L., trans. *A Lute of Jade*. London: John Murray, 1909.

Danielou, Alain. *Shiva and Dionysus*. Trans. K. F. Hurry. London: East-West Publications, 1982.

Dasenbrock, Reed Way. *Imitating the Italians: Wyatt, Spenser, Synge, Pound, Joyce*. Baltimore: Johns Hopkins UP, 1991.

———. *The Literary Vorticism of Ezra Pound and Wyndham Lewis: Toward the Condition of Painting*. Baltimore: Johns Hopkins UP, 1985.

Davidson, Martha. *A List of Published Translations from Chinese into English, French, and German*. 2 parts. Washington, D.C.: American Council of Learned Societies, 1957. Part 2.

Davie, Donald. *Ezra Pound*. Chicago: U of Chicago P, 1975.

Deng Shaoji, et al., eds. *Tang shi san bai shou* [*Three Hundred Poems of the Tang*]. Dalian: Dalian Chubanshe, 1992.

Deutsch, Babette. "And Again to Po Chü-i." *The Dial* (Sept. 1921): 280.

Diggory, Terence. "The Blue Nude and Mrs. Pappadopoulos." *William Carlos Williams Review* 18.2 (1992): 24–34.

Doyle, Charles. *Richard Aldington: A Biography*. Carbondale: Southern Illinois UP, 1989.

Edwards, Richard. *The World around the Chinese Artist: Aspects of Realism in Chinese Painting*. Ann Arbor: U of Michigan P, 1989.

Eliot, T. S. *After Strange Gods: A Primer of Modern Heresy*. New York: Harcourt, Brace, 1933.

———. "Ezra Pound: His Metric and Poetry." *To Criticize the Critic*. New York: Farrar, Straus, and Giroux, 1965. 162–82.

———. Introduction. *Ezra Pound: Selected Poems*. London: Faber and Faber, 1928.

Evans, Arthur. *The God of Ecstasy: Sex Roles and the Madness of Dionysos*. New York: St. Martins Press, 1988.

Fang, Achilles. "Fenollosa and Pound." *Harvard Journal of Asiatic Studies* 20 (1957): 213–38.

Fang Yurun. *Shi jing yuan shi* [The Original Shi jing]. Beijing: Zhonghua Shudian, 1986.

Farrer, Anne. *The Brush Dances & the Ink Sings: Chinese Paintings and Calligraphy from the British Museum*. London: South Bank Centre, 1990.

Fenollosa, Ernest. *Epochs of Chinese and Japanese Art*. 2 vols. London: William Heinemann, 1912.

Fletcher, John Gould. *Life Is My Song: The Autobiography of John Gould Fletcher*. New York: Farrar and Rinehart, 1937.

———. "Perfume of Cathay." *Poetry* 13 (1919): 273–81.

———. *Selected Essays of John Gould Fletcher*. Ed. Lucas Carpenter. Fayetteville: The U of Arkansas P, 1989.

Flint, F. S. "The History of Imagism." *The Egoist* 1 May 1915: 70–71.

Fogelman, Bruce. *Shapes of Power: The Development of Ezra Pound's Poetic Sequences*. Ann Arbor: UMI Research Press, 1988.

Fong, Wen C., et al. *Images of the Mind*. Princeton: Art Museum of Princeton University and Princeton UP, 1984.

Froula, Christine. *To Write Paradise: Style and Error in Pound's Cantos*. New Haven: Yale UP, 1984.

Gadamer, Hans-Georg. *Truth and Method*. Ed. and trans. Garrett Barden and John Cumming. New York: Seabury Press, 1975.

Gallup, Donald. *Ezra Pound: A Bibliography*. Charlottesville: UP of Virginia, 1983.

Gao Heng, ed. *Shi jing jin zhu* [New Annotated Shi jing]. Shanghai: Guji, 1980.

Gautier, Judith. *Le livre de jade*. 1867. Paris: Librairie Plon, 1933.

Giles, H. A., trans. *Chuang Tzu: Mystic, Moralist, and Social Reformer*. London: Bernard Quaritch, 1889.

———, trans. *Gems of Chinese Literature*. 1884. New York: Paragon Book Reprint Corp. and Dover Publications, 1965.

———. *A History of Chinese Literature*. New York: D. Appleton, 1901.

———. *An Introduction to the History of Chinese Pictorial Art*. 1905. London: Bernard Quaritch, 1918.

Goodwin, K. L. *The Influence of Ezra Pound*. London: Oxford UP, 1966.

Graham, A. C. Introduction. *Poems of the Late T'ang*. Baltimore: Penguin, 1965.

Granet, Marcel. *Festivals and Songs of Ancient China*. Trans. E. D. Edwards. New York: E. P. Dutton, 1932.

Hall, Donald. "Ezra Pound." *Writers at Work: The Paris Review Interviews*. Second Series. Introd. Van Wyck Brooks. New York: Viking Press, 1963.

Halladay, Terry G. "A Descriptive List of Books from the Library of William Carlos Williams Purchased by the William Reese Company, 1987." *William Carlos Williams Review* 16.2 (1990): 55–63.

Hamilton, Scott. *Ezra Pound and the Symbolist Inheritance.* Princeton: Princeton UP, 1992.

Hartley, Marsden. *Adventures in the Arts.* 1921. New York: Hacker Art Books, 1972.

Hawkes, David. *Ch'u Tz'u: The Songs of the South: An Ancient Chinese Anthology.* London: Oxford UP, 1959.

——. *The Songs of the South: An Ancient Chinese Anthology of Poems by Qu Yuan and Other Poets.* Harmondsworth: Penguin, 1985.

Heal, Edith. "William Carlos Williams' Personal Library at Fairleigh Dickinson University, Rutherford." *William Carlos Williams Newsletter* 4.1 (1978): 20–21.

Hirth, Friedrich. *Scraps from a Collector's Note Book.* Leipzig: Otto Harrassowitz; New York: G. E. Stechert, 1905.

Holaday, Woon-Ping Chin. "Pound and Binyon: China via the British Museum." *Paideuma* 6.3 (1977): 27–36.

Homberger, Eric, ed. *Ezra Pound: The Critical Heritage.* London: Routledge and Kegan Paul, 1972.

Hughes, Glenn. *Imagism & the Imagists: A Study in Modern Poetry.* London: Bowes and Bowes, 1960.

Hulme, T. E. *Further Speculations by T. E. Hulme.* Ed. Sam Hynes. Minneapolis: U of Minnesota P, 1955.

Jha, Ashok Kumar. *Oriental Influences in T. S. Eliot.* Allahabad: Kitab Mahal, 1988.

Jiang Jianyuan and Cheng Junying, eds. *Shi jing zhu xi* [The Annotated Shi jing]. Beijing: Zhonghua Shuju, 1991.

Jin Xuezhi. "Pictorial Beauty in the Poetry of Wang Wei." *Chinese Literature* 4 (1985): 160–78.

Jung, Angela Chih-Ying. "Ezra Pound and China." Diss. U of Washington, 1955.

Karlgren, Bernhard. *The Book of Odes: Chinese Text, Transcription, and Translation.* Stockholm: Museum of Far Eastern Antiquities, 1950.

Kenner, Hugh. *The Pound Era.* Berkeley: U of California P, 1971.

Knox, Bryant. "Allen Upward and Ezra Pound." *Paideuma* 3.1 (1974): 71–83.

Kodama, Sanehide. *American Poetry and Japanese Culture.* Hamden: Archon Books, 1984.

Kreymborg, Alfred. *Troubadour: An Autobiography.* New York: Boni and Liveright, 1925.

Legge, James. *The Chinese Classics.* 5 vols. Oxford: Oxford UP, 1892. Vol. 4.

Levy, Dore J. *Chinese Narrative Poetry: The Late Han through T'ang Dynasties.* Durham: Duke UP, 1988.

Li Bo. *Li Taibo quanji* [The Complete Poems of Li Bo]. Shanghai: Shanghai Shudian, 1988.

Liu, James J. Y. *The Art of Chinese Poetry*. Chicago: U of Chicago P, 1962.

Liu Wu-chi. *An Introduction to Chinese Literature*. Bloomington: Indiana UP, 1966.

Liu Yialing et al., eds. *Zhongguo lidai shige jianshang cidian* [A Companion to Classical Chinese Poetry]. Beijing: Zhongguo Minjian Wenyi, 1988.

Luh, C. W. [Lu Zhiwei]. *Five Lectures on Chinese Poetry*. Beijing: Foreign Language Teaching and Research Press, 1982.

Lyons, Elizabeth. "*Ming Huang's Journey to Shu*: The History of a Painting." *Expedition* 28.3 (1986): 22–28.

MacNair, Harley Farnsworth, ed. *Florence Ayscough and Amy Lowell: Correspondence of a Friendship*. Chicago: U of Chicago P, 1945.

Mariani, Paul. *William Carlos Williams: A New World Naked*. New York: McGraw-Hill, 1981.

Marquis d'Hervey-Saint-Denys, Marie J. L. *Poésies de l'époque des Thang*. 1872. Paris: Editions Champ Libre, 1977.

Martin, W. A. P. *The Lore of Cathay*. New York: Fleming H. Revell, 1901.

Meech, Julia, and Gabriel P. Weisberg. *Japonisme Comes to America: The Japanese Impact on the Graphic Arts 1876–1925*. New York: Harry N. Abrams, 1990.

Miller, J. Hillis. *Illustration*. Cambridge: Harvard UP, 1992.

———. "Williams' *Spring and All* and the Progress of Poetry." *Daedalus* 99 (1970): 405–35.

Monroe, Harriet. *A Poet's Life: Seventy Years in a Changing World*. New York: Macmillan, 1938.

———. "Waley's Translations from the Chinese." *Poetry* 15 (1920): 337–42.

Moore, Marianne. *The Complete Prose of Marianne Moore*. Ed. Patricia C. Willis. New York: Viking Penguin, 1986.

Murray, Gilbert, trans. *Euripides*. New York: Longman, Green; London: George Allen, 1912.

Naito, Shiro. *Yeats and Zen: A Study of the Transformation of His Mask*. Kyoto: Yamaguchi, 1984.

Nolde, John J. *Blossoms from the East: The China Cantos of Ezra Pound*. Orono: National Poetry Foundation, 1983.

Norman, Charles. *Ezra Pound*. New York: Macmillan, 1960.

Obata, Shigeyoshi, trans. *The Works of Li Po: The Chinese Poet*. New York: E. P. Dutton, 1922.

Okakura, Kakuzo. *The Ideals of the East*. London: John Murray, 1903.

Olson, Charles. *The Maximus Poems*. Ed. George Butterick. Berkeley: U of California P, 1983.

Oshima, Shotaro. *W. B. Yeats and Japan*. Tokyo: Hokuseido Press, 1965.

Owen, Stephen. *The Great Age of Chinese Poetry: The High T'ang*. New Haven: Yale UP, 1981.

Poirier, Richard. *Poetry and Pragmatism*. Cambridge: Harvard UP, 1992.

Pound, Omar S. *The Dying Sorcerer.* Nova Scotia (Canada): Antigonish, 1985.

Qian, Zhaoming. "Works from the Library of William Carlos Williams at Fairleigh Dickinson University: Addenda to the Descriptive List." *William Carlos Williams Review* 21.1 (1995): 53–67.

Rainey, Lawrence. *Ezra Pound and the Monument of Culture: Text, History, and the Malatesta Cantos.* Chicago: U of Chicago P, 1991.

———. "The Price of Modernism: Publishing *The Waste Land.*" *T. S. Eliot: The Modernist in History.* Ed. Ronald Bush. Cambridge: Cambridge UP, 1991. 91–133.

Read, Dennis M. "Three Unpublished Poems by William Carlos Williams." *American Literature* 58.3 (1986): 422–26.

Ruthven, K. K. *A Guide to Ezra Pound's Personae (1926).* Berkeley: U of California P, 1969.

Said, Edward W. *Orientalism.* New York: Random House, 1978.

Schmidt, Peter. *William Carlos Williams, the Arts, and Literary Tradition.* Baton Rouge: Louisiana State UP, 1988.

Schwartz, Sanford. *The Matrix of Modernism: Pound, Eliot, & Early 20th Century Thought.* Princeton: Princeton UP, 1985.

Sekine, Masaru. *Yeats and the Noh: A Comparative Study.* Buckinghamshire: Colin Smythe, 1990.

Singh, Amar Kumar. *T. S. Eliot and Indian Philosophy.* New Delhi: Sterling Publishers Private Limited, 1990.

Smoller, Sanford J. *Adrift Among Geniuses: Robert McAlmon: Writer and Publisher of the Twenties.* University Park: Pennsylvania State UP, 1975.

Sri, P. S. *T. S. Eliot, Vedanta, and Buddhism.* Vancouver: U of British Columbia P, 1985.

Stevens, Wallace. *Letters of Wallace Stevens.* Ed. Holly Stevens. New York: Alfred A. Knopf, 1981.

Stock, Noel. *The Life of Ezra Pound.* London: Routledge and Kegan Paul, 1970.

Su Xuelin. *Qu Yuan yu Jiu ge* [Qu Yuan and *The Nine Songs*]. Taipei: Wenjin Chubanshe, 1992.

Suzuki, Daisetz T. *Zen and Japanese Culture.* Princeton: Princeton UP, 1959.

Suzuki, Kei. *Comprehensive Illustrated Catalog of Chinese Paintings.* 5 vols. Tokyo: U of Tokyo P, 1982.

Taupin, René. *The Influence of French Symbolism on Modern American Poetry.* Trans. William Pratt and Anne Rich Pratt. New York: AMS Press, 1985.

Terrell, Carroll F. *A Companion to the Cantos of Ezra Pound.* Berkeley: U of California P, 1980.

Townley, Rod. *The Early Poetry of William Carlos Williams.* Ithaca: Cornell UP, 1975.

Tsukui, Nobuko. *Ezra Pound and Japanese Noh Plays.* Washington, D.C.: UP of America, 1983.

Upward, Allen. "Correspondence: The Discarded Imagist." *The Egoist* 1 June 1915: 98.

——. *The New Word*. New York: Mitchell Kennerley, 1910.

——. "Sayings of K'ung the Master: Selected with an Introduction." *The New Freewoman* 1 and 15 Nov., 1 Dec. 1913; *The Egoist* 16 Feb. 1914.

Waddell, Helen. *Lyrics from the Chinese*. Boston: Houghton Mifflin, 1913.

Waley, Arthur, trans. *The Book of Songs*. London: George Allen and Unwin, 1937.

——, trans. *A Hundred and Seventy Chinese Poems*. New York: Alfred A. Knopf, 1919.

——. *The Life and Times of Po Chü-i*. London: George Allen and Unwin, 1949.

——, trans. *More Translations from the Chinese*. New York: Alfred A. Knopf, 1919.

——. *The Nine Songs: A Study of Shamanism in Ancient China*. London: George Allen and Unwin, 1955.

——. *The Poetry and Career of Li Po*. London: George Allen and Unwin, 1950.

Wallace, Emily Mitchell. *A Bibliography of William Carlos Williams*. Middletown: Wesleyan UP, 1968.

Wang Bomin et al., *Zhongguo meishu tongshi* [A History of Chinese Art]. Jinan: Shandong Jiaoyu Chubanshe, 1987.

Wang, Jing. *The Story of Stone: Intertextuality, Ancient Chinese Stone Lore, and the Stone Symbolism of* Dream of the Red Chamber, Water Margin, *and* The Journey to the West. Durham: Duke UP, 1992.

Wang Jingzhi. *Shi jing tong she* [The Annotated Shi jing]. Taipei: Puren University, 1968.

Wang Wei. *Wang Youcheng ji jianzhu* [The Works of Wang Wei]. Shanghai: Guji, 1984.

Watson, Burton, ed. and trans. *The Columbia Book of Chinese Poetry*. New York: Columbia UP, 1984.

——, trans. *The Complete Works of Chuang Tzu*. New York: Columbia UP, 1968.

Wells, Henry W. "William Carlos Williams and Traditions in Chinese Poetry." *Literary Half-Yearly* 16.1 (1975): 3–24.

Whitaker, Thomas R. *William Carlos Williams*. Rev. ed. Boston: Twayne, 1989.

Wilhelm, J. J. *Ezra Pound in London and Paris: 1908–1925*. University Park: Pennsylvania State UP, 1990.

——. *The Later Cantos of Ezra Pound*. New York: Walker, 1977.

Winters, Yvor. *Yvor Winters: Uncollected Essays and Reviews*. Ed. Francis Murphy. Chicago: Swallow, 1973.

Witemeyer, Hugh. *The Poetry of Ezra Pound: Forms and Renewal, 1908–1920*. Berkeley: U of California P, 1969.

Wong, Kai-chee, Pung Ho, and Shu-leung Dang. *A Research Guide to English Translation of Chinese Verse (Han Dynasty to T'ang Dynasty)*. Hong Kong: Chinese UP, 1977.

Xia Zhuancai et al., eds. *Zhongguo gudai mingpian xuandu* [Anthology of Chinese Masterpieces]. 2 vols. Beijing: Yuwen, 1985. Vol. 1.

Xiao Difei et al., eds. *Tang shi jianshang cidian* [A Companion to Tang Poetry]. Shanghai: Cishu, 1983.

Yeats, W. B. *Four Plays for Dancers*. New York: Macmillan, 1921.

———. "William Butler Yeats to American Poets." *The Little Review* 1.2 (1914): 47–48.

Yip, Wai-lim. *Ezra Pound's Cathay*. Princeton: Princeton UP, 1969.

Yu, Pauline. *The Poetry of Wang Wei: New Translations and Commentary*. Bloomington: Indiana UP, 1980.

———. *The Reading of Imagery in the Chinese Poetic Tradition*. Princeton: Princeton UP, 1987.

———. "Wang Wei: Recent Studies and Translations." *Chinese Literature: Essays, Articles, Reviews* 1.2 (1979): 219–40.

Zhang Longxi. "The Myth of the Other: China in the Eyes of the West." *Critical Inquiry* 15 (1988): 108–31.

———. *The Tao and the Logos: Literary Hermeneutics, East and West*. Durham: Duke UP, 1992.

INDEX

Zhaoming Qian is Assistant Professor of English at University of New Orleans.

Library of Congress Cataloging-in-Publication Data

Qian, Zhaoming.

Orientalism and modernism : the legacy of China in Pound and Williams / Zhaoming Qian.

p.   cm.   Includes bibliographical references and index.

ISBN 0-8223-1657-9 (cloth). — ISBN 0-8223-1669-2 (pbk.)

1. American literature—Chinese influences. 2. American poetry—20th century—History and criticism. 3. Pound, Ezra, 1885-1972—Knowledge—China. 4. Williams, William Carlos, 1883-1963—Knowledge—China. 5. Modernism (Literature)—United States. 6. Exoticism in literature. 7. China—In literature. I. Title.

PS159.C5Q25   1995   811'.5209—dc20   95—6130   CIP